VIEWPOINTS
ON
SUPPLY-SIDE
ECONOMICS

VIEWPOINTS ON SUPPLY-SIDE ECONOMICS

THOMAS J. HAILSTONES

COLLEGE OF BUSINESS ADMINISTRATION
XAVIER UNIVERSITY
CINCINNATI, OHIO

Reston Publishing Company, Inc.
A Prentice-Hall Company
Reston, Virginia

ISBN 0-8359-8386-2

PRINTED IN THE UNITED STATES OF AMERICA

10   9   8   7   6   5   4   3   2

Designed and typeset by Publications Development Co. of
Crockett, Texas, Developmental Editor: Nancy Marcus Land,
Production Editor: Bessie Graham

PREFACE

In spite of some previous successes with the use of Keynesian and monetarists policies in stabilizing the level of economic activity, it became apparent in the mid-1970s that our usual demand management policies and measures were not successful in maintaining price stability, economic growth and a high rate of employment as required by the Employment Act of 1946 and the Full Employment and Balanced Growth Act of 1978.

Energy blackouts, crop shortages, OPEC embargos, oil price shocks, the demise of the gold standard, a changing international monetary system, continued balance of payments deficits, a flood of imports, double-digit inflation, sky-high and volatile interest rates, the decline of American productivity, the persistence of stagflation and three recessions within a 10-12 year period indicated trouble with our economic policies.

Whether Keynesian and monetary policies were mismanaged or no longer applicable in the changing, dynamic economy of the 1970s is still a question to be answered. Nevertheless, the changing economic environment of the 1970s and early 1980s opened the door for the emergence of the new philosophy of supply-side economics.

Supply-side economics means different things to different people. Since the principles, propositions, analyses and the pros and cons of supply-side economics are not fully incorporated into our principles of economics texts as yet, much of the supply-side literature remains scattered and fragmented. As a result, there is a need for a single source of information about the origins, propositions, claims and counter claims and analyses of supply-side economics.

It is the purpose of this readings book to bring a considerable amount of what has been written on supply-side economics together into a single book. This will permit those who desire to study and analyze various viewpoints and aspects of supply-side economics to readily and conveniently do so.

By the mid-1980s we should have better supply-side models and know much more about the effectiveness of supply-side measures as espoused by so-called Reaganomics.

By that time also supply-side thinking may be more crystalized and we will learn whether it is something temporary that will fade away, be widely accepted as the new economics replacing Keynesian demand analysis, or something to be continued but integrated with demand management and monetarism.

In the meantime it is hoped that this book will be helpful in your understanding and analysis of the new supply-side approach to economic policies.

A note of thanks is due to the many authors and publishers of the articles contained herein and to my secretary, Mrs. Marjorie Schmidt, for her stenographic assistance in compiling the book.

In addition to my earlier text, *A Guide to Supply-Side Economics,* other books about supply-side economics are listed in the Appendix of this book.

Thomas J. Hailstones
January 1982

CONTENTS

I

DOUBTS ABOUT KEYNESIAN POLICIES IN A CHANGING ECONOMIC ENVIRONMENT

The articles in Part I reveal the growing questioning and doubts about the application and effectiveness of economic policy based on Keynesian analysis in dealing with the continuing and new problems of the changing economic environment between mid-1960s and 1981.

1

The Death of Keynes*

ROBERT E. LUCAS. JR.

Today, I'd like to discuss where I think economics is going, particularly macroeconomics and monetary economics. This is a topic of interest to me—I'm an economist, and everyone is interested in developments in his own industry. But occasionally developments in economics do matter for non-economists, and I hope the ones I will talk about will be of some interest to you.

The main development already has occurred: Keynesian economics is dead (maybe "disappeared" is a better term). I don't know exactly when this happened, but it is true today and it wasn't true ten years ago. This is a sociological, not an economic observation, and so is the supporting evidence. For example: one cannot find good, under-forty economists who identify themselves or their work as "Keynesian." Indeed, people even take offense if referred to as "Keynesians." At research seminars, people don't take Keynesian theorizing seriously anymore; the audience starts to whisper and giggle to one another. Leading journals are getting fewer and fewer Keynesian papers submitted.

I suppose that I, along with many others, was in on the kill in an intellectual sense, but I don't say this as any kind of boast, or even with much pleasure. It's just a fact.

True, there are still leading Keynesians in academic and government circles: Keynesian economics is alive in that sense. But this is transient because there is no fresh source of supply. The only way to produce a

*Reprinted with permission of the author. Robert E. Lucas is vice-chairman and professor in the Department of Economics at the University of Chicago. This article is a condensation of his remarks during a panel discussion at the 27th Annual Management Conference in Chicago on April 26, 1979.

sixty-year-old Keynesian is to produce a thirty-year-old Keynesian and wait thirty years.

This disappearance of Keynesian economics is more than just industry gossip because Keynesianism mattered; it filled a very central ideological function. Now that it is gone, something is going to have to take its place, and we need to think about what that something is likely to be. I'd like to approach this by recalling the ideological function of Keynesian economics.

The central lesson of economic theory is the proposition that a competititve economy, left to its own devices, will do a good job of allocating resources. Of course, we need to make this proposition more precise, add necessary qualifications, etc., but this is the basic message of nineteenth century economics and has continued into the twentieth century. Recurrent depressions and occasional inflation were something of an embarrassment to this theory, but these tended to be brief and it was not unreasonable to hope that some reform of monetary institutions could be found that could eliminate or mitigate them. These beliefs were very widely shared in pre-1929 capitalist economies, not just by a few economists but by the public at large.

In the 1930s, all this went out the window. Next time you are at a cocktail party, ask people "Do you think our private economy, left to its own devices, could be trusted to do a good job of maintaining full employment?" An economist would probably ask you to spell out exactly what you mean by "left to its own devices," but a normal, literate person would say, "Of course not. Just think of the 1930s." Try it. If you try it enough times, I think you'll find the view that the economy needs to be managed on a year-in, year-out basis is almost universal, even fifty years after 1929.

But what do we mean by "managing" an economy? Prior to Keynes, "managing" was taken to involve a good deal of governmental intervention at the individual market level: socialism in Russia, fascism in Italy and Germany, the confusion of early New Deal programs in the United States. The fundamental shift was away from market allocation and toward centralized direction.

The central message of Keynes was that there existed a middle ground between these extremes of socialism and laissez-faire capitalism. (Actually, there is some confusion as to what Keynes really said: largely Keynes' own fault. Did you ever try to read the *General Theory?* I'm giving you Keynes as interpreted by Alvin Hansen and Paul Samuelson.) It is true (so the argument went) that the economy cannot be left to its own devices, but all that we need to do to manage it is to manipulate the general levels of fiscal and monetary policy. If this is done right, all that elegant nineteenth century economics will be valid and individual markets can be left to take care of themselves.

In effect Samuelson told his colleagues: "Face it, you live in a world where virtually nobody has any faith in this laissez-faire religion of yours. I'm offering a substitute ideology that concedes the inability of a competitive economy to take care of itself but also offers a management system that is, say 95 percent consistent with laissez-faire." These were hard times, and this was too good a deal to pass up. We took it. So did society as a whole. Conservatives were a little grumpy, but how bad off could we be in a country where Paul Samuelson was viewed as a leftist?

What I meant by saying that Keynesian economics is dead at the beginning of my talk is just that now this middle ground is gone—not because people don't like the middle ground anymore, but because its intellectual rationale has eroded to the point where it is no longer serviceable. There are many reasons for this, and it is a difficult problem to spell out the details. I think that the problem, in a nutshell, was that the Keynes-Samuelson view involved two distinct, mutually inconsistent theoretical explanations of the determination of employment. For a time, we thought we could find a new theory that would unify or reconcile these two explanations, but the more progress we made, the more difficulties came into view, dragging us farther under. By now, I think it is fairly clear that the attempt is hopeless. As a result, new talent is not attracted to refining and developing Keynesian economics. This is what we mean by the "death" of a scientific idea.

What happens now? In academic circles: total chaos. Everyone has his own theories, and since orthodoxy has no way of discriminating, all get a fair hearing. It's a great time to be a macroeconomist.

For social policy? Not so cheerful. The collapse means the end (for the time being, anyway) of consensus economics. Crackpot proposals like the Humphrey-Hawkins or Roth-Kemp bills get attention along with serious ones: there is no "establishment" with the influence to align the economics profession against such schemes. I expect public debate to grow increasingly more ideological, reverting to the pre-Keynesian lines of laissez-faire types versus socialist-fascist interventionist types. (Presumably both sides will select fresher labels, but old hands will recognize the arguments.)

What will the outcome be? Who knows? It certainly won't be settled by a few dozen academic experts. If the general reading of the '30s as the "failure of capitalism" continues to prevail, I see one outcome. If some combination of counter-argument or perhaps just passage of time overcomes this view, I see brighter prospects.

2

An Essay on Keynesian Economics*

IRWIN L. KELLNER

The lopsided election results may be open to several interpretations, insofar as economic policy is concerned. Clearly, the first is simply that the voters did not care for the policies pursued by the previous Administration and are hoping for something better from the incoming President and the new Congress. Beyond this statement, however, it becomes less certain what the voters had in mind. Did they reject Keynesian economics in favor of monetarism? Did they discard liberal economic policies in favor of conservative economics? Are they looking for someone who follows the concept of "rational expectations"? Or maybe is it "supply side" economics that the electorate yearns for as opposed to "demand management"?

For that matter, are they looking for *any* economic policy? More than once in recent months the media has severely criticized the economics profession, claiming it is anywhere from just "muddling through" to being in a "mood of exhaustion and inadequacy." In some ways the media cannot be blamed for criticizing economists since one eminent member of the profession was moved to remark some time ago that "the rules of economics are not working in quite the way they used to."

I don't profess to be able to read the voter's minds beyond the simple statement noted at the opening of this Report. That is—to paraphrase elections past, many people believed that it was "time for a change." For one thing, I don't believe that most people are aware that there are different economic philosophies, and that some have been tried and found wanting while others are waiting in the wings to show their efficacy. For another, I don't think that it should boil down to a question

*Mr. Kellner is Senior Vice President and Economist for Manufacturers Hanover Trust Company, New York. Reprinted with permission from *The Manufacturers Hanover Economic Report*, November 1980 and February 1981.

of rejecting one type of philosophy in favor of another because we haven't given *any* economic theory a chance to work.

In our collective efforts to make the present as comfortable as possible, we have neglected the future. Unfortunately, the future has finally arrived, and we are paying for our sins of the past. In other words—our economic problems (including the growing questioning of economists' abilities as well) do not stem from the rules of economics changing. Rather, we are in the mess that we are in because of our unwillingness to abide by the rules of economics that already exist.

WHAT'S RIGHT WITH KEYNES . . .

Since not a few people are interpreting the election as a "mandate" to get rid of Keynesian economics, I thought it would be appropriate to discuss this month just what has gone wrong with Keynesian economics—and what hasn't. Taking the latter first, the one part of Keynesian economics that, in my view, we should hold on to is the use of a balanced budget. Contrary to popular belief, Keynes never directly attacked the classical notion that the Federal government's budget must be in balance. What he said was that during periods in which the level of employment declines, the government "willingly or unwillingly" should run a budget deficit to provide unemployment relief. This deficit, quite naturally, would be financed by borrowing money—what Keynes called "loan expenditures." He believed that such actions would increase people's ability (and willingness) to consume, thus extricating the economy from recession.

Those who have written about Keynes in an effort to interpret his writings have drawn the conclusion that budget deficits are quite acceptable during periods of economic slack. I would agree. Some authors believe that Keynes had a cavalier attitude toward budget deficits, pointing to the views of many of his disciples who assert that deficits do not matter. With this I would disagree. If Keynes did not place great emphasis on the implications of a budget deficit beyond that of stimulating the economy, it is simply because he believed that deficits should not be used as a main tool of economic policy, and when they were, they were to be used during periods of economic slack. It is Keynes's followers, and the politicians whom they educated, that are to blame for the "cavalier" attitude toward budget deficits that subsequently developed in the 1950s and 1960s. I recall one argument vividly: "Why worry about debt, when it is simply money that we owe to ourselves?" That was used as a justification by many so-called Keynesian economists to run persistent budget deficits even when the pace of economic activity was strong. This kind of thinking was brought to its apex when the notion of the "full employment balanced budget" was advanced. This view held that, while the economy might have been nominally expanding, it would never reach its full potential if the budget, calculated at hypothetical full employment, were in surplus. You can see where this led to a further departure from Keynes's basic notion of running deficits in bad times and surpluses in good times. Since "good times" were some phase of economic activity that could only be described theoretically, rather than a measure of what was actually happening, one could easily justify continued deficits in the budget.

To liberal economists, this seemed to assuage their concerns about high unemployment and unequal distribution of income. They could recommend policies that they earnestly believed would make the economy run even better than it might have been doing at the time. But it was the politicians to whom the notion of a "buy now, pay later" budget system proved most appealing, in that it provided an important assist in getting them elected. Politicians could now parade before the American people and promise all kinds of things without presenting a bill. There always seemed to be Federal money available to remedy whatever local ailment existed. And if it was not increased spending that they promised, it was lower taxes. Budget deficits soon became "acceptable" as a way of life. Little wonder that we got into the mess that we are in today!

The table shows the sorry record of the postwar years as far as budget deficits and surpluses are concerned. As you can see, we have *not* followed Keynes's idea of running a deficit in bad times and a surplus in good times. Plainly, we have not had 12 recession years in a row. 20 out of the past 21 or 29 out of the past 37. Thus, before we are ready to cast off Keynesian economics altogether, we should observe that one aspect of his policies that might have worked—the idea of running budget deficits in bad times and surpluses in good times—was not allowed to because it was not adhered to.

What bothers me even more is that we have a new group of elected officials coming into Washington in January, committed to tossing out Keynesian economics in the name of fighting inflation—yet advocating what would amount to a substantial widening of the budget deficit. They want to cut taxes and increase defense spending before they can put into effect offsetting reductions in nondefense outlays. This simply will not work. Its near-term impact on the Federal government's financing needs will be devastating, since any policy that calls for more spending and less taxes—regardless of what their classroom results might be—will in the real world widen an already swollen budget deficit. This will, in turn, cause one or more of several possible adverse events to occur.

Federal Budget Receipts and Outlays: Fiscal Years 1945-81 (Billions of Dollars)			
Fiscal Year	Receipts	Outlays	Surplus or Deficit (−)
1945	45.2	92.7	−47.5
1946	39.3	55.2	−15.9
1947	38.4	34.5	3.9
1948	41.8	29.8	12.0
1949	39.4	38.8	.6
1950	39.5	42.6	− 3.1
1951	51.6	45.5	6.1
1952	66.2	67.7	− 1.5
1953	69.6	76.1	− 6.5
1954	69.7	70.9	− 1.2
1955	65.5	68.5	− 3.0
1956	74.5	70.5	4.1
1957	80.0	76.7	3.2
1958	79.6	82.6	− 2.9
1959	79.2	92.1	−12.9
1960	92.5	92.2	.3
1961	94.4	97.8	− 3.4
1962	99.7	106.8	− 7.1
1963	106.6	111.3	− 4.8
1964	112.7	118.6	− 5.9
1965	116.8	118.4	− 1.6
1966	130.9	134.7	− 3.8
1967	149.6	158.3	− 8.7
1968	153.7	178.8	−25.2
1969	187.8	184.5	3.2
1970	193.7	196.6	− 2.8
1971	188.4	211.4	−23.0
1972	208.6	232.0	−23.4
1973	232.2	247.1	−14.8
1974	264.9	269.6	− 4.7
1975	281.0	326.2	−45.2
1976	300.0	366.4	−66.4
Transition Quarter	81.8	94.7	−13.0
1977	357.8	402.7	−45.0
1978	402.0	450.8	−48.8
1979	466.0	493.6	−27.7
1980 (preliminary)	520.0	579.0	−59.0
1981 (estimated)	605.0	632.4	−27.4

Sources: Department of the Treasury, Office of Management and Budget, House-Senate Conference Committee.

If the Federal Reserve continues to adhere to its present course of trying to slow the growth of the money supply to noninflationary proportions, then Washington's increased financing needs will have to be met by funds drawn from the private sector. This would imply not only less liquidity for business and consumers initially, but also higher interest rates as well. Higher interest rates, of course, make it less attractive—if not outright difficult—for business and consumers to spend.

Of course, the Federal Reserve could always "give in" and expand the supply of money and credit to meet Washington's increased financing requirements while accommodating everyone else. In this event, interest rates might stay stable for a while (and they might not, at that, since the financial markets are so sophisticated these days that they would catch immediately the extra injection of money into the system and begin to anticipate its inflationary consequences), but at the expense of worsened inflation later on. A higher rate of inflation drains purchasing power, thereby constricting consumer spending, while the higher interest rates that would eventually result will further depress economic activity by discouraging both consumer and business spending.

...WHAT'S WRONG...

Without question, there are aspects of Keynesian economics that are no longer applicable in today's world. Keynes did not believe in the automatic adjustment process that was central to classical or orthodox economic theory. At the heart of his General Theory was the proposition that a modern economy was unstable. He labeled as outstanding faults of the modern economy what he called the failure to provide full employment and an equitable distribution of wealth and income. The maintenance of high demand, therefore, became the central object of his economic policy. This entailed two things: managing the economy by government and managing by manipulating demand.

Looking at the world as it existed when Keynes matured and began studying and writing about economics, it is easy to see how he came to the conclusion of an inherently unstable economy. There were many booms and busts in the United States in its formative industrial years during the late nineteenth and early twentieth centuries. And if these cycles weren't enough, the Great Depression, during which his General Theory was written, probably provided sufficient evidence to Keynes that the economy needed some guidance from government.

However, we have learned a lot about economic theories and policies during the past half century. Those deficiencies in the system that produced booms and busts such as the absence of a central bank, reliance on a gold standard whose liquidity-creating abilities were not consonant with the economy's needs and, in general, a lack of understanding of when to run budget surpluses and when not to, have been largely remedied. The creation of the Federal Reserve, along with the end of the gold standard, and the development of such automatic stabilizers as unemployment insurance, Social Security and welfare sharply reduced the economy's tendency toward instability.

As it has been translated into specific policy, the one aspect of Keynesian economics that we have followed over the years, demand management, is one that should be put aside at this time. Demand management economics might have been appropriate for an era when the economy was performing well below par and needed the stimulus of government to stimulate it. However, today's problem is not a lack of demand, but rather, insufficient supplies of goods—and more important, new productive machinery.

The Keynesian notion that supply increases will follow demand increases no longer holds true in a period of high inflation and high interest rates, both of which represent tremendous disincentives for business to invest. What is needed is a "new" economic policy that stresses supply instead of demand. ironically, this "new" economics is not new but rather, is very old—as old as Adam Smith himself. This is because its focus is on economic growth through the encouragement of investment and production, and it sees such growth arising from a free response to the economic incentives of a free market. What is more, it believes that only the private sector can bring us sustained growth, thus there is a need to reduce the role of the public sector.

. . . AND WHAT SHOULD BE DONE

Therefore, before we pin the pro- or anti-Keynes labels on ourselves,— or, for that matter, before we discard Keynes altogether—we should remember that one aspect of Keynesian economics that has *not* been used (budget surpluses in good times; deficits in bad times) is still relevant, while another of his theories that *has* been followed (government interference in the economy through the vehicle of demand management) is no longer appropriate. In other words, the rules of economics still work— provided that we know what they are and follow them.

3

Will It Work?*

IRWIN L. KELLNER

Contrary to the belief expressed in some quarters, President Reagan's economic proposals are neither an outright repeal of the economic theories of John Maynard Keynes, nor are based entirely on a new, untested economic theory. Rather, they are an amalgam of old and new. As such, the President's proposals are not as risky as their critics assert. On the other hand, their likelihood of success may not be as great as the Administration hopes.

KEYNES RESURRECTED

First and foremost in the President's plan is the need to balance the Federal government's budget. The President wants to do this in order to make the Federal Reserve's job of slowing money growth easier. That is—when the budget is in or near balance, the Federal Reserve can slow the rate of increase of money and credit without precipitating a credit squeeze. And as I will discuss below, slower money growth is the *sine qua non* for permanently reducing the rate of inflation.

As I pointed out in my November Economic Report, Keynes never directly attacked the classical notion that the Federal government's budget must be in balance. He was very much in favor of balanced budget during periods in which the economy was growing. He advocated the use of a budget deficit to provide unemployment relief during peri-

*Reprinted with permission from *The Manufacturers Hanover Economic Report*, February 1981.

ods in which the level of employment declined. However, he did not place great emphasis on the implications of a budget deficit beyond that of stimulating the economy. This is because he believed that deficits should not be used as a main tool of economic policy, and when they were they were to be used during periods of economic slack. The record of the postwar years shows that we have departed from Keynes's basic notion of running deficits in bad times and surpluses in good times. The last time we had a surplus in the Federal government's budget was in 1969; the time before that was 1960. In the 37 years since the end of the second World War, we have had deficits in 29.

The President has wisely recognized the implications of this spate of budget deficits. Not only has it forced the Federal Reserve to expand the supply of money and credit faster than the economy's ability to grow thus producing the basis for inflation, it has opened the door for the Federal government to intrude in many aspects of American life. The "buy now, pay later" budget system that characterized fiscal policy during most of the postwar era provided a boon to elected officials. Politicians began parading before the American people, promising everything without presenting a bill. There always seemed to be Federal money available to remedy whatever local ailment existed. Little wonder that we got into the economic mess that the President says we are in today. Thus, far from repealing Keynes, I would say that the President is adhering to one of Keynes's basic tenets—the use of budget deficits only to provide unemployment relief.

MONETARISM RETAINED

Another aspect of the President's economic plan deals with monetary policy. The Administration would like the Federal Reserve to restrain money growth. Quoting from the President's State of the Union message: ". . . Our plan requires a national monetary policy which does not allow money growth to increase consistently faster than the growth of goods and services. In order to curb inflation, we need to slow the growth in our money supply. We will . . . vigorously pursue budget policies that'll make (the Federal Reserve's) job easier in reducing monetary growth. A successful program to achieve stable and moderate growth patterns in the money supply will keep both inflation and interest rates down and restore vigor to our financial institutions and markets."

There is nothing new and untested about this aspect of the President's plan. It takes into account what monetarists in particular and most economists in general have said for a long time: The basic, fundamental cause of inflation is too much money chasing too few goods. While individual prices change all the time, the overall price level can only go up if there is an excess amount of money and credit in circulation. Through the years, the Fed has had difficulty holding money growth to the growth of real goods and services. This is because of the influence of the Federal government and its policy of running budget deficits year after year. When the Federal government runs a deficit in its budget, it has to borrow to make up the difference, just like when you or I spend more than we take in. The Treasury, being the top-rated borrower, gets the first shot at the credit markets, and everybody else has to fall in line for the rest. As I observed before there have been only eight times since the end of World War II in which the Treasury did not have to increase its borrowing from the financial markets, because there were eight surpluses in the budget. The rest of the times there were deficits.

Because the economy generates only a certain amount of loanable funds each year, the more the government borrows, the less is available for the private sector. This does not affect the top-rated corporations, which have access to funds from various sources. It does affect those at the bottom of the credit totem pole, where people like you and I might stand if we were buying a house, a car or any other item that requires credit. If the Federal Reserve stood idly by and did not replenish the money that Washington took out at the top, we would get closed out of the markets. In this situation, a money panic would ensue, interest rates would go sky-high; a credit crunch would develop followed by widespread business failures and bankruptcies.

Because the Fed was created to put an end to the repeated panics that caused the economy to have many severe downturns, and because the Fed, like the Supreme Court during Franklin Delano Roosevelt's era, reads the newspapers, it has felt constrained to provide additional liquidity to the financial markets so that the private sector can get what it wants after the public sector has financed its needs. This is why the Federal Reserve over the years has produced more money than the economy has goods. In turn, this is why we have the inflation rates that we do. Quoting from testimony that Paul A. Volcker, chairman of the Federal Reserve, gave last year before Congress, "There is little doubt that inflation can not persist in the long run unless it is accompanied by excessive expansion of money and credit." To this the monetarists would add: Control the quantity of money and you control inflation. The President is relying on the Fed to do just that, hence my statement that he is drawing from monetarism in the construction of his economic plan.

SUPPLY MANAGEMENT "DISCOVERED"

One of the greatest misconceptions perpetrated by the popular press is the notion that supply-side economics is new. Nothing could be further from the truth! Supply-side economics has its roots in no less a person than the classical economist, Adam Smith. Some 200 years ago, Smith warned that "high taxes, sometimes by diminishing the consumption of the taxed commodities and sometimes by encouraging smuggling, afford a smaller revenue to government than what might be drawn from more moderate taxes." Another classical economist, Jean Baptiste Say, in his Law of Markets, developed the notion that "supply creates its own demand." This theory holds that there can never be a serious and continuing shortage of purchasing power because production automatically returns to producers the wherewithal to buy the goods that are produced. If goods are left unsold, the classical economists argued, prices would fall to the level where all the items would evenually be sold. Moreover, the presence of unsold goods means that consumption is falling and savings are rising. The increase in savings, in turn, forces interest rates down and pushes investment up. Thus slack in consumption is automatically offset by investment. Classical theory, therefore, holds that the cyclical ups and downs of an economy are merely phases in the process of an adjustment that tends toward full employment.

The Great Depression, with its lack of demand amid plentiful supplies, scotched this theory. Prices did not fall very rapidly, and savings failed to generate offsetting investment. Keynes argued that a shortage of purchasing power could grow progressively worse as consumers cut back expenditures and business responded by curtailing production and investment. Indeed, the economy could settle at exceedingly depressed levels of economic activity and high unemployment. This led him to come up with the notion that the government could boost demand by spending more than it takes in. In other words—Keynes believed that demand creates its own supply.

This worked for a while—until deterrents developed and began to outweigh the incentives created by increased demand. One of these deterrents was inflation, caused by years of deficit spending. Besides boosting interest rates, inflation distorted corporate balance sheets and pushed individuals into higher tax brackets. Thus our tax code, which at one time was neutral in its effects on investment conditions, had become a significant deterrent by retarding capital formation. In subsequent years other deterrents appeared. Businessmen became concerned with energy availability, the threat of controls and ever increasing rules and regulations.

Several years ago a study by the Joint Economic Committee of Congress recommended removing these deterrents in order to slow inflation without having to keep economic growth at a reduced level. Signed by conservatives and liberals, Republicans and Democrats alike, this unanimous report was remarkable in its espousal of supply-side economics. Focusing on economic growth through the encouragement of investment and production, supply-side economists see such growth arising from a free response to the economic incentives of a free market. What is more, they believe that only the private sector can bring us sustained growth, thus there is a need to reduce the role of the public sector. This hardly seems like a new, untested economic theory.

Central to the supply-siders in the Reagan Administration is a change in tax rates. The aim of President Reagan's tax cut is to stimulate supplies—not demand, as has been the case in the past. High tax rates are seen as a roadblock to economic growth, as a disincentive to labor and capital. The Administration is trying to alter economic behavior by expanding the rewards for production. People will have the incentive to work harder if they can keep more of their incremental wages. This would be accomplished by people working overtime, withdrawing from tax shelters, foregoing consumption, rejecting leisure, selling gold, purchasing stocks, starting a business, taking extra training or otherwise accepting additional risk to earn more money. Not only are workers supposed to work harder for incremental dollars, but investors are supposed to limit their consumption in order to earn more dollars in the future. The tax cuts are supposed to reduce the rewards of sheltering income from taxes through investments in untaxable activities or through work "off the books."

To me, this aspect of supply-side economics makes a lot of sense. As I have said in the past, we have long paid too much attention to demand management and not enough to conditions that generate increased supplies. More supplies of goods and services will not only hold down inflation by matching demand, but the newer, more modern machinery and equipment that produces these goods, by increasing labor productivity, will further help slow the rate of inflation by providing an important offset to ongoing wage increases.

So far so good. These three aspects of the President's economic plan are neither new in nature nor unreasonable in objectives. If and as the budget is brought into balance, the Fed will be able to slow money growth without precipitating a credit squeeze and high interest rates. This will allow the rate of inflation to slow while at the same time removing a major deterrent to new investment in the form of high interest rates. With an assist from tax cuts aimed at generating increased supplies, this new investment will bring forth a faster rate of growth for the economy, more goods and services, more jobs and profits. It is when we get to the fourth part of the basis for the President's economic proposals that I encounter some difficulty. Interestingly, this is the "new" aspect that I referred to at the outset.

RATIONAL EXPECTATIONS: NEW AND RISKY

Simply stated, rational expectations theory suggests that individuals respond not only to specific stimulus connected with actual events, but also to expectations about the future effects of current events and policies. To me, this is separate from the other theories that the President has espoused. This is because entirely different results can be predicted if one has reason to believe that the public's attitude will change, for whatever the reason.

For example, tax cuts are normally viewed as contributing to additional expenditures by those receiving the tax relief. If these cuts were to be considered as a means toward reducing inflation, people would not spend more, they would save more, instead. As for investors, they would shift their preferences from precious metals, real estate and other tangible assets to such financial assets as corporate bonds and Treasury securities, if they thought inflation was set to recede. This portfolio shift would increase the supply of funds to the capital markets so that interest rates would not rise—even if the Federal Reserve maintained a very tight rein on money growth.

This increase in savings and investment is supposed to work in the following way: First, if people really believe that inflation will abate, they will be less tempted to buy goods simply to avoid paying higher prices later. At the same time, they (and others with investable funds) would view the current level of interest rates as a great investment opportunity, since less inflation usually brings with it lower interest rates. Thus they would buy government and corporate bonds either for their high rate of return, or with the hope of selling later with a capital gain. Either way, this theory goes, the cut in government revenues that would accompany a reduction in taxes would be financed largely out of savings and not by the Federal Reserve creating new money.

For this to work, two key elements must occur. The first is that an across-the-board tax cut must be enacted. This would allocate much of the benefits toward the upper income groups that pay the most taxes and have the greatest propensity to save. If the President's tax cut proposals are altered by Congress so that upper-income families don't get as much tax relief as the President would like, it is possible that, rather than savings, consumption might be stimulated, since the tax cuts would be going largely to those with the greatest tendency to consume.

More important is the notion that people have to believe that the government will be able to reduce inflation. It is here that I have even more difficulty, since there has been a general distrust of government in recent years. I guess this goes back to the Vietnam War, and the efforts by President Johnson to conceal its scope from the American people while he was escalating it. In the 1970s people did not believe the government when it told them there was an energy crisis. People in the parched Northeast don't believe their local governments today when they tell them that water supplies are dangerously low. And, I would bet, a good many people don't believe that President Reagan will be able to balance the budget any more than his predecessor, Jimmy Carter, who "promised" the electorate in 1976 that he would balance the budget by 1980.

Plainly, if the people do not believe that the President's policies will slow inflation, then they will spend, not save, and will not provide the wherewithal for the increased budget deficit to be financed. In the absence of this increased savings, one of two things will happen: Either the Federal Reserve will stand fast, in which case interest rates will rise, choking off both investment and consumption, or if the Fed accommodates, then inflation expectations will worsen with the same negative effects.

To make matters worse, many people have grown to accept inflation as a way of life, and have made significant adjustments to it. These include such people as those whose incomes are linked to the consumer price index, people who have bought homes, people who borrow money and even people who lend money and save money. It would seem to me that the President has to recognize that he has to address this "inflation constituency" first, and convince people that inflation is something that should not be adjusted to, before he can get people to believe that the government is really going to slow its pace.

In the main, I think that if the President's program survives the inevitable alterations by Congress, it stands a pretty good chance of succeeding. However, its probability of success would be greater if less attention were paid to the relatively new and untested rational expectations theory and more emphasis were placed on the traditional, well-known and respected theories of balancing the budget, slowing money growth and providing additional economic incentives for business investment. It has taken a long time for the public to become aware of inflation and especially the government's role in it. I don't think it is reasonable to assume that the public's attitude is going to change overnight—especially on the basis of words, as opposed to deeds.

It would seem to me that people will change their attitudes toward inflation and the expectation of inflation only when they see a fiscal policy that contains a credible schedule for reducing the budget deficit, and a monetary policy that follows up with progressively lower growth targets for the supply of money and credit. If and as this occurs, it will first show up in a reduction of interest rates in both the short- and the long-term markets, for financial market participants will then demand less of an inflation premium for commitments of funds. At this point, it would be safe for the Administration to ask the Congress to pass its program of across-the-board tax cuts. For only then will there be a chance that people will save the proportion of the tax cut that its proponents hope for, in order to prevent the resulting increased budget deficit from forcing either interest rates or the rate of inflation higher.

4

Excerpts from Congressional Hearing On the 1980 Mid-Year Review of the Economy*

Opening Statement of Senator Bentsen, Chairman

Senator Bentsen. Mr. Schultze, we are going to start this hearing on time. I know you've got a tight schedule.

Let me say this is the first of two hearings to be held by the Joint Economic Committee on the Midyear Review of the Economy. We will also look at today's figures in the Consumer Price Index for June. Our witness this morning is the Honorable Charles L. Schultze, Chairman of the Council of Economic Advisers.

Mr. Schultze, this is an election year, and history shows that in election years most Presidents up for reelection tend to let economic policy be molded by political needs. So when you find a President who has made up his mind about the economy and what he wants to achieve, and then sticks to his plan regardless of what the polls or his opponents say, you have to admire the President whether or not you agree with every aspect of the plan.

I think President Carter ought to be commended for resolving not to play politics with our economy.

During the recent past, our economy has been wracked by an inflation that reached an 18-percent annual rate during the first 3 months of the year. President Carter decided on a program of fiscal and monetary restraint to fight that inflation, and he has stuck with that program. Now, whether or not this is good politics, we are not going to know until November. Whether or not it is good economics is a question we want to address today, particularly in light of the deepening recession.

One of my main concerns is the shortrun issues that may divert our attention from the important longrun aspects of economic policy. The tax cut issue, which has been injected into this campaign, is an excellent example.

For the past 2 years, the Joint Economic Committee has argued that an investment-oriented tax cut is needed in order to improve our productivity and to help reduce the

---

*Reprinted from Document 67-472 0, "The 1980 Midyear Review of the Economy," from *Hearing Before the Joint Economic Committee*, Congress of the United States, July 23, 1980.

underlying rate of inflation. That is the way you really get it down, by putting more goods on the shelf at a cheaper price, and by producing them more efficiently.

The most recent forecast by Data Resources, Inc., indicates that you are going to have a real investment decline in our economy of 11.9 percent during this recession. And that shows that investment stimulus is needed now more than ever.

Although President Carter opposes a tax cut, I believe our differences are more a matter of form than a matter of substance. I am not arguing for a tax cut that would stimulate the economy, because I don't believe that, at this late date, we can have a tax cut that is going to have any effect on the timing of this recession's end. What we do need, though, is a tax cut that will give us a much higher quality and a much less inflationary-prone recovery than the recovery from the 1974-75 recession.

I believe we can enact a tax cut this year. I think we should. Or we can wait until next year, as President Carter advocates. But in either case, at least half that cut ought to go for stimulating new investment and improving productivity. That is what this committee has been saying for a long time. And our recommendation still holds on that, Mr. Schultze, and we would like to hear your testimony now.

I would like to insert for Congressman Brown, ranking minority member, at his request, who will be along in a minute, his opening statement in the record at this point.

[The opening statement follows:]

Opening Statement of Representative Brown

We sit here today to perform a postmorten on the balanced budget of 1981. It was stillborn. Everyone outside the administration knew it would be. If the administration does not at long last learn something from this autopsy, if the administration does not take action, we shall soon be performing the last rites for the whole U.S. economy.

The great tragedy is that the inflation and the recession were both totally unnecessary. Economists outside the administration have warned against excessive spending and money creation in each year of the Carter administration. But we had the inflation anyway, because the administration blamed OPEC and American workers and businesses instead, and pretended its own policies were not involved.

Then we had quantum leaps in taxes and in regulations. Economists outside the administration warned that this was leading to recession, and that there was no hope of a balanced budget in a recession. But again the administration blamed OPEC, and the American people, and pretended its own policies were not involved, and pretended the budget would be in balance long after everyone knew better.

For 2 years the Joint Economic Committee has been warning against all of these excesses. The administration has ignored all of these warnings.

Any modest attempt to control Federal spending, by taking just 3 to 5 percent off each of the last three budgets, would have reduced spending and money growth enough to have avoided this inflation. And the $25-$30 billion in noninflationary supply side tax cuts recommended by Senator Bentsen and myself in a joint news conference more than a year ago, and urged by many leading economists, and by this committee, would have prevented this recession.

Tax cuts are not all alike. They are not all inflationary. There are many ways to cut individual taxes to encourage saving. Saving is anti-inflationary and pro-growth.

The same thing applies to business tax cuts. This committee heard from the Chairman of the SEC and the Chairman of the Financial Accounting Standard Board that inflation has drastically increased business taxes, crippled depreciation, and strangled investment. This has been known for years. And for 2 years the Congress has been ready to do something about deprecaition, only to be blocked by the administration. The administration has nit-picked every congressional depreciation proposal to death.

The administration has had 3½-years to come up with a savings and depreciation proposal of its own. I am tired of this dog-in-the-manger attitude. There is something much, much worse than a slightly-less-than-perfect depreciation bill—and that is no depreciation bill at all.

The administration has addressed the issue of progrowth, anti-inflationary personal and corporate tax reduction with all the vigor and flexibility of advanced rigor mortis.

If this administration is defeated in November, it will be because it has understood nothing, learned nothing, admitted nothing, and done nothing about the economy of this country.

Senator Bentsen. Please proceed, Mr. Schultze.

STATEMENT OF HON. CHARLES L. SCHULTZE, CHAIRMAN, COUNCIL OF ECONOMIC ADVISERS, ACCOMPANIED BY DAVID MUNRO, SENIOR STAFF ECONOMIST

Mr. Schultze. Thank you, Mr. Chairman, and thank you for those remarks. I guess, given those remarks, I am pretty close together with you on your remarks as you are pretty close together with us on policy. And where we differ is, I think, a matter of technical judgment.

pretty close together with us on policy. And where we differ is, I think, a matter of technical judgment.

I also welcome the emphasis which you placed, Mr. Chairman, and I think properly placed, and which your committee has placed for some time, on looking at our problems in the longer run perspective. In fact, if I may, I'd like to put my testimony in that context. While this Mid-Session Budget Review that the President has sent to the Congress is an occasion to review the short-term economic outlook, and I will do that for the committee, I'd like to put that in the context of a longer term review, and very briefly do so by looking backward at it through the decade of the 1970's and maybe forward to the decade of the 1980's.

Controlling the Growth of Demand Through Monetary and Fiscal Policy

If inflation is to be reduced in the long run, monetary and fiscal policies have to be geared toward reducing the growth of total public and private spending combined. That is, over time we must reduce the growth of nominal GNP, GNP measured in current dollars.

Now in one sense this is simply a truism, it's arithmetic. The rate of growth of nominal GNP is simply equal to the rate of growth of output, plus the rate of growth of inflation. If, for example, real output grows by 3 percent and inflation is 10 percent, then the money value of the GNP, or nominal GNP, is going to grow by 13 percent.

Given a fairly steady advance in real output, a long-term reduction in inflation necessarily requires a decline in the growth of total spending measured in dollar terms. That is, it requires a decline in the growth of nominal GNP, but it's more than a truism. There's a momentum to inherited inflation as prices and wages chase each other, influenced by expectations about inflation in the future. Unless some force actively works against that inherited inflation, it tends to keep going unabated. The longrun reduction of the underlying rate of inflation requires that economic policy aim on the average to produce restraint on the growth of spending and thus a decline in the annual growth of nominal GNP.

This need for long-term restraint in monetary and fiscal policy doesn't imply that policies can't respond to changes in economic conditions, but, on the average, more restraint and greater caution will be required over the years than would have been warranted or required, were we in a period of price stability.

In that context, long-term supply and structural policies take on a new meaning. Supply-side economics is not an alternative to demand restraint, but it is a complement. To the extent that supply and structural policies can speed up productivity, reduce the growth of costs and increase the competitiveness and flexibility of the economy, they thereby reduce inflationary momentum. The long-term demand restraint that's necessary to lower inflation becomes more and more compatible with the sizable growth in output and employment. Or, to say it another way, to the extent we can speed up the growth of supply and increase the flexibility of the economy, the needed slowdown in nominal GNP can result in quicker reductions in inflation and faster growth in output.

Similarly, the long-term anti-inflation requirement for demand restraint has important implications for any tax measures which might be adopted to help speed recovery. In particular, it is not enough to pay attention to the immediate year's budgetary consequences of a proposed tax reduction. It's essential that the longer term revenue losses be carefully evaluated in terms of budget prospects over a number of years in the future.

You have to bend over backward to assure that the out-year revenue losses from any proposed tax reduction are consistent with long-term fiscal and budgetary restraint. Otherwise, immediate gains in output and employment from such a cut may be dissipated in later years by renewed inflationary pressures.

Let me spend just a moment on supply and structural policy. A substantial and a durable increase in the flexibility of the American economy and the growth of its productivity will require a number of supply and structural measures over the years ahead. Among these will be policies, some of which have already been enacted, to adjust our economy to higher energy prices and reduce its vulnerability to supply and price decisions made abroad.

Improving long-term economic performance also demands a continuation of deregulation and regulatory reform efforts already underway. Mr. Chairman, it will most assuredly require us to take steps to increase the Nation's capital formulation. We do not know all the reasons for the recent decline in the growth of American productivity, but we do know that reversing that trend will demand significant increases in the share of the Nation's output devoted to investment. That investment share will have to grow in the 1980's for a number of reasons. There will be substantial new needs for direct investment in alternative energy sources. The adjustment to higher energy prices will also levy substantial investment requirements on the economy indirectly, as the Nation replaces large parts of its capital stock made obsolete by higher energy prices. Environmental and related objects will continue to require significant investment.

In addition to all of these requirements, we have to speed up the increase in capital stock per worker as a prerequisite to an increase in the growth of productivity.

It is not likely that the requisite investment will be forthcoming without tax measures aimed at increasing investment incentives. Restraint in Federal spending, if steadfastly pursued, will free national resources for such use through tax reductions to increase investment.

Mr. Chairman, we have to recognize that supply-side economics cannot provide a quick and painless way to cure inflation and speed growth. We cannot raise Federal revenues by cutting taxes. Federal revenues do indeed tend to rise year after year as nominal incomes grow. In the year after a typical tax cut, revenues will usually continue to rise since tax cuts are seldom large enough to offset the effect of income growth.

Senator Bentsen. Mr. Schultze, this committee at no time has said that supply-side economics is going to bring us a quick and painless way to cure inflation and speed up growth. We didn't get into this mess overnight, and we're not going to get out of it overnight. It's going to take some time, and it's going to take some very targeted tax cuts to go on that path. We've got to look beyond this next election to the years ahead.

It will not be a dramatic turnaround. Unfortunately, there's just no quick fix that anyone's been able to find.

Mr. Schultze. Mr. Chairman, I couldn't agree more, and I am sure you are aware that I know enough about what this committee has done that these remarks were not addressed to this committee.

But on the other hand, I think you're also aware that there have been a number of claims made with respect of pulling oneselt up by one's bootstraps, free lunches, and the like.

Senator Bentsen. Well, this is an election year.

Mr. Schultze. Mr. Chairman, those who do say that a tax reduction will increase GNP by such a large amount as to eliminate the revenue loss simply haven't looked at the arithmetic, if I may spend one more paragraph on this. I'm speaking to the converted, I realize.

Roughly speaking, an additional dollar of GNP will produce about 20 to 25 cents of additional revenue. That is, the relationship is about 1 to 4 or 5. So a $40 billion tax cut must generate $160 to $200 billion of additional GNP to provide enough additional income so that the initial tax loss is wiped out, and, of course, it doesn't do any good to produce hundreds of billions in additional spending unless it is matched by hundreds of billions of additional supply. Otherwise, we will simply get inflation. There's absolutely no body of evidence which suggests that for $1 of tax cuts, however carefully designed, we can expect $4 to $5 of increase in the GNP supplied to the economy.

Mr. Chairman, as I said earlier, this administration is deeply concerned by the economic prospects that face the Nation. The prospective rise in unemployment and the fact that it fails to decrease in 1981, is highly troubling because of the human suffering it entails, the social dangers it poses, and the debilitating effect of prolonged slow growth on investment and productivity. The rate of inflation that we foresee for 1981 and future years will also be too high in the absence of further policies to correct the situation. We intend, therefore, Mr. Chairman, to work closely with Congress toward the development of policies on both the demand and supply side of our economy to meet the problems I have outlined.

With respect specifically to taxes, Mr. Chairman, the administration believes that a tax cut may turn out to be appropriate and desirable in 1981. But by waiting to make a final decision we gain several important advantages.

First, we will have a better picture of the economic situation on which to base judgments about the magnitude and pattern of a tax program.

Second, before deciding on the magnitude of a tax reduction we ought to make sure that the spending restraints proposed by the President last March and contained in the first concurrent resolution of the Congress are actually being achieved.

Finally, and most importantly, we think we will get a much better tax cut by taking the time for responsible action. The tax cut we want must be a carefully designed part of a long-range economic improvement program, not simply a traditional antirecession fix. As I have been at pains to point out, we need to pay close attention to both demand-side and supply-side economic and to make sure that any tax reduction does not have excessive "out year" costs.

Otherwise, by violating the demand-side conditions of economic policy, that tax cut will lead to inflation. Tax burdens are rising and will need to be reduced. But it is absolutely essential in the long run, however, that when tax burdens are reduced, we put additional dollars back into the private economy in a way which accomplishes long-term structural objectives.

Mr. Chairman, I'll take your questions.

Senator Bentsen. Thank you very much, Mr. Schultze.

[The prepared statement of Mr. Schultze follows:]

Prepared Statement of Hon. Charles L. Schultze

The Mid-Session Review of the Budget offers a time to review the economic outlook and to take stock of where our economy is. I will of course set forth the immediate economic outlook and prospects facing our country, but I would like to put those economic problems and challenges in a longer-term context by looking backward at the developments of the 1970's and forward to the challenges for policy in the 1980's. . . .

This set of facts has an important implication that we should bear in mind when designating policies to improve what would otherwise be an unsatisfactory recovery: The problem of the U.S. economy is not an inability to generate large increases in jobs and production. Indeed, in this respect we have far outperformed other major countries. Rather, our problem is to produce additional jobs in ways that are consistent with a simultaneous reduction of the inflation and an increase in productivity. The major challenge therefore is not to produce a traditional short-run economic stimulus aimed solely at increasing sales and output but a longer-run tax and economic program that, in the process of generating jobs, also contributes toward lower inflation and higher productivity.

I would like to discuss briefly with you some of the considerations which ought to go into the design of a longer term economic policy aimed at improving performance.

While the rate of inflation has been brought down substantially from the 13 percent of 1979 and the 18 to 20 percent of early this year, the core or underlying rate of inflation probably now runs at something like 9 to 10 percent a year. The most important task of economic policy will be to encourage a healthy growth in jobs and output during the economic recovery while at the same time unwinding that underlying rate of inflation which remains far too high. Meeting this very challenging objective will require two approaches:

First, long-run monetary and fiscal policies to control the growth of spending, to keep reasonable restraint on the growth of aggregate demand in the economy, and so to help bring about a gradual slowdown in the growth of hourly wages, salaries, and other costs;

Second, supply and structural policies designed to raise productivity and efficiency and to increase the rate at which output and employment can increase without setting in motion inflationary pressures.

In other words, we need to have both demand policies and supply policies.

Controlling the Growth of Demand Through Monetary and Fiscal Policies

If inflation is to be reduced in the long run, the Nation's monetary and fiscal policies must be geared toward reducing the growth of total public and private spending. That is, we must over time reduce the growth of nominal GNP. In one sense this is simply a truism. The rate of growth of nominal GNP is equal to the growth of output plus the rate of inflation. If, for example, real output grows by 3 percent and inflation is 10 percent, then nominal GNP will grow by 13 percent. Given a fairly steady advance in real output, a long-term reduction in inflation necessarily requires a decline in the growth of total spending measured in dollar terms, that is a decline in the growth of nominal GNP.

But this is also more than a truism. There is a momentum to inherited inflation as prices and wages chase each other, influenced by expectations about inflation in the future. Unless some force actively works against that inherited inflation, it tends to keep going unabated. So if monetary and fiscal policy year after year simply aim at a continuation of the price year's growth in nominal GNP, or total spending, then inflation is likely to perpetuate itself. Indeed because our business-men, consumers, and financial markets have become infected with inflationary psychology after a decade of inflation, such a policy might lead to an acceleration of inflation. Long-run reduction of the underlying rate of inflation therefore requires that economic policy aims on the average, to produce restraint on the growth of spending and thus a decline in the annual growth of nominal spending.

This need for long-term restraint in monetary and fiscal policy does not imply that policies can-not respond to changes in economic conditions from year to year. However, on the average, more restraint and greater caution will be required over the years ahead than would have been warranted or required were we in a period of price stability.

In that context, long-term supply and structural policies take on new meaning. Supply-side eco-nomics is not an alternative to demand restraint, but a complement. To the extent that supply and structural policies can speed up productivity and reduce the growth of costs and increase the com-petitiveness and flexibility of the economy, they thereby reduce inflationary momentum. The long-term demand restraint that is necessary to lower inflation becomes more and more compatible with sizable growth in output and in employment. Or, to say it another way, to the extent that we

with sizable growth in output and in employment. Or, to say it another way, to the extent that we can speed up the growth of supply and increase the flexibility of the economy, the needed slow-down in nominal GNP can result in a quicker reduction in inflation and a faster growth in output.

Similarly, the long-term anti-inflation requirement for demand restraint has important implica-tions for any tax measures which might be adopted to help speed recovery. In particular, it is not enough to pay attention to the immediate year's budgetary consequences of a proposed tax reduc-tion. It is essential that the longer term revenue losses be carefully evaluated in terms of budget prospects over a number of years in the future. We must bend over backwards to assure that the "out-year" revenue losses from any proposed tax reduction are consistent with long-term fiscal and budgetary restraint. Otherwise, any immediate gain in output and employment from such a tax cut may be dissipated in later years by renewed inflationary pressures.

Supply and Structural Policies

A substantial and durable increase in the flexibility of the American economy and of the growth of its productivity will require a number of supply and structural policies over the years ahead. Among these will be policies—some of which have already been enacted—to adjust our economy to higher energy prices and to reduce its vulnerability to supply and price decisions made abroad. Improving long-term economic performance also demands a continuation of deregulation and regu-latory reform efforts already underway. It will most assuredly require that we take steps to increase the Nation's capital formation.

We do not know all of the reasons for the recent decline in the growth of American productiv-ity, but we do know that reversing that trend will demand significant increases in the share of the Nation's output devoted to investment. That investment share will have to grow in the 1980s for a number of reasons. There will be substantial new needs for direct investment in alternative energy sources. The adjustment to higher energy prices will also levy substantial investment requirements on the economy indirectly as the Nation replaces large parts of its capital stock made obsolete by higher energy prices. Environmental and related objectives will continue to require significant in-vestment. In addition to all of these requirements, we must speed up the increase in capital stock per worker as a prerequisite to an increase in the growth of productivity.

It is not likely that the requisite investment will be forthcoming without tax measures aimed at increasing investment incentives. Restraint in Federal spending, if steadfastly pursued, will free national resources for such use through tax reductions to increase investment.

However, we must all recognize that supply-side economics cannot provide a quick and painless way to cure inflation and speed growth. You cannot raise Federal revenues by cutting taxes. Federal revenues do indeed tend to rise year after year as nominal incomes grow. In the year after a typical tax cut, revenues will usually continue to rise since tax cuts are seldom large enough to offset the effect of income growth. Moreover, income growth tends to speed up somewhat after a tax cut so the net loss of revenues is less than the initial tax cut. But it is utter nonsense to attribute to the tax cut the absolute rise in revenues in the year after the cut was made. Faulty analysis of this point has plagued us ever since the 1964 tax cut.

Those who say that a tax reduction will increase GNP by such a large amount as to eliminate the revenue loss simply have not looked at the arithmetic. Roughly speaking, an additional dollar of GNP will produce about 20 to 25 cents of additional revenue. That is, the relationship is about one to four or five. A $40 billion tax cut, for example, must generate $160-$200 billion of additional GNP to provide enough additional income so that the initial tax loss is wiped out. Moreover, it does no good to produce additional spending unless it is matched by additional supply. Otherwise, we will simply get inflation. There is absolutely no body of evidence which suggests that for $1 of tax cuts, however, carefully designed, we can expect $4 to $5 of increase in GNP supplied to the economy.

Moreover, supply-side tax cuts cannot raise productivity by a large enough amount or quickly enough so that we can ignore the demand-increasing effect of such tax cuts. Investment-oriented tax reductions, by stimulating investment, can indeed improve the prospects s for productivity growth. But the payoff is a long-term one. The magnitude of the productivity improvements is likely to be moderate in terms of how far it reduces the inflation rate or raises the Nation's potential growth rate. Raising the historical 2 percent rate of productivity growth by say ½ percentage point represents a 25 percent increase in the productivity growth rate. It is unlikely to be achieved by some modest investment incentive. When realized it would itself tend to lower the underlying inflation rate from say 9 percent to say 8½ percent—a highly worthy but hardly revolutionary accomplishment. This country does need responsible measures to increase investment. But exaggerated claims, which suggest that we will get such a large supply response that we can ignore demand-side economics, do disservice to the cause of supply-side economics.

We cannot use supply-side tax cuts to escape the need for long-term demand restraint and for careful attention to the long-term budgetary consequences of tax reductions.

Mr. Chairman, as I said earlier, this Administration is deeply concerned by the economic prospects that face the Nation. The prospective rise in unemployment and the fact that it fails to decrease in 1981 is highly troubling because of the human suffering it entails, the social dangers it poses, and the debilitating effect of prolonged slow growth on investment and productivity. The rate of inflation that we foresee for 1981 and future years will also be too high in the absence of further policies to correct the situation. We intend, therefore, Mr. Chairman, to work closely with the Congress toward the development of policies on both the demand and supply side of our economy to meet the problems I have outlined.

With respect specifically to taxes, the Administration believes that a tax cut may turn out to be appropriate and desirable in 1981. But by waiting to make a final decision we gain several important advantages.

First, we will have a better picture of the economic situation on which to base judgements about the magnitude and pattern of a tax program.

Second, before deciding on the magnitude of a tax reduction we ought to make sure that the spending restraints proposed by the President last March and contained in the First Concurrent Resolution of the Congress are actually being achieved.

Finally, and most importantly, we will get a much better tax cut by taking the time for responsible action. The tax cut we want must be a carefully-designed part of a long-range economic improvement program, not simply a traditional anti-recession stimulus. As I have been at pains to point out, we need to pay attention to both demand-side and supply-side economics; and to make sure that any tax reduction does not have excessive "out-year" costs. Otherwise, by violating the demand-side conditions of economic policy, that tax cut will lead to inflation. Tax burdens are rising and will need to be reduced. But it is absolutely essential to the long-run health of our economy that when tax burdens are reduced we put additional dollars back into the private economy in a way which accomplishes long-term structural objectives.

5

The Bankruptcy of
Keynesian Economic Models*

MICHAEL K. EVANS

Keynesian models cannot deal with current economic ills because they
concentrate on questions of demand. We need models that stress the
supply side, centering on the stimulation of productivity.

The U.S. economy is in sad shape. The rate of inflation is at an all-
time postwar high, and we are now in the beginning phases of a recession which promises to be more severe than the 1974-75 debacle. Unemployment and personal bankruptcies are up sharply. The value of the
dollar sways precariously, dependent on the whims of Arab potentates.
The personal "discomfort" index, defined as the sum of the rate of
inflation and the rate of unemployment, reaches new peaks every
month.

How did all this come about?

The complete answer goes all the way back to 1965, when we tried
to have massive tax cuts, the Great Society, and the Vietnam War all
at the same time. But much of the blame can be placed on the economic architects of the past three years.

During the latter half of 1976 the U.S. economy was neither well nor
sick. The growth rate slowed to a puny 3.3 percent, and the unemployment rate seemed to be stagnating at 8 percent. On the other hand, the
rate of inflation had diminished sharply from the 12.2 percent increase
of 1974 to an average rate of only 5.4 percent.

When confronted with this set of statistics, the Carter administration
decided that unemployment was the primary, if not the only, economic
problem they faced. Implicit in this decision were the assumptions that:

*Reprinted by permission of M. E. Sharpe, Inc., Armonk, N.Y. 10504, from *Challenge*, Jan-
uary-February 1980. Michael K. Evans is President, Evans Economics, Washington, D.C.

- Federal budget deficits didn't count. State and local governments and foreign central banks were willing to buy any additional government securities, since they had surpluses.
- A weaker U.S. dollar didn't count. Indeed, in a *bon mot* which ranks with Herbert Hoover's "prosperity is right around the corner," Treasury Secretary Blumenthal declared that "a weak dollar is good for America."
- Money supply growth didn't count. Monetary policy should accommodate the growth in the economy which would be caused by fiscal policy stimulus, and should not work to restrain this growth.
- Inflation didn't count, or at least not very much. Once the economy returned to full employment, we would begin worrying about a buildup of inflationary pressures.

Thus the Carter administration policy-makers viewed the economic problems of the country as unidimensional. They would cure high unemployment and handle everything else later.

The purpose of this preamble is not so much to make fun of the Carter economists, although they clearly are not blameless for what has transpired, as to indicate that they—and a goodly part of the entire economics profession—were basing their actions on forecasts which were far from the mark. For 1978, the average forecast for inflation was 6.1 percent, but the actual figure was 7.7 percent. Similarly, the 1979 forecast called for 7.6 percent inflation; yet the actual figure is now sure to be in excess of 11 percent.

MODELS AND MODEL-BUILDERS

The models which generated these forecasts can, in general, be considered Keynesian models. The purpose of using this term is not to debate whether each and every model faithfully follows the exact language which Keynes may or may not have used on page 236 of *The General Theory*; it is to indicate the type of model which is in accordance with the general tenets developed by Keynes. The most important of these may be summarized as follows: spending stimulates aggregate demand whereas savings retards it; when private sector demand slackens, it should be supplemented by greater public sector spending; demand can be increased without any noticeable effect on inflation; and an increase in government spending will stimulate the economy more than an equivalent decline in taxes.

As it turns out, the subpar performance of economic forecasters over the past two years has sent model-builders frantically scurrying to deny that their models really do embody these concepts. The new buzzword these days is "supply-side" economics. Taken at its face value, this term simply means that economists must take into account the ability of the economy to produce goods and services as well as the ability of consumers and businesses to purchase them. If income increases and consumers spend more, the economy is eventually going to run into capacity shortages and bottlenecks unless productive capacity increases apace. However, as might be expected, supply-side economics is a good deal more complicated than just a simply balancing algorithm between demand and production, and the rest of this article is an attempt to discuss some of these relationships and contrast them with the state of existing econometric models.

Before doing this, however, a small biographical insertion may be in order. Readers are always entitled to know the biases of the author, so let me clear up any lingering curiosity at the outset. I built the original version of the Wharton model, and subsequently built the macroeconomic models at Chase Econometrics. Thus two of the so-called "big three" econometric models contain defects for which I was responsible. On the other hand, as it began to become clear that these models were not equal to the task of predicting the current pattern of economic activity, my model-building horizon began to expand, and I was eventually selected by the Senate Finance Committee to construct a supply-side model. Much of what follows draws on the work which has already been completed on that project.

The fundamental problem which has plagued the U.S. economy for the past decade has been the slowdown in the growth of productivity. This slowdown has been responsible both for the higher rate of inflation and the lower rate of growth in real GNP. Productivity, or the amount of output per unit of labor input, increased about 3 percent a year during the first 20 years of the postwar period. Since then it has diminished to 1 percent a year, and has actually declined since 1977. Concomitantly, the annual rate of inflation has zoomed from 2 percent to 8 percent and the rate of growth has slowed to under 3 percent from an average 4 percent a year in the 1950s and 1960s.

Yet all the major econometric models currently used for forecasting and policy analysis have played down, if not ignored, the critical role of productivity in determining the economic environment. The effects of changes in policy variables such as government spending and personal and corporate income tax rates are measured primarily through changes in demand. Yet it is clear that demand-oriented policies, far from being able to reverse the productivity slowdown, have exacerbated it. Supply-side economics, on the other hand, deals with the effects of changes in fiscal and monetary policy on productivity and incentives. For example,

lower tax rates will not only increase spending by raising disposable in-
cme, but they will increase output by raising investment, productivity,
and work effort.

SPENDING AND SAVING

We now return to the four basic tenets of Keynesian models listed
above. First, in all existing models, spending stimulates demand whereas
saving retards it. Under this hypothesis, a redistribution of income from
upper-income to lower-income individuals through higher tax rates for
the rich and higher transfer payments for the poor would raise spending,
output, and employment, since poor people spend a larger proportion
of their income than rich ones do.

In terms of the initial impact—what happens right away—the above
statement is correct. Such a move would increase consumer spending,
which would raise output and result in the hiring of additional workers.
In the Keynesian models, that is the end of the story. Everyone is better off, with the possible exception of the rich who are left grumbling
about the inequity of the progressive income tax system.

If economist ever thought life was that simple, they certainly ought
to be disabused of that notion by now. The decline in savings does not
materialize out of thin air, but represents a reduction in assets which
would be used for productive purposes. Maybe, during the days of the
Great Depression when short-term interest rates were zero and occasionally even negative, the rich really did keep their money under the
mattress; and when taxes were raised they paid them with some of that
idle cash—although there is grave reason to doubt that even in the 1930s
this occurred. However, with interest rates at 15 percent it is clear that
no rational person keeps his money squirreled away at home. The decline in savings which would stem from higher taxes results in an increase in interest rates and a reduction in funds available for capital
formation.

Hence, the increase in taxes results in a decline in assets of the rich,
which reduces the flow of funds to the banking system, stock market,
and corporations. As a result, firms bid for a smaller available supply
of funds, and interest rates rise. Eventually this reduces capital formation and housing construction.

Even though this argument sounds logical, it is not accepted by large
numbers of economists, including most econometric model-builders.
First, it is argued that the rich will not reduce their savings because of
higher taxes but will simply reduce consumption by the same propor-

tion that the poor increase it, thereby leaving aggregate demand unchanged. Indeed, in existing models the rate of taxation has no independent effect on saving other than the changes it causes in disposable income. However, we have found that the personal saving rate is affected by the after-tax rate of return earned on savings, a result which may appear obvious but is not included in any of the existing macroeconomic models. In particular, a 10 percent reduction in tax rates would generate about a 2 percent increase in personal savings; this finding is in line with recent work done on the subject by Michael Boskin and others.

Even if personal savings are increased, these additional savings are not translated into a higher level of investment in many existing models. In these models either interest rates are determined by Federal Reserve policy rather than by fundamental demand and supply factors, or investment is unresponsive to changes in interest rates. But we have found that both these linkages are quite strong. An increase in savings will indeed lower interest rates, which in turn will raise investment.

In addition, the tax rate will affect work effort. If taxes are increased for upper-income individuals, they may decide to take more vacations or reduce the number of hours they work, particularly if they are independent professionals—doctors, lawyers, accountants, and so forth. Indeed, even at the lower end of the income scale, several studies have found a significant relationship between tax rates and work effort. In a number of income maintenance projects funded by the government, it was found that every 10 percent increase in tax rates resulted in about a 1 percent decline in the amount of labor offered. In some cases, employees chose to work fewer hours; in other cases, they simply dropped out of the labor force. Thus an increase in taxes may also lower the quality and quantity of labor supplied, which would reduce output even further.

Thus in existing econometric models, an increase in transfer payments (such as social security benefits or welfare payments) and an equal reduction in taxes generated by lower personal income tax rates would have the same effect on the economy. Since the amount of additional funds received by consumers is the same, the effect on consumption, output, and employment would also be identical.

The supply-side approach, however, claims that the results would be far different. An increase in transfer payments results in lower saving, once the increase in the federal budget deficit is taken into account, while a reduction in tax rates results in higher saving. Thus the combination of higher transfer payments and higher tax rates would result in lower investment and a slower growth in productivity. Finally, an increase in transfer payments would at best leave the amount of work effort unchanged and might diminish it, whereas a reduction in tax rates would actually improve it.

To look at the same phenomenon from a slightly different angle, an increase in transfer payments would raise total consumption without increasing total productive capacity. If excess slack existed in the economy, problems would not arise immediately, but as the economy approached full employment and capacity, it is clear that such a move would be inflationary. On the other hand, a tax cut would not only increase demand, but would at the same time provide additional stimulus to aggregate production. Thus the economy would exhibit balanced growth and inflationary pressures would not arise.

This logic has been vehemently attacked by many Keynesian economists, who argue that the increased demand will in and of itself generate an increase in labor supply and investment, since the demand for more goods will create the incentive for higher production. In this sense they are as intellectually deficient as the followers of Say's Law.

LAWS OF SAY AND KEYNES

Jean Baptiste Say was a nineteenth-century French economist who believed that supply created its own demand. According to Say and his disciples, we could never have recessions of any major duration, since if firms produced more goods, consumers would ultimately buy them and hence the economy would return to full employment. As might be expected, Say's Law sold at a heavy discount during the Great Depression and has never really recovered.

Before dismissing Say as a complete crank, it may be worth one brief paragraph to explain whatever logic lay behind his "law." Say's basic idea was that in order to produce goods it was necessary to purchase materials, hire labor, and invest in plant and equipment. The money spent for these inputs would be used by its recipients to purchase additional goods and services. If more workers were hired, labor income and hence consumption would rise. The fatal flaw in this argument occurs when individuals or businesses decide to shift their spending patterns, or when the value of their assets declines because of a stock market crash or bank closings.

In any case, Say's Law has, in many econometric models, been replaced by what has loosely become known as Keynes' Law, namely, that demand creates its own supply. Just as with Say's Law, the logical underpinnings can be defended to a point but it too contains a fatal flaw.

The logic behind Keynes' Law is that as demand rises, stimulated perhaps by government spending or an increase in handouts, the rate of return on invested capital will rise because firms will be producing more goods per unit of capital. As this happens, they will expand their productive facilities and thus increase total capacity. If more labor is needed, it can be attracted by offering higher wage rates. Thus productive capacity will increase apace with rising demand, and Keynes' Law is fulfilled.

It is indeed the case that investment will rise if output increases and other factors involving the rate of return are unchanged. Keynesian economics assumes this. However, as we have already pointed out, a decline in savings will raise the interest rate, which will reduce the equilibrium capital-output ratio, hence lowering rather than raising investment. In addition, if firms need to attract additional labor due to the combination of greater demand and lessened work effort, this will raise wages and unit labor costs, which leads to a higher rate of inflation.

LOW PRODUCTIVITY, HIGH INFLATION

The fatal flaw in Keynes' Law is that it ignores the effects of lower productivity and higher inflation. Inflation reduces the rate of growth for several reasons. First, it moves individuals into higher tax brackets, thereby reducing their real disposable income. Second, this reduction causes wage earners to bargain for larger raises, thus worsening the inflationary cycle. Third, it reduces investment through raising interest rates and lowering the real rate of return. Fourth, it worsens our net export position by making exports more expensive and imports relatively cheaper.

The first of these phenomena is well known to virtually all taxpayers and hence does not require an extended discussion. Consider a taxpayer with an income of, say, $30,000 who receives a 10 percent raise in a year in which the rate of inflation is also 10 percent. He has not kept abreast of inflation, for his marginal tax bracket has increased and the proportion of taxes to income has risen. Thus even if wage hikes keep up with price increases—as they have most asuredly not done in 1979, with wages lagging behind prices by some 5 percent—consumers are worse off with inflation and the present tax system.

Wage bargains are usually set so that workers keep even with rising prices; sometimes they also receive part of the increase in productivity, but since these increases have all but disappeared during the past decade, wage hikes are now designed primarily to keep workers abreast of inflation. However, since inflation pushes workers into higher tax brackets, they try to bargain for even larger increases, and the entire inflationary spiral is accelerated.

Conversely, if tax rates are cut, workers are better off if wages and prices rise by the same proportion. Consequently, they would not push quite as vigorously for further wage gains, hence slowing the inflationary spiral. Thus tax cuts also contribute to lower inflation by reducing the demands for wage increases. None of the existing econometric models contains this important link.

The argument that inflation causes lower investment hinges primarily on the fact that depreciation allowances are valued in terms of historical cost rather than replacement cost. As a result, when inflation rises, profits appear to increase in nominal terms—and firms must pay taxes on these increased profits. However, this phony accounting fools no one. Since the cost of replacing the capital good at the end of its useful life will far exceed the funds which have been accumulated for this purpose, firms must set aside additional funds from their profits in order to pay for replacement. But these funds must be set aside from aftertax dollars; the federal government first takes its 46 percent and state and local governments take about another 5 percent. Hence profits must rise about twice as fast as the rate of inflation in order for firms to generate sufficient reserves to buy replacement equipment at higher prices. If profits do not rise this rapidly, firms simply raise the required rate of return on any given investment project, which results in lower capital spending. This phenomenon has become particularly acute during the past five years, and as a result the ratio of productive capital spending to GNP has declined to its lowest level in the entire postwar period.

Finally, inflation reduces real growth by worsening our net foreign trade balance, since exports cost more and imports cost relatively less. Even demand-side models recognize this, but their answer—as echoed by former Secretary Blumenthal—is to redress the imbalance by lowering the value of the dollar. This turned out to be a colossal mistake. The dollar fell over 30 percent between mid-1977 and late 1978 relative to the Deutsche mark, the Japanese yen, and other strong foreign currencies. Yet the U.S. trade balance is still deeply in deficit and the inflationary impact of a lower dollar is now all too evident. For every 10 percent decline in the dollar relative to strong foreign currencies, wholesale prices increase about 1 percent and consumer prices rise about 0.5 percent. Thus the 30 percent decline which occurred added about 1.5 percent to inflation in 1978, with the effects continuing to spill over into 1979.

Thus we find that increasing aggregate demand without simultaneously providing adequate incentives for greater supply invariably leads to higher inflation, which retards real growth, output, and employment.

Since Keynesian models assume that higher demand will be automatically translated into higher supply, they do not incorporate the linkages which we have just described.

ROLE OF GOVERNMENT SPENDING

We now come to the last of the four major tenets given above, namely that government spending will lead to a larger increase in demand and output than an equivalent reduction in taxes. All of the popular econometric models incorporate this assumption, a fact recently documented in a study by the Congressional Budget Office.

Their reasoning is straightforward, if inaccurate. If the government increases its spending, the entire dollar goes for additional demand. If taxes are cut, however, some of the dollar is used for saving, and hence demand does not rise as much. Since savings are a useless residual and do not contribute to increased investment or lower inflation, the economic effect of tax changes is smaller.

Furthermore, these models also state that a personal income tax cut has a larger effect than a corporate income tax cut, and for much the same reason. Individuals spend a larger proportion of the extra money they get from reduced taxes than do corporations, and once again, that left-over saving does not contribute to economic growth or prosperity.

The supply-side work which we have undertaken gives exactly the opposite result: a corporate income tax cut has a larger effect on the economy than does a personal income tax cut, which in turn has a larger effect than an increase in government spending. The reasoning stems entirely from the supply-side effects, which we can enumerate and summarize as follows:

1. A reduction in tax rates increases the incentives of individuals to save by raising the rate of return on assets held by individuals. This higher savings leads to lower interest rates and higher investment.
2. Corporate tax rate cuts or similar measures, such as increasing the investment tax credit or liberalizing depreciation allowances, improve investment directly by increasing the average after-tax rate of return.
3. Higher investment leads to an increase in productivity, which means that more goods and services can be produced per unit of input. As a result, unit costs do not rise as fast and inflation grows more slowly.

4. The transfer of resources from the public to the private sector increases the overall growth rate in productivity, since productivity gains in the public sector are small or nonexistent.
5. The faster growth in productivity provides the needed capacity to produce additional goods and services demanded because of the tax cut, thus leading to balanced growth without bottlenecks or shortages.
6. Lower tax rates result in more modest demands for wage increases, since real income has risen by virtue of the tax cut and workers do not suffer a loss of real income by moving into higher tax brackets.
7. Lower inflation leads to an increase in real disposable income, and hence a rise in consumption, output, and employment.
8. Lower tax rates improve work effort, resulting in an increase in the quality and quantity of work. This in turn raises productive capacity still further, thereby contributing to the slowdown in the rate of inflation.
9. The lower rate of inflation causes an increase in net exports, which strengthens the value of the dollar. This leads to further reductions in the rate of inflation because imported goods decline rather than advance in price.
10. The increase in capacity also permits the production of more goods for export as well as domestic consumption, thereby providing additional strength for the dollar and less imported inflation.

NO ONE-DIMENSIONAL SOLUTION

One must be careful not to expect too much from reducing the rate of taxation on personal and corporate income. We are not subscribers to the theory that all of the ills of the economy can be cured simply by cutting taxes without regard to any of the other dimensions of fiscal or monetary policy. Solutions to economic problems are seldom unidimensional. We can no more cut taxes without restraining government spending than we could singlemindedly reduce the rate of unemployment, as was tried in 1977. To the extent that the increase in private sector saving generated by tax cuts if offset by a decrease in public sector saving, additional funds will not be available for investment. Thus tax cuts need to be accompanied by a reduction or at least a slower growth rate in government spending for the next several years. This was the critical ingredient missing in the original Kemp-Roth bill, and probably one of the major reasons why it did not pass.

However, even this solution is not admissible under old-style Keynesian models. For these models state that the efficacy of government spending is greater than tax cuts, and hence a simultaneous reduction in spending and taxes would lead to a decline in economic activity, output, and employment. Our results suggest that just the opposite is true. Inflation is raised by higher government spending but diminished by lower tax rates, and the total productive capacity of the economy expands with tax cuts but remains stagnant or oven contracts with higher government spending. Hence tax cuts will result in both faster growth and lower inflation than would be the case for an equivalent increase in government spending.

Our current policy-makers are so wedded to the past that a change in their behavior must be considered extremely unlikely in 1980. However, a fresh team of advisers in 1981, coupled with the availability of supply-side econometric models, suggests that we can at least look forward to more rational fiscal and monetary policies during the 1980s.

6

Kennedy's Supply-Side Economics*

WALTER W. HELLER

The goal was full employment, economic growth, and price stability. The means included supply-side measures like investment tax credits, liberalized depreciation rules, wage-price guideposts, and an initial restraint on tax cuts.

The economics of the Kennedy years and of the 1964 tax cuts have become a born-again issue in the current debate over President Reagan's economic program. As seen through the inverted prism of the supply-side revisionists, successful Kennedy tax cuts "prove" the case for broad-scale personal tax reduction as the key to a great leap forward in the economy's capacity to produce—in other words, as the key to self-financing and anti-inflationary tax cuts. As objectively as I can, and at the risk of repeating things I have been saying for nearly twenty years, let me review the rationale and record of Kennedy economics.

What was so new about the "New Economics," as the press quickly dubbed the Economics of the New Frontier in 1961? Not the theory— much of that went back nearly a quarter of a century to John Maynard Keynes. What *was* new, however, was the translation of modern economics into practice under the leadership of a willing and responsibe President (who, at the very outset, directed his Council of Economic Advisers to "return not just to the letter but to the spirit of the Employment Act of 1946").

*Walter W. Heller is Regents' Professor of Economics at the University of Minnesota, and was Chairman of the Council of Economic Advisers under Presidents Kennedy and Johnson. This article is adapted from remarks made to the Conference on the Presidency of John F. Kennedy, University of Southern California, November, 1980. Reprinted with permission of M. E. Sharpe, Inc., Armonk, N. Y. 10504, *Challenge*, May-June 1981.

THE MAIN ELEMENTS

The main elements of the new stamp that the Kennedy administration put on policy and policy-making were the following:

The translation of the fuzzy mandate of the Employment Act of 1946 to achieve "maximum employment, production, and purchasing power" into the concrete goals of full employment, price stability, more rapid growth, and external payments equilibrium (under the constraints of maintaining freedom of economic choice and promoting greater equality of economic opportunity).

• Even more important was the Council's conversion of the key qualitative goals into specific quantitative targets, and the President's endorsement of those targets. Thus, in place of a general but vague commitment to "full employment," the Kennedy administration adopted a specific target of 4 percent unemployment (at a time, by the way, when the 1960 recession had boosted unemployment to 7 percent). The target for economic growth—that is, the growth in the economy's potential to produce—was set at 4 percent per year in place of the 3 percent to 3.5 percent rate of growth in potential GNP in the Eisenhower years (and the 2.5 percent actual rate of expansion of real GNP in those years). As to price stability, the goal was to maintain the very low rate of inflation (just over 1 percent per year) left as a welcom legacy of the Eisenhower era at the heavy cost of three recessions in eight years, high unemployment, and low rates of growth. Once these numerical targets were adopted, they exerted a discipline on policy that the more abstract and qualitative goals could not achieve.

• Equally significant was the concomitant shift in policy focus from moderating the swings of the business cycle to achieving the full-employment potential of the economy. It was not enough simply to reverse recessions and temper expansions. Success was to be measured in terms of hitting a moving target, namely, the economy's rising full-employment potential. The point was to close the gap between actual and potential output, without triggering inflation.

• The concepts of full-employment potential and gap-closing were not brand new—they trace back to the bold and innovative Truman Council under the leadership of Leon Keyserling. But until Kennedy came along, the country never had a President who was willing to embrace such seemingly unorthodox doctrines and unabashedly move modern economics to the front burner.

• Also new and different was a positive policy of voluntary wage-price restraint. The Kennedy wage-price guideposts were introduced in January 1962 to induce labor and business to hold wage and price increases within the bounds of productivity advances and thus help ensure that fiscal-monetary stimulus would not run off into higher prices and wages but would instead express itself in higher output, jobs, profits, and investment. Indeed, the 1961-65 record shows that the guideposts played their part: wage increases in manufacturing stayed within the bounds of productivity increases, thus contributing to continued price stability and a sustained advance in real wages and living standards. Corporate profits doubled in those years.

• Less tangible, but no less important, was the orchestration of policy through skilled White House management, utilizing such instruments as the Troika (Treasury, Budget, and the Council of Economic Advisers [CEA]), and the Quadriad (adding in the Federal Reserve Chairman). Economic policy differences were ironed out and presented to Congress and the public as a united and coherent effort.

• The vital ingredient in this was the leadership by a sagacious President, quick to accept sound new thinking and to reject the old clichés that had hobbled policy. Banished were the beliefs that deficits in a weak economy were instruments of the devil and that public debt was a "burden on our grandchildren." John F. Kennedy was the first President to free us of these shibboleths, to relate budget-balance not to the calendar year but to full employment as a target, and thus to facilitate a more activist economic policy.

• Side by side with the new activism was the President's use of the White House "as a pulpit for public education in economics" (a use he urged on us even before his inauguration). Just as he advised his staff to explain and clarify the goals, concepts, and policies of the "New Economics" to the press, on television, and so on, the President himself provided a sense of direction through his own speeches to business and financial groups, national TV programs, press conferences, and the famous Yale commencement speech in June of 1962.

• Finally, one should mention the quality of economic thinking that President Kennedy attracted throughout his administration, not just in the CEA but in such outstanding economic and financial leaders as David Bell in the Budget Bureau, Douglas Dillon and Robert Roosa in the Treasury, and George Ball in the State Department. The CEA had as Council members Kermit Gordon, James Tobin, Gardner Ackley, and John Lewis; as staff members, Kenneth Arrow, Robert Solow, Arthur Okun, George Perry, William Capron, Lloyd Ulman, Nancy Teeters, Vernon Ruttan, Warren Smith, and Richard Cooper; and as close-in consultants, the likes of Paul Samuelson, Charles Schultze, Joseph Pechman, Otto Eckstein, and John Meyer.

THE FIRST YEAR: SUPPLY-SIDE ECONOMICS

Except for a quick but mild dose of demand stimulus in an early 1961 anti-recession package, the first year was essentially a year of supply- and cost-side measures. We did not use the catch phrase, "supply-side economics," but that's exactly what it was:

First, introduction of the investment credit, to this day the backbone of tax incentives for growth through business capital formation. It was proposed in 1961 but not enacted until 1962, largely because of the misgivings and often hostility of both the business and labor communities. (Either because of its novelty or because of its form, the investment tax credit was at first opposed by many business leaders. Secretary Douglas Dillon was fond of telling the story of a man who asked him to explain it, step by step, and at the end added, "One last question: Why am I against it?")

Second, the liberalization of tax depreciation guidelines.

Third, the "monetary twist," designed to make funds available for long-term investment and decrease long-term interest rates, while holding up short-term rates to cut outflows of funds overseas.

Fourth, the bolstering of worker training and retraining programs.

Fifth, the development and introduction of the wage-price guideposts to help ensure that stimulative measures would not run off into wage and price inflation.

Sixth, and perhaps least well recognized, the decision in late 1961 to go for the "Cambridge-New Haven Growth School" formula of holding off on tax cuts in the hope that the economy could struggle up to full employment under the then existing burden of taxation and thus produce a full-employment surplus. The purpose? To channel funds from consumption to investment via the debt repayment that would provide funds for private capital formation.

Let me pause here to note two oft-misunderstood points. The first is that while the supply-side effects of tax cuts on work effort and on saving are murky at best, there's no doubt that running a surplus at full employment would have salutary supply-side effects. Let me be more specific:

The evidence does show an impressive investment response to sharply targeted measures like investment tax credits and more liberal depreciation.

• But on work response, the evidence is ambiguous. Countless studies show that existing workers' responses to tax cuts are an amalgam of (a) added work by some—the "eager beavers"—as they keep a larger proportion of their rewards for work effort and thus see the cost of leisure going up; (b) no change by those who are locked into a pattern of fixed hours; and (c) reduced work by those laid-back members of the labor force who ease off because they can now achieve their income-after-tax targets with fewer hours of work. Contrary to loose—but ever-confident—assertions by some supply-side economists, painstaking research has not yet established for sure even the sign—plus or minus—of workers' net response, let alone the magnitude. (Studies do show a significant positive response of labor effort by spouses and other second earners to increases in take-home pay.)

• Similarly, on savings, we are not sure which response dominates: to save *more* in the light of lower taxes on savings or to save *less* since lower taxes enable the saver to achieve a given target living standard with less saving. Most economists would agree that, on net balance, there is a modest positive response of saving to tax cuts, especially at the outset.

• We do know that when governments cut their deficits or run surpluses in a high employment economy, *that* constitutes net saving (that is, either reduced dissaving or positive saving) and releases funds for business investment and housing, provided the monetary authorities do not offset the effect by single-minded pursuit of the wrong target.

The second point is that although President Kennedy sought some significant expenditure increases from Congress, both for social programs and defense, his batting average on civilian programs was not high, and total defense spending as a percentage of GNP declined steadily during his administration. I underscore the latter point because the idea that he got the economy moving again through a defense buildup is a canard that dies mighty hard.

Recently a *New York Times* guest columnist confidently asserted that "the higher growth rates of the 1960s were achieved only after President Kennedy succeeded in persuading Congress that, in light of the Berlin crisis, defense spending should be increased by 50 percent." In *absolute* terms, national defense expenditures rose less than 10 percent in the early sixties, from $46 billion in 1960 to $50 billion by 1965. More important, in *relative* terms, defense outlays actually fell as a percentage of GNP, from 9 percent in 1960 to about 7.5 percent in 1965, just before escalation in Vietnam. So much for the notion that defense powered the 1961-65 expansion.

THE TAX CUT: THE DEMAND-SIDE FOLLOW-THROUGH

The shift to demand-side economics came in 1962 when it became painfully apparent that the overburden of taxes was so heavy that the

economy could not achieve prosperity under its yoke. Alas, the Cambridge-New Haven hope for full employment surpluses had to go by the
boards. With economic expansion faltering in 1962, with Congress in
no mood to provide economic stimulus from the budget-spending side,
and with top individual income tax rates still at 91 percent—far too
high—we launched the offensive for a big tax cut in March of 1962. Its
main purpose was to step up the pace of expansion and bring the economy up to its full-employment potential.

From March 1962 on, the Council campaigned for a $10 billion, later
a $12 billion, tax cut. The treasury was initially willing to go along with
$3 or $4 billion of it, mainly to facilitate tax reform. But it was not
until we hammered out an agreement in the Cabinet Committee on
Growth late in 1962 that the President adopted the $12 billion tax cut
goal.

The tax cut's nine-month White House gestation period was then followed by 15 months of labor in Congress. To be pushing a large tax cut
in the face of a sizable deficit and a rising economy was unprecedented.
It was a rocky road. I remember all too vividly in early 1963 when Con-
gresswoman Martha Griffiths asked me, at a Joint Economic Committee
hearing, why the American people were so loath to accept a tax cut. After I suggested that it might just be their Puritan ethic, Congressman
John Byrnes of Wisconsin let me have it: "I'd rather be a Puritan than a
Heller."

Fairly early in the game, the President had to drop much of his reform package in order to clear the track for the cut itself. And much
of the Kennedy Cabinet voiced only lukewarm support (and some, privately, opposition or apprehension) lest the tax cut deprive them of
revenues needed for their programs. That it would stimulate the economy and provide a sounder basis for later increased appropriations was
not an easy case to sell.

That calls for another word about the bizarre notion that a tax cut
will pay for itself by so stimulating supply (work, savings, and investment) that the reflow of tax revenues will match the initial tax loss.
When an economy is operating far below its potential, as in the early
1960s, a tax cut's demand-side effect boosts purchasing power and puts
both idle machines and factories and idle workers back to work, thus
broadening the tax base—not enough fully to pay for itself, but enough
to cut the revenue loss very significantly.

The notion that a tax cut's prompt demand stimulus, let alone its
long-delayed supply stimulus, could generate enough revenue to pay for
itself is unfortunately not supported by the statistical evidence. (Once,
in an exuberant response to a leading question by the late Senator
Hubert Humphrey, then Chairman of the Joint Economic Committee,
I suggested that the tax cut had paid for itself; but on more careful

inspection of the evidence, I publicly recanted later in a letter to the *Wall Street Journal*.)

In any event, the tax cut—20 percent for individuals and, in combination with the earlier tax breaks for business, 20 percent for corporations—became law after President Kennedy's death. To a remarkable degree, it "delivered the goods" until it was overtaken by Vietnam events:

• Enacted in March, 1964, it stimulated a more vigorous expansion of the economy and reduction of unemployment without agitating inflation. The specific numbers: by July of 1965 (just before escalation of the war in Vietnam), the unemployment rate had dropped to 4.4 percent, while the consumer price index was rising at a rate of only 1.5 percent per year.

• Dropping top individual tax rates from 91 percent to 70 percent helped to weaken somewhat the incentives for tax avoidance and strengthen the incentives for investment, while easing of low-bracket rates and tightening of the capital gains tax helped improve the equity of the tax structure.

• In a two-track policy emphasizing both demand and supply stimulus, the combined tax cuts gave a powerful boost to demand while at the same time providing strong incentives to increase risk-taking and enlarge the flow of investment funds. In point of fact, the ratio of private investment to GNP reached a new postwar peak in 1965.

• As later events proved, the surest path to more adequate financing for government programs was, paradoxically, through tax reduction. With the acceleration of expansion through the tax cut, the economy soon returned to full prosperity. Both the atmosphere thus created and the resulting generous flows of federal, state, and local revenues led the country to a more sympathetic attitude toward expansion of government social programs. As President Kennedy put it in a conversation just 11 days before his death, "First we'll get your tax cut, and then we'll get my expenditure programs." And on November 19, he assured me that a direct attack on poverty would be part of his 1964 program. The 17 percent rise in GNP in the two years after the tax cut—between the first quarters of 1964 and 1966—made possible a 13.5 percent rise in government spending at lower average tax rates.

The tax cut proved the flip side of the Kennedy dictum that success has a thousand fathers, but failure is an orphan. In a perverse way, I treasure an April, 1964, release by the American Taxpayers Union of New Jersey assuring one and all that it had "planned, initiated, and spearheaded the crusade that resulted in the recent [federal] tax cut." Showing a nice sense of proportion, it went on to note its support of legalized off-track betting.

Successful as the tax cut was, one has to add a disappointing postscript. When, with Vietnam, the time came for President Johnson and the Congress to turn the "New Economics" around—to use tax increases to cut aggregate demand and subdue inflation—the political process was found wanting. It was not until mid-1968 that a tax increase was finally enacted. Meanwhile, the superimposing of some $25 billion per year of Vietman expenditures on an economy already programmed for full employment had done its malevolent work, overheating the economy and letting the inflationary tiger out of its cage.

Against the great human and political tradegy of Vietnam, the economic cost may not loom so large. But without the tragic war, I doubt very much that we would have been blown so far off the course of economic-growth-with-price-stability on which President Kennedy had set us in his exhilarating thousand days.

II

AN INTRODUCTION TO SUPPLY-SIDE ECONOMICS

Articles in Part II provide an introduction to the relatively new concept of supply-side economics. They explain what it is, how it works, and what is new and not new about supply-side propositions.

7

Supply-Side Economics: An Introduction*

RONALD A. KRIEGER

Editor's note: With a suddenness that has startled even some of its ardent proponents, an approach to economic policy stressing "supply-side" tax incentives for businesses and individuals has penetrated the nation's consciousness. Supply-side concepts influence the thinking of many presidential advisers, and these ideas lie at the heart of the taxcut program proposed by President Reagan. The assumptions behind this approach are straightforward enough, but they raise many complex issues. A year ago, Chase's *Business in Brief,* the predecessor of *The Chase Economic Observer,* took a careful look at some supply-side propositions as they related to productivity, the inflation rate, and business tax cuts. Now that these tenets promise to have a significant impact on national policy, the *Observer* would like to provide its readers with a more extensive view of the questions involved.

In the article below, the first of a series, we briefly explore some of the basic concepts of the supply-side approach and the controversies that surround it. Future issues of the *Observer* will discuss the response of work effort to taxation; the effects of tax incentives on saving and investment; supply-side economics and inflation; and the intellectual basis for the supply-side approach.

The new emphasis in Washington on the supply side of the economy is one of the most encouraging developments in economic policy in many years. It promises a badly needed shift of priorities away from managing total demand—the traditional emphasis of federal stabilization

*Reprinted with permission from *The Chase Economic Observer*, March/April 1981, May/June 1981, and July/August 1981. Ronald A. Krieger is Editor in Chief of The Chase Economic Observer.

policy—and toward stimulating elements of the productive process: capital investment, saving, productivity, work effort, and enterprise. Moreover, it focuses welcome attention on the detrimental effects of a rising tax burden on productive effort. And, although it is often criticized for lacking a solid foundation, it in fact relies on a time-tested proposition of microeconomics—encouraging productive behavior through increased incentives at the "margin," where people make decisions. That is, it zeroes in on the *additional* costs and benefits associated with the tax treatment of an additional dollar of saving or investment or an additional hour of work.

Nevertheless, there is a very real danger that this highly promising approach will be discredited by a failure to live up to the more extreme claims of some of its advocates. For one thing, the supply-side response to tax incentives is likely to be much more modest—at least in the short run—than many of its supporters expect. Furthermore, some enthusiasts have claimed that supply-side economics is in itself a sole cure for inflation, rather than one of several tools that can contribute to a reduction in the inflation rate over a period of years. This claim is unfortunate, because it can lead to a neglect of the restrictive demand-side measures that most economists feel are also necessary to reduce inflation significantly. In this more cautious view—apparently reflected in the Reagan program of balanced tax and spending cuts—drastic tax-slashing unaccompanied by restraint in monetary policy and federal spending can lead to enormous increases in the federal deficit, with potential inflationary consequences.

THE LAFFER EFFECT

Such caution is not shared by all supply-siders. Some invoke a curve (see diagram) popularized by Professor Arthur B. Laffer to argue that tax cuts need not reduce revenues or increase deficits. The Laffer curve indicates that there are always two tax rates that will generate the same amount of government revenue—a low rate (point A, for example) and a high rate (point E). As tax rates increase from zero, total output—the tax base—falls off because of the disincentive effects on productive effort. But the tax take still increases up to a point, since the higher rates more than offset the declining output. Beyond point C, however, the combined effect of tax avoidance and production disincentives will predominate, and higher tax rates actually reduce tax revenues. In that zone (shaded blue in the diagram), the tax base has been eroded by high taxes to the point where the so-called "Laffer effect" occurs: Tax reve-

The Laffer curve: How tax rates affect the tax take

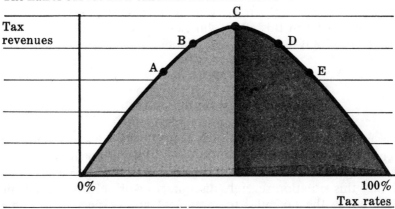

The Laffer curve portrays the presumed relationship between tax rates and tax revenues. Revenues are zero, of course, when the tax rate is zero. But they are also zero when tax rates rise to 100%; the tax base depends upon production and income, and at a 100% tax rate there would be no incentive to produce. Revenues are maximized at some intermediate point, labeled "C" in the diagram. Beyond that point, in the zone shaded blue, rising taxes discourage effort to such an extent that revenues fall—the higher rates are more than offset by reduced output. The curve is hypothetical, and nobody knows either its shape or the location of point C. These will vary with the type of tax; it is not likely either that the true curve is symmetrical or that the point of maximum revenue will lie at a tax rate halfway between 0% and 100%.

nues can be increased by *reducing* tax rates, say from point E to point D. Investment, labor supply, or work effort will respond so strongly to the incentive of lower tax rates that tax revenues will actually rise.

Critics have been quick to point out, however, that it is difficult to know in advance where the economy is located on the Laffer curve. They suggest that rather than boosting revenues from point E to point D, a tax cut is more likely to stimulate only a weak production response and reduce tax receipts from, say, point B to point A. Even if the economy is in the Laffer-effect zone—perhaps at point D—a large tax cut could move it to point A, again lowering revenues.

Thus, the economy's position on the Laffer curve—indicating the *extent* of the response of work effort, investment, and production to a tax cut—has emerged as the key controversy in the debate over supply-side economic policy. If the response is so weak that a tax reduction generates larger federal deficits, then the resulting spurt in government borrowing will either crowd private borrowers out of credit markets or—if financed through excess money creation—accelerate the inflation rate. Either result is likely to weaken the tax cut's supply-side stimulus. Subsequent articles in this series will examine the nature and probable extent of this supply-side response in detail.

WORK AND TAXES

High marginal rates of taxation under the progressive income-tax system ensure that the government takes an increasing share of labor income as wages and salaries rise. A major tenet of supply-side economics holds that this situation severely discourages work effort in the United States. Reduce the tax bite, the argument goes—especially the sharp, progressive rate increases on increments to personal income—and workers will respond with a much greater effort. They will work more hours because they will be able to keep a larger share of the added income.

It is not at all certain, however, that workers will put in longer hours when their tax rates are cut. Indeed, the opposite may well be true. It is possible for lower marginal tax rates on additional labor income to *reduce* total work effort. The key to this apparent paradox is the dual nature of the response to a change in net income resulting from a change in the tax rate. Two forces pull workers in opposite directions when taxes fall: the "substitution" effect and the "income" effect.

OPPOSING FORCES

The substitution effect is what supply-siders have in mind when they cite the incentive effects of tax cuts. Anyone who works for a living sacrifices free time that could have been spent in leisure pursuits. An increase in the tax rate reduces the net wage and therefore lowers the cost of substituting leisure for work. Since more of any "good" will be demanded when its cost falls, leisure time will expand and work effort will contract. A reduction in the marginal tax rate on additional labor income will have the opposite effect. The higher take-home pay will make leisure more costly, leading work effort to expand and leisure time to contract. This is the substitution effect.

But there is an opposing effect from a tax cut that is often ignored by supply-side advocates. Leisure can be considered a "normal" good, in the sense that more of it is demanded at higher incomes, less at lower incomes, other things being equal. Higher taxes reduce hourly disposable income and cause less leisure to be "demanded." That is, as taxes rise, workers have to put in more hours to take home as much income as before. By the same token, a cut in marginal tax rates will reduce the amount of work required to earn a given disposable income. Net hourly income rises and so does the demand for leisure. Thus, the higher net wage will tend to reduce work effort. This is the income effect.

Any cut in the marginal tax rate on labor income will have both substitution and income effects. The net effect on labor supply will depend on the respective intensities of these opposing forces. If the substitution effect predominates, a tax cut will induce more hours of work. If the income effect is stronger, fewer hours will be worked. In principle, either effect could prevail in a given situation.

INTENSITY OF RESPONSE

Most empirical research indicates that substitution effects will generally outweigh income effects for the labor force as a whole, although the opposite may be true for prime-age male workers alone. But even though the response of labor supply to a tax cut will generally be positive, the question remains: How strong is this response? Supply-side advocates often maintain that higher taxes so discourage work effort that, above a certain rate, rising taxes actually reduce tax revenues from labor income (see chart). That is, substitution effects overwhelm income effects to such a degree that the rising tax rates are more than offset by the shrinking tax base. Extreme supply-siders assert that the response of labor is so strong that even a very low tax rate will elicit this so-called "Laffer effect." Thus, they argue, it is likely that a cut in taxes from current U.S. rates will induce a major increase in work hours and generate tax revenue—the outcome represented by the movement from point T_A to point S_A in Panel A.

Critics of this position maintain that income effects, on average, are almost strong enough to offset substitution effects, so that rising taxes induce only a slight reduction in labor supply. In their view, tax rates would have to be exceedingly high—much higher than they are at present—for rising taxes to reduce the tax take. Thus, a tax cut from current rates would increase work effort only slightly, so that the expansion of the tax base would not be sufficient to offset the lower tax rate, and revenue would fall. This is illustrated in Panel B by the movement from T_B to S_B.

How labor response affects the tax take

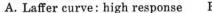 A. Laffer curve: high response

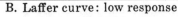 B. Laffer curve: low response

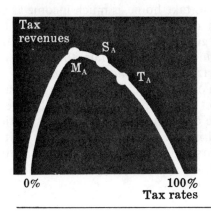

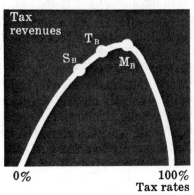

The Laffer curve represents the presumed relationship between tax rates and tax revenues (see the *Observer*, March/April 1981). The curves above depict this relationship for taxes on labor income. As tax rates increase from zero, work effort and economic activity are progressively discouraged and leisure is increasingly substituted for work. At first, the rising rates bring in increased revenues, despite the fall-off in work hours and labor income. But at some tax rate below 100%, the tax take eventually peaks. Beyond this point, rising rates discourage effort to such an extent that the sharp shrinkage of labor income causes total revenues from the tax on this income to fall.

If the amount of labor supplied is highly responsive to changes in after-tax income—as many supply-siders claim—then even a minimal tax rate on labor income will severely discourage work effort. In this situation (Panel A), the point of maximum tax revenue (M_A) may come at a relatively low tax rate. On the other hand, if the labor-supply reaction to reduced after-tax income is weak (Panel B), as many critics assert, then work effort and labor income fall off very slowly as taxes rise. Only beyond point M_B, as the tax rate approaches 100%, will further rate hikes discourage labor enough to reduce the tax take.

EMPIRICAL WORK

Most research into the response of labor to tax incentives in the United States casts doubt on the extreme supply-side view. For example, in a recent study for the Office of Tax Analysis of the Treasury

Department, Princeton's Don Fullerton found that, as in Panel B, current U.S. taxes are far below the rates necessary to elicit the Laffer effect. For the labor force as a whole, workers will increase their hours on the job by only 0.15% for each 1% rise in after-tax pay. With that low degree of responsiveness, Fullerton found, total tax revenues will increase as tax rates on gross labor income rise, up to about 72%—far above the highest marginal tax rate on earned personal income in the United States. Other studies have come to similar conclusions, although there is still some disagreement. Researchers typically have found that the work hours of prime-age males show only a weak tendency to increase in response to a tax cut, while those of female workers are highly responsive. This may be because, when they provide the second paycheck in a family, women's earnings are added to those of their husbands and thus are taxed at a higher marginal rate.

In any event, the questions raised by empirical research about the shape of the Laffer curve do not invalidate the basic thrust of the supply-side case. From a policy point of view, cuts in marginal tax rates on labor income may still be warranted, whatever their effects on total revenues. For one thing, however much or little they may have to do with the *quantity* of work, they may induce a higher *quality* work effort. Lower marginal rates may result in a somewhat greater willingness of entrepreneurs, professionals, and salaried employees to take more risks, undergo further education and training, and work more conscientiously and productively in the hope of advancement. Lower tax rates may also serve to return some "off-the-books" economic activity to the tax rolls, enhancing the revenue-producing potential of a tax cut. In addition, tax legislation to reduce the "marriage penalty" would help to increase the work effort and labor-force participation rate of married couples.

In sum, reduction of marginal tax rates on labor income is likely to enhance both the quantity and the quality of work in the United States. The effects, however, may turn out to be fairly small. A potentially more promising avenue for supply-side approaches is the stimulus the tax cuts can give to saving and investment. This will be the subject of the next article in this series.

TAXES AND SAVINGS

The centerpiece of the supply-side approach to economic policy is the use of tax incentives to stimulate personal saving and business investment in plant and equipment. These are key elements in the Reagan administration's strategy of promoting capital formation to foster economic growth, and they are well provided for in the 1981 tax act. The main features of the legislation that affect saving and investment include:

- Lower personal income tax rates. The maximum rate will fall from 70% to 50% on income from interest and dividends, and from 28% to 20% on capital gains. Marginal tax rates on ordinary income will decline by a total of 23% in three stages, and tax brackets will be indexed to the Consumer Price Index beginning in 1985.
- Personal income exclusions. Within certain limits, new or expanded exclusions from taxable income will apply to reinvested dividends from public utility stocks, to interest on certain one-year savings certificates, to contributions to Individual Retirement Accounts, and—beginning in 1985—to net interest income.
- Corporate income tax cuts. The act provides for accelerated depreciation of structures and capital equipment, reduced rates in the two lowest corporate tax brackets, and expansion of the investment tax credit.

Of course, tax reduction is only one element of President Reagan's total economic program, which also features federal spending cutbacks, encouragement of monetary restraint, and easing of the regulatory burden on business. Viewing the program as a whole, economists can find ample reason to predict that it will indeed stimulate a great deal of private capital formation in the United States over the next several years. There is considerable dispute, however, over how much of a role the tax cuts will play in that process—at least in the case of personal saving.

THE INCENTIVE TO SAVE

Saving, in the sense of refraining from consumption, is needed to free resources for private investment. Some of this is accomplished by businesses—for example, by retaining earnings for reinvestment. The remainder has to come from household saving. U.S. personal savings rates have been close to their postwar lows in recent years, and they are far below those of most industrial countries. Supply-side enthusiasts have predicted a big spurt in personal saving as a result of the tax cuts. Critics, however, argue that the degree of response may be low.

Cuts in taxes on investment income—interest, dividends, and capital gains—increase the returns to individual savers and investors. These cuts may induce people to save either less or more. Just as in the case of labor income (see the *Observer*, May/June 1981), the magnitude and di-

Did the 1964 tax cut pack a supply-side punch?
(percent)

Investment rate* ■■
Savings rate** ■■

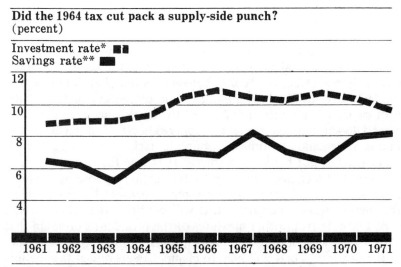

* Real non-residential fixed investment as a percentage of real GNP
** Personal savings as a percentage of disposable personal income

Data: U.S. Department of Commerce

rection of the response will depend on the relative strength of two op-posing forces generated by the tax cuts: substitution effects and income effects.

By increasing the future reward for current saving, a lower tax rate on investment income raises the relative cost of choosing to consume rather than save, thereby encouraging households to substitute a certain amount of saving for a portion of their consumption. This is the substitution effect. But lower tax rates also allow people to save less from current income and still receive the same stream of future earnings. Thus, a tax reduction on investment income can serve to discourage personal saving. This is the income effect. In principle, either effect can predominate.

THE DEBATE

Supply-side proponents stress the substitution effect. They maintain that, by cutting *marginal* tax rates and thereby increasing the after-tax rate of return to additional savings, the 1981 tax cut will revitalize personal savings. They argue that the rise in the savings rate after the 1964 Kennedy-Johnson tax cut (see chart) was a direct supply-side response to the incentives of lower marginal tax rates, just as the increase in business investment was spurred by direct incentives for capital spending.

Critics of the supply-side view express doubt that tax cuts will induce a large increase in the supply of savings. They argue that the income effects of falling *average* tax rates will just about cancel out the substitution effects of lower marginal rates, so that changes in the return to capital will have little net effect on savings behavior. Some skeptics insist that even the 1964 tax cut had only a modest—and temporary—effect on the supply of savings. They attribute most of the improvement in the economy after 1964 not to the tax cut's supply-side effect on saving but to its stimulus of demand at a time of economic slack.

The debate will not be easily resolved. It is true that most empirical studies support the critics, generally finding little response by personal saving to higher rates of return. But some recent research by supply-siders disputes these results. In any event, it will be difficult to separate the effects of tax cuts from other measures of the president's program that have little to do with supply-side prescriptions. For example, lower tax rates in the upper brackets will help to channel assets out of tax shelters and into productive business investment. But higher real rates of return on financial assets that stem largely from demand-side monetary policies are already having that effect. Moreover, it is likely that corporate tax reforms and reduced regulation will further increase rates of return and free resources for capital spending, while lower inflation and cutbacks in federal spending will greatly improve the investment climate. Thus, whatever the ultimate effect of tax cuts on personal saving, it is probably safe to predict that the Reagan economic program as a whole will serve to accelerate capital formation.

SUMMING UP

Just a few months after enactment of the Economic Recovery Tax Act, soaring federal-deficit projections have given rise to second thoughts among policymakers over the timing and extent of the tax cuts. Under grim but realistic assumptions, the administration now expects deficits of as much as $109 billion for fiscal 1982, $152 billion for 1983, and $162 billion for 1984. These projections have given added impetus to calls for further slashes in government spending and for a reversal or modification of the tax reductions even before many of them have gone into effect.

Little is heard anymore around official Washington of the questionable argument that massive cuts in marginal tax rates would actually increase revenues collected. Instead, tax reductions are spoken of these days mainly in terms of their putative inflationary role in expanding the federal deficit. It would appear that the supply-side approach to economic policy has fallen out of favor, a victim in part of the exaggerated claims made on its behalf.

LONG RUN AND SHORT RUN

If this is indeed the case, it is an unfortunate development. The administration should not let short-run considerations weaken its commitment to a program designed to provide long-term solutions to some intractable economic problems. Productivity growth has been stagnant in recent years, while inflation rates have soared (see chart). Conventional demand-management approaches have failed to turn the economy around and often appear to have made the problems worse. Meanwhile, high marginal tax rates have served to discourage enterprise, saving, investment, and work effort.

In this environment, tax cuts cannot legitimately be viewed as an inflationary force serving only to hike the federal deficit. In the first place, there is little evidence that larger deficits by themselves increase the inflation rate. If the deficit is not financed through monetary expansion, the inflationary effect will be small. The restrictive monetary policies pursued by the Federal Reserve in recent months will—if maintained—minimize the inflationary impact of the federal deficit.

Furthermore, although tax reductions inevitably have demand-side as well as supply-side effects, it is misleading to equate the two. Supply-

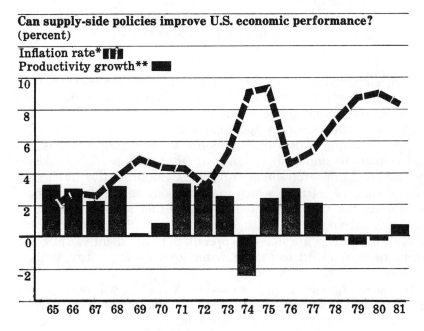

**Can supply-side policies improve U.S. economic performance?
(percent)**

Inflation rate*
Productivity growth**

65 66 67 68 69 70 71 72 73 74 75 76 77 78 79 80 81

* Year-over-year percentage change in implicit gross domestic product price
deflator for private business sector.
** Year-over-year percentage change in output per hour worked, private business sector.

Data: U.S. Department of Labor; Chase estimate for 1981

side principles are derived from a "general equilibrium" approach that considers the long-run tendencies of the economy after prices and wages have adjusted to eliminate excess demand and supply in all markets. Demand-side concerns over the deficit, on the other hand, reflect a short-term "disequilibrium" model of the economy that deals with problems of *adjusting* prices, wages, output, employment, and financial variables to the economy's long-term path. Policies designed to enhance long-run economic growth potential should not be judged by criteria used to evaluate short-run measures aimed at bringing the economy up to that potential.

Finally, it should be kept in mind that supply-side policies can indeed serve to *reduce* inflationary pressures in the long run. To the extent that they are able to boost productivity growth beyond the rate of wage inflation, businesses will be obliged by competitive pressures to moderate their prices in line with lower unit labor costs. These disinflationary effects will emerge only in the long run, and they will not be large in any given year. Over time, however, they could take several percentage points off the inflation rate. The key to the strength of this effect is the magnitude of the responses of work effort, saving, and investment to tax incentives.

DEGREE OF RESPONSE

Both empirical evidence and theoretical analysis suggest that some claims for these responses have been exaggerated. As earlier articles in this series have pointed out, tax cuts can set opposing forces in motion, and the outcome is not always clear. For example, reductions of taxes on earned income will usually give rise to substitution effects, which lead workers to supply more hours of labor because higher take-home pay makes leisure—refraining from work—more costly. But they can also have income effects, which cause workers to supply less labor because lower tax rates reduce the amount of time it takes to earn a given disposable income. Research suggests that for the labor force as a whole, substitution effects are likely to prevail, but only slightly. Thus, the response of work effort to the tax reductions, while positive, is likely to be small.

The small arguments apply to saving. A tax cut will raise the net return to saving, increasing the benefit to household from postponing purchases in order to boost future buying power. But it will also have income effects, reducing the amount of savings needed to produce a given future income. The evidence indicates that a positive response of saving to the 1981 tax measures can be expected, but here too, the magnitude is not likely to be large.

A more certain road to productivity improvement probably lies in the direct incentives for business investment established by the new tax law. Accelerated depreciation and expansion of the investment tax credit are likely to provide a strong stimulus to capital spending in the long run, although the effects will be minimal as long as economic activity is weak and business has substantial excess capacity.

In sum, supply-side economics can work, given time for long-run effects to make themselves felt. These effects will be neither as potent nor as quick as exaggerated claims by supply-side enthusiasts have led policymakers to believe. Nor can they do it all alone. But combined with the demand-side remedies that form an integral part of the president's economic package—substantial budget cuts and restrictive monetary growth—the supply-side approach can make a significant contribution toward conquering inflation and restoring health to the nation's economy. It should be given a chance to prove itself.

8

Norman B. Ture on
Supply-Side Economics*

DAVID RABOY

Supply-side economics is being discussed with increasing frequency, yet many people confuse its basic principles with those put forth by economist John Maynard Keynes. How do the two economic theories differ? And why should one be constructive and the other unworkable in the long run? For answers, *Enterprise* turned to the economist who, in cooperation with NAM's Tax Impact Project, developed the first econometric model for measuring the effects of tax changes on the supply side.

There is more talk nowadays about "supply-side" economics. Just what is it and how does it differ from the prevailing Keynesian economic theory?

Ture: Supply-side economics is shorthand for a way of analyzing the effects of government policies and actions on the economy. Based on the principles of economics as developed by such classical economists as Adam Smith, J. B. Say and Alfred Marshall, its basic concepts predate the Keynesian economic theory by a century and half. What's new about "supply-side" economics is its application to public economic policy problems, particularly tax and fiscal policies.

In essence, supply-side economics holds that government tax and spending policies influence the economic behavior of households and businesses by changing the relative costs they confront. In contrast, the Keynesians believe fiscal policy affects the private sector's activities by changing disposable income. The supply-side economics shows that there can't be any changes in total income resulting from a government tax or

*Reprinted with permission from *Enterprise*, magazine of National Association of Manufacturers, June 1980.

spending action until people react to the change in relative costs the actions involve by changing the amount of labor services supplied or the amount of saving and investment they undertake.

A simple illustration shows why fiscal actions can't initially affect aggregate demand, as the Keynesians insist.

Suppose we pretend the government's budget is balanced and assume that income taxes are reduced. According to the aggregate demand approach, this results immediately in an increase in disposable income, most of which will go to increase consumption demand. Supposedly, this increases business demands for production inputs—both labor and capital—which result in additional employment of labor and capital services and, as a result, an increase in total output.

But since the tax cut, by assumption, is not matched by a government spending cut, the loss in tax revenues must result in an equal deficit. Then the additional disposable income resulting from the tax cut must be used to buy the additional government debt. If some people use their additional disposable income to finance additional spending for goods and services, then others will have to reduce their spending in order to buy the additional debt instruments. Although some redistribution of spending will occur, there can be no increase in the total amount of spending—no change in total demand.

A tax cut cannot, in and of itself, increase the economy's aggregate income because it does not, in and of itself, increase the amount of productivity of production inputs. A tax cut may increase income, but this is a "second-level" effect, which occurs only because the tax cut induces an increase in the supply of labor and capital services, which in turn results in more output and income. To have this result, the tax cut must reduce the relative cost of market-directed effort and of saving. A tax cut which doesn't reduce these costs, such as the infamous rebates of a few years back, has no effect on the economy.

Raboy: What are the implications of supply-side economics for taxing and spending policies? How does supply-side theory relate to employment and capital formation?

Ture: Applying the supply-side analysis to taxing and spending policy results in a much different cast of policy from that of the past several decades. In contrast with the Keynesian focus on changing effective tax rates and disposable income, the current emphasis in the supply-side policy is on reducing *marginal* income tax rates, directly and indirectly, in order to reduce the existing tax biases against work and saving and investing.

There are many ways in which taxes can be cut in order to reduce marginal tax rates. Allowing businesses to write off their investments in production facilities more rapidly is the equivalent of reducing the marginal rates of tax applicable to the income they produce with these facilities. The supply-side analysis shows, for example, that the 10-5-3 capital cost recovery system, [embodied in pending legislation H.R. 4646 and S. 1435] makes it less costly, in terms of the amount of current consumption that must be given up, to save and to add to the stock of capital in the business community. Similarly, it shows that cutting taxes on capital gains reduces the cost of saving and investment and leads to an increase in capital formation.

In the same way, the supply-side analysis shows that government spending programs raise the costs of using labor and capital services by the private sector. It demonstrates that many government transfer programs, although not intended as such, actually are rewards for not working. They operate to reduce the supply and employment of labor.

The supply-side economics offers a guide for analyzing how government spending affects the allocation of the economy's production resources and for determining priorities in spending and in spending cuts.

Raboy: Much of contemporary federal economic policy has been directed toward "fine tuning" of the economy, that is, pumping up the economy in periods of recession and attempting to cool the economy in inflationary times. How does supply-side theory relate to short-term attempts at fine tuning?

Ture: The supply-side theory shows that fine tuning is at best irrelevant and is highly likely to be hazardous to the economy's health over the long run. Trying to prop up the economy during a recession by increasing government outlays, particularly transfer payments, principally serves to increase costs to business and thereby to impede the expansion of business activity. Increasing transfer payments as part of a counter-recession fine tuning program is perverse strategy—it raises the cost of working, discourages employment, hence restricts gains in production.

In boom periods, fine tuning efforts seldom take the form of cutting government spending, which would release resources to the more productive private sector and lead to expansion of output. Far more often, fine tuning in these circumstances takes the form of income tax rate increases which, perversely, make it more costly for people to work and to save and invest. This, in turn, limits production and increases inflationary strains. In short, supply-side economics holds that fine tuning tends to make matters worse. Supply-side economics calls for a "steady-as-she-goes" approach to policy, characterized by continuing progress in reducing the growth—if not the absolute amount—of government spending and reducing marginal tax rates, by one kind of tax change or another.

Raboy: In light of this, what are the short and long-term responses to supply-side-oriented changes?

Ture: The basic analytical framework of supply-side economics specifies that the initial effects of tax and spending changes take the form of changes in the relative costs and prices people face. The way people respond to these changes in relative prices is likely to result in changes in the amount of work and saving and investing, therefore in the amount of output and income produced. These changes in output and income, in turn, will lead to additional changes in employment and in capital formation.

But these changes take time. Economic adjustments are not completed instantaneously, even though they are likely to get under way very promptly. For example, simulations with our econometric model show that although there would be significant economic changes—gains in supply and output, investment, etc.—in the first year in which 10-5-3 became effective, the full adjustment and the largest gains in the economy would be several years down the road.

Raboy: Some supporters of supply-side economics claim that supply-side tax cuts will stimulate long-term growth without short-run inflation. What is your view on this prospect, and how does monetary and budget policy relate to the likely outcome?

Ture: The right kind of tax cuts will lead to increases in the supplies and employment of production inputs, hence increases in output. In and of themselves, these developments should ease inflationary pressures. Bear in mind that the root cause of inflation today, as always, is too fast a growth in the quantity of money relative to the growth in real output. If the growth in the stock of money isn't changed, tax cuts which lead to production increases will ease inflationary strains.

The view that tax cuts will accentuate inflation comes from the Keynesian notion that tax reductions serve only to increase demand and have no effects on supply. The supply-side theory, on the other hand, shows that tax cuts—of the right sort—first lead to changes in supplies of labor and capital, then output. Of course, these increases in output themselves are not likely to be large enough to eliminate inflation. To do the job right, we must keep to a very restricted growth in the supply of money.

Sometimes its argued that tax cuts, by creating or adding to the government's budget deficit, will, for that very reason, increase inflationary pressures and/or crowd out private investment. An increase in the budget deficit, however, does not necessarily mean either a crowding out of private investment or an accentuation of inflationary pressure.

Crowding out would occur only if the increase in the government's deficit (or the reduction in its surplus) were not at least offset by an increase in private sector saving. If private saving were not to increase at least by as much as the deficit, gross national saving—which is the sum of the saving of households, businesses, and the excess of government revenues over expenditures—would decline.

Since gross national saving necessarily equals the sum of gross private domestic investment and net exports, a decline in gross national saving means that either or both capital formation or the trade balance must decrease. Then, crowding out would occur. But if household and/or business saving increases by as much, if not more, than the government's deficit, gross private domestic investment and/or the excess of exports over imports will increase. Crowding out, therefore, is not an inevitable outcome of an increase in the government's deficit. It depends on whether the increase in the deficit is associated with a decline or a smaller increase in private saving.

For example, the principal initial effect of 10-5-3 would be a substantial increase in business and in individual saving. The initial increase in business saving, i.e., the decrease in business income tax liabilities, would be just equal to the initial increase in the government's deficit. Additional saving by both business and households would be forthcoming and great enough to finance, in real terms, both very large gains in capital formation and the additional federal deficit (or reduction in surplus).

On the other hand, some tax cuts do not reduce the cost of saving relative to consumption and, therefore, do not lead to an increase in the aggregate amount of saving. That type of tax reduction and the deficit it generates is likely to displace private sector uses of the economy's production capability, particularly for capital formation.

A tax cut like 10-5-3 would not itself be responsible for augmenting inflationary pressures. In the Keynesian system, only the increase in investment spending resulting from 10-5-3 is taken into account; the increase in the input of capital and labor services is ignored. If only the additional spending occurred, more intense inflation would result. But spending can never exceed output in real terms. Nominal—current dollar—spending, to be sure, can exceed real output and real income, provided this inflationary excess is financed by an increase in the stock of money.

The danger of additonal inflation from a tax cut is that the monetary authorities might quicken the pace of monetary expansion in order to finance the budget deficit of the federal government. If they were to do so, this untoward and unnecessary monetary expansion might well impel an upward surge in the price level. Any deficit which might result from the tax cut doesn't itself generate the inflation. It's the monetary authorities' mistaken effort to finance the deficit which does the dirty work.

Raboy: Some economists, notably Alice Rivlin of the Congressional Budget Office, are vehemently suspicious of supply-side theory. To what do you attribute these views?

Ture: I don't believe Mrs. Rivlin is "vehemently suspicious" of supply-side theory. On the other hand, it is likely that she is not fully cued in to the theory, and her misunderstandings, which regrettably are widely shared, are likely to impede her acceptance of the theory and its policy implications.

Of course, embodying supply-side economics in the budgetary analyses of the Congressional Budget Office would entail a sharp shift in the policy focus of that organization's work. Mrs. Rivlin might be quite unsympathetic to shifting concerns from managing aggregate demand by budget manipulations toward devising ways to reduce the burden of government on the private sector.

Raboy: You have been a pioneer in the area of supply-side economics. What forces pushed you in this direction against the mainstream of Keynesian thought?

Ture: I began to move toward the supply-side in the mid-1960s when I found the Keynesian analysis less and less useful in supplying answers conforming with reality. It was a commonplace observation at that time, for example, that the structure of the tax system was of far less consequence for the growth of the economy than the amount of taxes collected relative to the amount the government spent. I found this view less and less satisfactory during the late '60s, and turned to neoclassical price theory to find explanations of why different tax changes affect the economy in the different ways they do. Supply-side economics really is just the application of price theory to the analysis of governmental fiscal actions.

Raboy: In cooperation with NAM's Tax Impact Project, you developed the first econometric model to measure the effects of tax changes on the supply side. Now many other models, both traditional and otherwise, claim to have the same capabilitiy. How is your model different from the others?

Ture: The fundamental difference is that most, if not all, of the other models claiming to be supply side really are the old Keynesian aggregate demand models to which some supply equations have been added. They still rely on first-level disposable income effects of fiscal actions to activate their simulations. In doing so, they necessarily misrepresent how fiscal changes affect the economy. For example, some of these models treated the capital gains tax reductions provided in the 1978 tax legislation as increasing disposable income which would lead to increases in consumption, hence in GNP, which in turn would lead to some increase in investment. In no way did these models pick up the simple fact that the cut in the capital gains tax made it less costly to save and invest. In contrast, our model relies on first-level price effects to set adjustments in motion. In fact, the model has the capacity to identify these price effects of an enormous variety of tax changes and to distinguish among those differing tax changes in terms of the magnitude and nature of the economic effects and the effects on tax revenues.

Raboy: Considering the current economic situation, is there justification for a supply-side tax cut? How should it be structured?

Ture: A supply-side tax cut is urgently needed—the sooner the better. There is a very large inventory of such cuts that could be useful in removing the fetters from the private sector and revitalizing the nation's economy. At the top of the list I'd place 10-5-3 (which would replace the existing depreciation system with a capital cost recovery system), across-the-board individual and corporate income tax rate cuts, and some form of broadly applicable indexing. The tax on capital gains also should be reduced. These measures do not exhaust the list, but should get top attention.

9

Analyzing Supply-Side Economics: A Symposium*

Reagan Administration victories on taxes and spending signal the most fundamental shift in government economic policy since the Great Depression. The vehicle for change: supply-side economics.

How does it work? Can it cure inflation? Are its economic claims reasonable—or extravagant?

*Reprinted from the August 1981 issue of The Morgan Guaranty Survey published by Morgan Guaranty Trust Company of New York.

To find answers, Morgan Guaranty Trust Company invited four leading proponents of the supply-side doctrine to a symposium at the end
of June. The panelists (see box) were in agreement on many issues. But
sharp differences arose on topics ranging from the impact of tax cuts
and the politics of supply-side economics to the convertibility of the
dollar into gold. Excerpts follow.

Moderator: What is meant by the term supply-side economics? Is it
really as revolutionary as some claim?

Rutledge: Supply-side economics is part of a bigger revolution in the
economics profession which recognizes that the basic unit under study—
the human being—can think, calculate, speculate, and respond to market
incentives. In this sense, supply-side economics shares the stage with
"rational expectations" and "efficient markets" as concepts which
sharply distinguish economics from the physical sciences by focusing on
the human element of economic agents. The basic points of the supply-
side arguments are very important. First, output is the direct result of
inputs. Second, these inputs respond to incentives. Clearly, taxes on
productive effort and on the accumulation of capital represent a serious
impediment to output, employment, and our living standards. I worry
sometimes, however, that many supply-siders focus on too narrow a
definition of "taxes."

The tax burden, of course, is not only personal and corporate taxes.
And its scope goes beyond the burden of government spending. In reality,
the tax burden should be defined as the amount of resources that the
government accumulates, acquires, and destroys—with the emphasis on
the third.

Resources are destroyed by the government when its policies force
up the price level so fast that it wipes out the market value of securities—
the inflation tax. The way I measure taxes is by adding the inflation
taxes on securities and the inflation taxes on money holdings to standard measures of taxes. When I do, I find that something like two thirds
of all such taxes are not taxes shown in the government budget. It then
follows that the number one supply-side priority, in my view, is inflation control.

Laffer: Supply-side economics is nothing more than classical economics in modern dress. It basically looks to incentive. People alter their
behavior when incentives change. If you make an activity more attractive, people will engage in more of that activity. If you make an activity
less attractive, people do less of that activity. And through the implementation of changes in taxation, regulation, government spending, and
through all sorts of government actions on the economy, you change

these incentives and you change people's behavior. As far as I can tell there is nothing libertarian about the supply-side program. It can be run as a state enterprise just as well as a private enterprise.

Moderator: Why is it that so many economists disparage the supply-side approach?

Roberts: Two reasons, I suppose. Many economists used to feel that economic success can only be achieved if government manipulates and pulls levers. These "interventionists" feel threatened. Secondly, Keynesianism was a convenient way for the government to acquire larger and larger claims on the economy's resources without having to legislate higher tax rates. So in that sense, the supply-side approach is politically threatening to the kinds of vested interests which benefit from large spending programs. Between the two, you have a great deal of opposition.

Moderator: But Keynesians believe in cutting taxes, too . . .

Roberts: But their reasons for cutting taxes are profoundly different from ours. Keynesianism has taught everyone for so long that to have a tax cut is to have a stimulative fiscal policy, and a stimulative fiscal policy means more spending, more demand, probably higher inflation, and in the Keynesian context it always means a budget deficit. Indeed, the very reason for cutting the taxes was to produce a budget deficit in order to add to aggregate demand.

That is the way tax cuts are perceived, given the dead hand of the past. Now the Reagan Administration's thinking is totally different. The reason we are cutting taxes is to reduce the marginal rate of taxation. That is, we are trying to cut taxes on additions to income, and the reason we want to do that is to change relative prices rather than raise total demand.

Let me explain how changes in two relative prices can influence the supply side of our economy. First, relative prices influence how people allocate their income between current consumption and saving. A decision to allocate additional income to current consumption is simultaneously a decision to forego a future income stream generated by saving. The value of the foregone future income is affected by the marginal rate of taxation. The higher that marginal tax rate is, the cheaper it is for a person to engage in additional current consumption.

Moderator: Can you illustrate that point?

Roberts: Yes, with what I call the parable of the Rolls Royce. It is the case of an Englishman facing the 98% marginal tax bracket on earned income. With $50,000 he must decide whether to buy a car or to invest the money and earn 17% interest.

On a pre-tax basis, he is looking at a future income stream of $8,500 a year from the $50,000. On an after-tax basis, he is looking at a future income stream of $170 a year. So, after tax, the price of the Rolls Royce is simply to forego a mere $170 a year of interest income. Consumption, in this instance, is clearly more alluring than saving.

Another important relative price governs how people allocate their time—for work, leisure, entertainment, or to pick up additional skills.

Here again, if you allocate a unit of your time to leisure you must forego some amount of current income that could be earned by working. The value of the foregone current income is a function of marginal tax rates. The higher the marginal tax rate, the cheaper it is to engage in leisure.

Since 1965, there has been an enormous increase in marginal tax rates. For a median income family, that family has experienced a 65% increase in marginal tax rates as inflation has pushed people into higher tax brackets.

The family with twice the median income has experienced almost a 100% increase in marginal tax rates. This means that every year leisure and current consumption are becoming cheaper and cheaper in terms of foregone income from working or saving. This affects things like work attitudes, absenteeism rates, willingness to accept overtime, saving rates, and willingness to assume risks.

The whole approach of this Administration is to remove deficits from being an instrument of policy. That change ought to be very attractive as compared to the Keynesian approach, where an unbalanced budget has traditionally been a principal instrument of policy.

IMPACT OF A TAX CUT

Moderator: What makes you optimistic that tax cuts can be such a wonderful force? Is there an historical precedent?

Laffer: Puerto Rico, with its 30% across-the-board tax cut, is a good example. Chile is another case of what can be accomplished in an economy by reinstating private incentives. Take California and Proposition 13. Or what Governor Ed King has accomplished in Massachusetts. Or here in New York State, where marginal rates have been cut and forecasts of a budget deficit of $850 million are turning out to be a surplus of $100 million in the state budget for the current fiscal year.

Also, if you look at countries like West Germany and Japan, where marginal tax rates have been cut, their performance has been superior. Moreover, there is a huge body of evidence generated in the 19th century that shows that incentives do play a major role in growth and employment.

Moderator: More recently, the tax cut by President Kennedy in 1963 . . .

Roberts: Yes, indeed. Let's examine that experience.

Consumer spending as a percentage of income fell after the Kennedy tax cut. The personal saving rate moved up strongly. Indeed, the immediate gain in real personal saving was about three-fourths the size of the tax cut. As a consequence, the growth in business capital spending, in real terms, which had expanded at a 4.2% annual rate between 1959 and 1963, jumped up to 12.9% annually through the next three years. The empirical footprints of response to incentive are there and they are rather clear.

Moderator: But the Kennedy tax cuts came at a time of hardly any inflation. How can you expect a similar response in today's inflationary times?

Roberts: It is true that the value of these tax cuts depends importantly on success in pulling down the inflation rate. But if inflation comes down as fast as we expect it will, there most certainly will be a significant cut in the "inflation tax" burden mentioned earlier by Dr. Rutledge. Even more significant, in the Kennedy years the great majority of taxpayers were positioned at the bottom of the tax brackets. Today the picture is considerably different. Average, ordinary people are more heavily burdened by being in the middle tax brackets. This argues that the effects of the proposed tax cuts should be even more powerful than they were in the Kennedy years. Moreover, the reduction in the top rate from 70% to 50% cannot be offset by the inflation tax.

Moderator: What kind of results do you expect from the Reagan tax plan?

Roberts: We do not necessarily anticipate massive effects on individual behavior. But the cumulative effect could be very substantial. For instance, if the saving rate goes up two percentage points, you are talking about an additional $42 billion annually available to the private capital markets at current income levels. As for the supply-side effects on work attitudes or work performance, if the willingness to accept overtime rises enough that the work week is lengthened by a half hour, then you are talking about an additional $25 billion in output. If absenteeism rates drop by one half a percentage point, you are talking about an additional $10 billion of GNP. So relatively small changes or relatively low responses by individuals can have large aggregate effects.

Moderator: Dr. Rutledge, your views on the tax cut are somewhat different. Why?

Rutledge: The "whopping" tax cut, which everybody plays up, is not really much of a cut at all. Federal taxes are now about 21% of GNP. Three years from now, after all this massive tax cutting, taxes will be about 20% of GNP. So the tax load gets reduced by only one percentage point. If real GNP grows by more than 1% over the next few years, the total tax burden will rise. That is not a big tax cut. It's really a tax freeze. To be sure, it is a necessary one, and the Reagan tax approach does provide needed restructuring by lowering the top brackets and providing incentives for savers. But I wouldn't expect much economic "juice" from such a small reduction.

Actually, about eight out of the ten bullets in the supply-side program are aimed at trying to pull down demand coming from the government sector by either cutting spending, or cutting the rate of growth of the money supply, or freeing up business resources through less government regulation. I would characterize the program as an interest rate/inflation control plan geared to get investments going by providing longer-term funds in financial markets.

Kristol: What we are getting is a freeze on individual tax rates over the next two and a half to three years. That is it. Sure, we are getting a lot of other things—this "Christmas tree" Congress is giving us for business—and that is better than nothing. But I believe this tax cut is too small and I myself do not perceive it as especially ideological.

Moderator: Have political considerations crept into Administration policies?

Kristol: I think the political aspect—one which I call the populist element in supply-side economics—is absolutely crucial. An interesting question is: Why did Ronald Reagan hitch his horse to supply-side economics? I think it is because he has very good political instincts. He did not want to put the economy through the wringer, since there is no way that a Republican president can create a Republican majority in this country by beginning with a recession. For him that is the key consideration.

Moderator: Will the process of political compromise dilute the potential of the supply-side strategy?

Rutledge: It could. I think Administration officials have really blundered in their marketing effort. They have continued to advertise tax cuts that will stimulate the economy. But actually they have emasculated a key element in the supply-side program. As I said earlier, there is no big tax cut. The principal avenue of stimulus is inflation control. Administration officials should go ahead and admit that there really isn't much in the way of added fiscal stimulus. Such an admission in my view would exert a positive influence on the bond market.

ATTACKING INFLATION

Moderator: Could we probe a bit more deeply into the linkage between supply-side economics and a cure for inflation? Specifically, might Administration projections on lower inflation (see box) take longer to achieve than forecast?

Rutledge: Prices can and do move very quickly. And the reason they move quickly is that people are not stupid. They set prices with an eye on the government.

Kristol: I don't think anyone ever claimed supply-side economics in and of itself is a solution to inflation. If the government wants to inflate, it can still do so even if it adopts supply-side policies.

Laffer: In my view, this Administration has in fact not done anything to really impact inflation. Therefore, bond-market participants are correctly concluding that until the Administration does do something, they will be disbelievers.

The heart of the problem is this: The government has a quasi-monopoly on the liabilities of the monetary authority, and as such it has been operating all along trying to control the growth rate and the quantity of these liabilities in order to bring inflation under control.

I don't think that approach can work. Being a classicist in my own perception, I think the only thing government should do is to produce a *quality* product—the money supply—as opposed to regulating the quantity of that product in the marketplace. I think the government should guarantee the purchasing power of the U.S. currency. Until

OFFICIAL FIVE–YEAR FORECAST

THE Reagan Administration forecasts a significant improvement in U.S. economic performance over the next five years (accompanying table). The growth of "real" GNP is expected to average 4¼ % over the 1982-86 period—considerably faster than the 3¼ % average growth over the preceding five years. Inflation is anticipated to be below 5% by 1985, and a sharp reduction is also expected in market interest rates. Moreover, the unemployment rate is seen dipping below 6%, and the budget of the federal government is projected to be in balance by the 1984 fiscal year.

Supply-side tax policy is to play a critical but not exclusive role in generating this success story. Tight monetary policy, regulatory relief, and control over government spending are also stressed as essential ingredients of the Reagan strategy.

	1982	1983	1984	1985	1986
"Real" GNP growth (%)	3.4	5.0	4.5	4.2	4.2
Consumer prices (%)	7.0	5.7	5.2	4.6	4.2
Unemployment rate (%)	7.3	6.6	6.2	5.8	5.5
Interest rates: Three-month Treasury bills (%)	10.5	7.5	6.8	6.0	5.5
Budget surplus or deficit (billions of dollars)	−42.5	−22.9	0.5	5.8	28.2

NOTE: Real growth and consumer prices are year-over-year percentage changes. Unemployment and interest rates are average levels. Budget figures are for fiscal years. SOURCE: Mid-session Review of the 1982 Budget, Office of Management and Budget, July 15, 1981.

that is done we will not have a serious anti-inflation policy in this country.

Moderator: Are you suggesting convertibility of the dollar into gold?

Laffer: Yes, I am. Make the dollar as good as gold.

Moderator: Do you expect that to happen any time soon?

Laffer: I think the Administration is going to go back to gold convertibility. I think it is going to do it sooner rather than later. Ronald Reagan has made it very clear that he believes very much in a convertible currency.

When the Administration makes the dollar attractive by guaranteeing its value, then the bond market will perform very, very well. Until that time, any stream of monetary claims is highly suspect. Inflation is a monetary phenomenon, and the only monetary solution I know of is to make the dollar convertible, to guarantee its purchasing power.

Rutledge: I agree with the basic point: The problem of inflation is that there is no discipline over governments. So whether you get the discipline through a gold standard or some other arrangement is fine with me. But I am very skeptical that it is going to happen. I think the chances of a return to gold happening this year are about zero. After all, what government wants to put itself in a straitjacket? And even if it did, financial markets might still be skeptical. What a government has done about gold it can decide to undo.

Moderator: Participants in financial markets seem concerned about the continuance of large deficits in the federal budget. Dr. Roberts, would you address that concern?

Roberts: Everything is fine, they say, except the budget isn't balanced quickly enough. Why doesn't the Administration take money out of the tax cut and put it in revenues, and thus balance the budget more quickly?

Now, it doesn't work that way. You can't look at the government budget as if it were an accounting document, in which you can move something from one line to another. If you take the approach of "let us raise taxes and balance the budget first," you inhibit economic growth, increase the need for more government spending, and therefore the deficit stays where it is.

And the crucial difference is that this approach moves you further away from the path that will bring you to a balanced budget. You stay in the mode of the permanently unbalanced budget, because of the persistence of a weekly performing economy.

I think that is something that has been widely overlooked. People— and, unfortunately, many financial-market participants—are so conditioned by the past approach to deficits that they haven't quite caught on that in this new policy the deficit is an almost irrelevant side effect of restructuring the tax code. As I said earlier, in our approach deficits are removed from being an instrument of policy.

Moderator: Is the program fair or does it favor some segments of society over others?

Kristol: If the program leads to economic growth, it will be good for everyone. I think that is fair. But if you identify fairness with equality then obviously you have another point of view. In a society such as ours, some people simply will do better than others.

Laffer: I think fairness is a very important concept. I would be upset with a program if I felt for a moment that the lowest echelons of our society were not going to improve enormously. The supply-side model is a prescription for a beneficial government in such a way as to make all of us better off.

Kristol: Obviously, I expect low-income people to benefit. But one of the interesting things about economic growth is you never know who will benefit most. It is not predictable.

Moderator: A number of economists are concerned that the Administration's economic growth plans will clash with an unaccommodative Federal Reserve intent on restricting credit expansion in order to curb inflation. Do you lie awake at night worrying about that?

Roberts: Yes, I do. But then I worry about what things would be like if we had a program calling for larger deficits to stimulate consumption and to fight unemployment, and for more public-sector programs to deal with inequalities by redistributing income and expanding CETA jobs to make up for the private sector jobs that were not being provided. And I think if I had that program to defend I would be even more worried.

10

Supply-Side Effects of Fiscal Policy *

ROBERT E. KELEHER

Reductions in tax rates tend to increase the supply of labor because of shifts from leisure to work and from non-market to market activity. They also increase the supply of capital because of shifts from consumption to savings and investment activity and from tax shelters to more productive uses of capital.

In a paper published in June 1979 as part of the Federal Reserve Bank of Atlanta's Research Paper Series, Robert E. Keleher discussed some key issues surrounding tax cuts, and, in particular, examined the effects of tax cuts on the "supply-side." A longer article based on the Research Paper appeared in the September/October 1979 *Economic Review*, but because of the recent, increased attention to the topic, a brief outline of some of the paper's major points may be of interest to some readers.

In particular, the political campaign and the "tax revolt" have focused attention on the economic effects of a major tax cut. Opponents of a tax cut fear that increased consumer spending and an increased government deficit will result in higher inflation. In the debate over the effects of cutting taxes, many economists of both Keynesian and monetarist persuasions have focused almost entirely on how tax cut policies affect aggregate demand. Because of this preoccupation with aggregate demand, these economists do not distinguish between the economic effects of tax cuts and government spending increases or between tax rate changes and tax revenue changes.

According to economists (including Keleher) who support the so-

*Reprinted with permission from the *Economic Review*, Federal Reserve Bank of Atlanta, September/October 1980.

called "supply-side" view, tax rate cuts not only affect disposable income but also may induce changes in the supplies of factors of production such as labor and capital and hence changes in aggregate production, supply and economic growth. Tax rate changes, they argue, are relative price changes and thus will affect choices between work and leisure, consumption and saving-investment, and market and non-market activity. These changes in the supply of factors of production to the market economy consequently affect aggregate supply and economic growth. Supply-side effects, in their view, are a key to the long-term growth of the economy. For those economists, then, these effects are more relevant to growth theory and policy than to stabilization theory (which seeks to control short-term, cyclical fluctuations in the economy).

Although most economists agree that the supply-side effects of fiscal policy exist and that these effects have long been neglected in macroeconomics, Keleher says there is still much disagreement about the policy implementation of these ideas. If the economy is on the upper portion of the so-called "Laffer Curve," for example (when, theoretically, rising tax rates diminish incentives to work and to supply capital and eventually reduce tax revenues), then the substantial increase in tax rates in recent years has induced a slowdown in aggregate market production that, together with undiminished monetary expansion, has produced "stagflation" (i.e., the coexistence of high rates of inflation and sluggish real economic growth).

Accordingly, supporters of this view recommend a reduction in tax rates which they contend will increase production (aggregate supply), the tax base, and, consequently, tax revenues. They argue further that if such policies are coupled with a gradual deceleration in the growth of the money supply, such tax cuts can contribute to slowing the rate of inflation.

Other economists have questions about the location of the economy on the "Laffer Curve," the magnitude of the supply-side effects, and the timing of the effects. Empirical tests of refutable tax cut hypotheses, they argue, have not been conducted. Tax cuts, in their view, could create pressures to monetize the increased deficit and thus create inflationary pressures in the short run. Supply-side theorists respond that these are short-term uncertainties which do not invalidate the long-term supply-side effects of a consistent fiscal and monetary policy.

Proponents of the supply-side theory include those economists who support tax cutting policies in order to slow the increase in total government spending (as a proportion of GNP). Instead of making decisions about government spending in isolation from decisions about revenue collection and taxation (as is currently the case), they argue, the electorate should first decide about levels of taxation and then allow its representatives to allocate these revenues.

Keleher's study analyzes specifically how these "supply-side" tax cuts influence (a) incentives, (b) the market supplies of factors of production, and (c) aggregate supply. Although the study is in the nature of "some preliminary hypotheses," Keleher concludes that reductions in tax rates tend to increase the supply of labor services because of shifts from leisure to work and from nonmarket to market activity. They also increase the supply of capital because of (a) shifts from consumption to savings and investment activity and (b) from tax shelters to more productive domestic uses of capital. Consequently, such restrictions in tax rates are likely to increase the economy's aggregate supply of real goods and services. In a concluding section, Keleher also summarizes some of the criticisms and various implications of the "supply-side" position.

11

A Rational Expectation Approach to Supply-Side Economics[*]

PAUL A. ANDERSON[†]

Regardless of who was elected President, we are likely to have some kind of tax cut in the United States in 1981. Almost surely, the tax package which will be enacted will include some provision designed to encourage capital investment by business.

For an economist, there are (at least) two interesting questions to consider:

1. What is the best policy to encourage capital formation and real growth?
2. What will be the effect of the policy actually taken?

As business economists, most of us have probably spent some time analyzing the first question. However, the real world being what it is, I suspect that most of us get paid for informing our employers or clients about the answer to the second question. If so, we are well-advised to concentrate our limited resources on that second question.

I am here today to express my opinions on both questions. In doing so, I speak from a somewhat different point of view from that of most discussants, the rational expectations point of view.

The rational expectations hypothesis is the cornerstone of the monetary policy prescriptions championed by the Minneapolis Federal Reserve Bank, but it has important implications for fiscal policy as well. I will explain, briefly, why the rational expectations hypothesis is important to the analysis of both questions, and then proceed to discuss our two questions.

*Reprinted with permission from *Business Economics*, March 1981.

†Presented September 15, 1980 at the 22nd Annual Meeting of the National Association of Business Economists in Los Angeles. The opinions expressed here are solely those of the author and do not necessarily represent the views of First Bank Minneapolis, its management or staff.

RATIONAL EXPECTATIONS AND TAX POLICY

The rational expectations hypothesis is important to fiscal policy analysis because of the increasing use and influence of econometric models for policy purposes. More and more frequently, decision-makers at all levels of government are confronted with econometric simulations of the expected effects of the alternative measures they are considering. The policy-makers then choose between the alternatives by deciding which econometric consequences they prefer.

The main point of the rational expectations research is that this sort of econometric policy evaluation using today's models does not provide reliable guidance for policy-makers. This is because today's models do not capture behavior which will remain unchanged when economic policies change. Let's not be abstract, let's consider a concrete example.

How many companies make an investment decision by considering only past interest rates, past tax rates, past costs, past sales and past prices? You and I (and the architects of econometric models) know that is not the most relevant information for a capital decision. Yet those data are what determine the level of investment spending in a garden variety investment equation from one of today's econometric models.

Investment decisions are based on forecasts of the future, on expectations of the stream of future after-tax profits which a building or a piece of equipment can provide. The equation from our econometric model is meant to represent the linkage:

- Investment is a function of expectations
- Expectations are a function of past data therefore, Investment is a function of past data.

This investment equation may be a useful representation of actual investment behavior over a period of time when the relationship between expectations and past conditions remains relatively static.

But when an important change in government economic policy is made, the expectations held by many firms change—and they change quickly. A firm's forecasts of future sales, future prices, future interest rates can be changed drastically. Moreover, those forecasts will depend not only on the present policy change but also on the firm's perception of what policy will be in effect next year and the year after.

In short, the investment response of the firms in the economy will depend on their expectations of *future* policies as well as actual *current* economic policies. For example, the investment response to a change in Federal Reserve policy is a reaction to not only the current market action by the Fed but also to the expected future moves, which today's action makes more likely.

Even if the standard investment equation can represent the *qualitative* response to a policy change it is unlikely that it will be able to give a good picture of the *quantitative* response in investment. And for many policy decisions, the quantitative effects—how much, how fast—are most important to the final choice.

A recent article by two economists at the Minneapolis Fed lays out the rational expectations critique of current methods of policy evaluation in more detail. The authors argue that the current methods of econometric policy simulation have contributed to generating higher inflation and have encouraged economic policies which have been too activist in nature. Both of these problems impact the capital formation process adversely and eliminating or compensating for those effects is an important element in a comprehensive capital growth policy.

Question 1: What is the Best Tax Policy?

From the rational expectations point of view, current econometric models are not of much help in answering the first question, but the question can be answered without relying on an econometric model.

I consider the objective of the various policies sometimes labeled "supply-side" economics to be the acceleration of the process of capital formation and, ultimately, of real growth. To be sure, capital formation has been unsatisfactory in recent years. I would like to focus on two factors which have had important adverse impacts on capital formation: current tax treatment of depreciation cost and the growing trend of stop-and-go economic policy.

Current tax treatment of depreciation inhibits capital spending during a period of inflation because allowable historical depreciation costs understate true economic depreciation costs. If a company's revenues and other costs keep pace with inflation, its taxable income (and hence its taxes) will grow faster than inflation because its depreciation costs on existing equipment are unchanged by inflation. Therefore, the attractiveness of a proposed capital investment in an inflationary environment is lessened by depreciation tax treatment.

Secondly, the inconsistency of government economic policy—both regulatory and stabilization policy—increases the uncertainty of the forecasts of future revenues and costs. The usual reaction of a business firm to an increase in the uncertainty surrounding future conditions is to take a more cautious approach to capital spending. And I think the net effect of the conduct of economic policy over the last fifteen years has been to increase the skepticism of business planners with respect to the assumptions about future policy which they must make as part of capital budgeting.

A successful tax policy to encourage capital formation must address both of these shortcomings of current policy. The first shortcoming, the treatment of depreciation, could be solved quite simply. We just need to make the corporate tax system neutral with respect to inflation. The accelerated depreciation proposals currently being discussed in Congress fall short of this objective. By shortening the official useful lives of different classes of capital assets, these proposals do raise the inflation "break even point" for investment and, hence, will provide an incentive for increased investment. But these proposals still leave us with a system in which high inflation can exert a drag on capital spending.

A simpler, more permanent remedy for this problem would be the Jorgenson-Auerbach depreciation proposal. Under this scheme, businesses would be able to expense the present value of future depreciation expenses in the year the initial investment is made. The present value calculation would use the existing schedule of useful lives (possibly somewhat simplified) and a "real" discount rate. This policy would not allow inflation to distort the investment choice and would not require some future legislative remedies if inflation escalates in the future.

The second problem—the uncertainty growing out of unpredictable economic policy—does not lend itself to such a quick easy solution. The main ingredient of a tax policy to stimulate capital formation should be to remove government policy as a source of uncertainty in business planning to the extent that this is possible.

To make headway on this second problem, the next administration, be it Republican, Democrat, or Independent, must announce (and follow) a consistent economic strategy which aims at explicitly stated long-term goals. The administration must state where it really thinks the economy is going, and what actions it is prepared to take (or consider) if subsequent economic events do not shape up as expected. While this strategy has sizable short-term political risks, the longer-term gains (both economic and political) of such an approach would be substantial. Obviously, not every contingency can be analyzed by economic policy strategiest, but there would be sizable benefits accruing from a policy of sending as clear a signal as possible about the course of future policy.

Whether the next administration will have the courage to undertake such a departure from past practice is, of course, a matter of conjecture. No econometric simulation can be produced to quantify the effects of such a strategy, but from a rational expectations point of view I believe such a bold step is necessary to make consistent progress to encourage capital formation.

Question 2: What Effect Will the Actual Policy Have?

At present, there are at least two ways of incorporating the insights of the rational expectations literature into predictions of the effects of "supply-side" tax policies.

The first option would be to modify an existing econometric model to reflect rational adjustment of expectations and its effects on market decisions. This modified model could then be used to simulate policy effects.

I carried out such an exercise while working in the Federal Reserve System, but I would not choose that option for my current work for several reasons. First, the internal structure of today's models is not really robust enough to give reliable forecasts when modified piecemeal. Second, such experiments are valid only under the twin assumptions that policy authorities will stick to their guns and that economic agents have confidence that the authorities will do so. (In recent history, instances of *either* assumption being a reasonable basis for analysis have been rare.) Finally, the resources costs of such an approach are substantial.

The second option, the one I have chosen to use, is a more efficient employment of resources from my point of view. I consider the econometric simulations from existing models and then analyze whether the picture they provide is really consistent with a rational expectations view of the behavior of the firms and individuals in the economy. I then modify the quantitative effects of the particular model at hand in line with my answers to several questions like:

- Is this policy change likely to be perceived as temporary or relatively long-lived?
- Are agents likely to expect the effects on interest rates, prices, and demands which are shown in the simulation?
- If these future economic conditions were known with certainty, would I as a firm or consumer react as the equations of the model predict?
- Are there significant risks which would cause me to take a different strategy of investment from the certainty alternative?

The results of such a process is a view of the macroeconomic effects of alternative policies which broadly reflects the outlines of the rational expectations viewpoint. While the specific "supply-side" policies to be put in place in 1981 are not yet known, some conclusions can be drawn at this point.

If the policies enacted have the appearance and reality of permanence, I feel that the standard econometric models (even most of the newer "supply-side oriented" models) are likely to under-predict the short-run and long-run increases in investment which will result. However, if the 1981 tax changes are not enacted in a way that seems to guarantee continued future policy support for investment, the resultant investment growth will be slower than most econometric models will predict.

CONCLUSION

Current "supply-side" economic policy proposals are designed to correct some of the (correctly) perceived failings of the last 15 years of economic stabilization policy. From a rational expectations point of view, the recent problems of standard policy are more the result of inappropriate activism than of the "Keynesian" choice to operate on the demand side of the economy.

A rational expectations approach to "supply-side" economics would stress that the most important element of a successful investment stimulation program is to make future policy as predictable as possible. It is very important that policy-makers take a more long-term, less activist approach. To be sure, there will be tempting econometric simulation results which will promise short-term gains from zigging and zagging on the supply-side of economic policy. Almost surely, attempts to reap those short-term gains will fail.

Supply-side advocates must therefore be painfully realistic in promising the benefits that will accrue from their approach. From the rational expectations point of view, one can confidently predict that Congress and the public will be much quicker to abandon an approach which overpromises and fails to deliver than they were last time around.

12

The Politics of Supply-Side Economics*

ORRIN G. HATCH

We have, in the Congress, a thing called a "budget process." You may not have noticed it, but it's there. It was the subject of heated debate when it was established in the middle 1970s, when many legislators who were worried about spending voted for it on the grounds that it would force us all to think about the financial consequences of our various programs, to reconcile them, and to set priorities.

It hasn't done that. In fact, deficits have gotten worse since the budget process began, and government spending is now approaching proportions of the GNP previously reached only in wartime. What the budget process did achieve was an infallible method of providing rationales for increased spending, usually in terms of an alleged rise in unemployment should government spending be reduced in the economy, but sometimes by means of specialized studies on technical issues. I might add here that the one area where the budget process did act to inhibit spending was defense, where it tended to challenge the specific requests made by the Pentagon and its friends in Congress. By coincidence, this reflected the political priorities of the party controlling Congress at the time and the predilections of the staff members coming onto the Hill during the Vietnam era.

All this happened in spite of the fact that the Congressional Budget Act of 1974 set up a body called the Congressional Budget Office, which was supposed to provide politicians in both Houses with dispassionate, objective, and professional assessments of policy proposals. As it turned out, it was the CBO that provided the arguments for increased spending,

*Reprinted from *The Supply-Side Effects of Economic Policy*. Federal Reserve Bank of St. Louis and the Study for the Center of American Business, May 1981.

and it backed them up with an imposing array of evidence from a variety of econometric models, much of it written in Greek and emanating from computers—which, as you know, never lie. For that matter, since economics is a science, many legislators, although puzzled, concluded that economists couldn't lie either, and that if they said deficits were OK, they must be.

There are in reality value judgments at the heart of the Keynesian orthodoxy, and particularly at the heart of the Keynesian proponents. This is not just a matter of Alice Rivlin (the supposedly impartial head of the CBO and one of what *Newsweek* magazine called the "half dozen leading liberal economists") dining with Senator Kennedy to prepare him for his challenge to Mr. Carter last year. (Another CBO projection bites the dust!) It isn't even just a matter of the faulty underlying assumptions contained in the CBO projections, although these are often rather odd. The CBO, as you all know from reading the literature, has for years systematically favored spending increases over tax reductions as a means of stimulating the economy, and, at one time, it was even using a model which assumed that a decrease in corporate taxation would reduce GNP.

Where the element of faith in the Keynesian orthodoxy really comes into its own is in the CBO's steady resistance to any sort of analytical or empirical debate about its assumptions. We had a particularly graphic example of this in the spring of 1980. There is abroad in the Western world at the moment, a particularly lethal weapon that has totally altered the balance of power between employers and the employed. This weapon is called the Xerox machine, and some anonymous dissident on the Budget Committee staff used it to send us a copy of a memo (written to Ed Muskie, then Chairman of the Budget Committee, from his staff director) discussing detailed collaboration between the CBO head and the Democrats on the Committee to suppress Republican efforts for a hearing on the econometric models CBO uses. These models, of course, are under severe attack for ignoring the incentive effect, and we were hoping to get CBO to consider some of the supply-side thinking now going on, of which this conference is a symptom.

The memo told Muskie: "Alice [Rivlin] doesn't really want to have hearings and would like to put Hatch off somehow. She says—and Susan Lepper (the Majority Economist) supports her in this—that the critics of the models CBO uses for forecasting are an extreme right wing claque who should not be given an audience, lest it legitimize their views and give Hatch a forum which should be denied him if we could. If we are to hold hearings, Alice believes they should involve noted economists telling the Committee that Hatch's witnesses are wrong. . . ."

Later on in the memo, the staff director told Muskie: "I am tempted to have him[me] off on this tangent, which few people know or care about outside the economics profession, rather than leave him with time to become involved with something that might be more serious. . . ."

None of this looks particularly objective or dispassionate, or for that matter even scientific, to me. Of course, I'm just a lawyer. I think the sad thing about all of this is that the people involved, whether political appointees like the Democratic staffers or civil servants like the CBO functionaries, are not in themselves dishonest or conniving people. The nature of the system causes them to act in this way because their own short-term interests are so very clearly involved.

Although bureaucrats and politicians—at least certain politicians—do benefit from continual deficits and pervasive inflation, the system is unstable. Inflation is only a temporary answer to the problem of separating the taxpayers of this world from their earnings. For one thing, the dislocation it causes annoys and distresses them. For another, the combination of inflated incomes carrying more individuals into higher tax brackets, and government expenditures which are steadily mounting, means that the underlying resistance to taxes is steadily increasing. More and more people are being pushed into the fiscal free-fire zone. They are reacting by digging fox-holes, constructing tax shelters, and generally refusing to obey orders.

This is a particularly acute problem for the economists of our "ruling class"—because that's what the Keynesians, in effect, are. Their system is entirely set up to suppress insurrections from people who believe in balanced budgets—and there are still a lot of them about, incidentally. All they have to do is show that balancing the budget will cause economic disruption, besides requiring either tax increases or spending reductions. But they don't have any way of dealing with the negative incentives of their system, except more government intervention to divide up the pie or to treat the symptoms of rising prices and wages. This is why we hear so much now about "zero-sum societies," lowered expectations, spiritual malaises, and so on. Tacitus said the Romans made a desert in Germany, and called it peace. We can say of the economic establishment that it has made a stagnant pond, and called it the Great Society. Still, it has been good for real estate prices in Georgetown. And it is causing us to rejoin the human race—with a command economy, with welfare for people and corporations.

In other words, supply-side economics has arrived in exactly the situation the late Harry Johnson diagnosed as existing at the time of the advent of Keynes, at the onset of the Depression:

> . . . On the one hand, the existence of an important social and political problem with which the prevailing orthodoxy was unable to cope, on the other hand, [a new theory with] a variety of characteristis that appealed to the younger generation of that period—notably the claim of

the new theory to superior social relevance and intellectual distinction, its incorporation in a novel and confusing fashion of the valid elements of traditional theory, the opportunity it offered to bypass the system of academic seniority by challenging senior colleagues . . . [and] the advancement of a new empirical relationship challenging for econometricians to estimate.

This may sound cynical, but it isn't really. As we have seen, economic policy is an area where even the most qualified professionals seem to have trouble keeping their minds open to new and inconvenient ideas. In that respect, it's unlike academic life—I hope. If any theory is to flourish in this environment, it must be protected by its political mentors. Keynes, incidentally, was fully aware of this and used every trick he could think of to advance his views. He had an extremely active mind, so he thought of a lot of tricks.

The best way of thinking about economic policy is by comparing it to a dog fight between World War II fighters. You have to aim at some point other than at the target itself in order to hit it, given your relative motion and so on. This is something that Keynes understood. He told Friedrich von Hayek that he realized his policy prescription would be inherently inflationary, but that when the moment came he would step in and turn public opinion around in six weeks. When Hayek tells this story, he always adds, with an ironic grin, that six weeks later Keynes was dead. But the point is that Keynes wanted to solve certain problems and he wanted to change policymakers' thinking about them, and the importance they put on them. In a sense, you could argue that there's an element of myth about all economic policy proposals—as defined by the French historian Sorel, who said many years ago that myths in human society were not factual statements, but were instead expressions of intentions to act.

Keynes was successful in getting all of us—not merely liberals—to accept his values. And I believe that those who have developed the supply-side theories will be successful in shifting our attention once again to incentives and production and the economic applications of liberty. As I say, this isn't merely an academic achievement. It is a political achievement of no small merit. What the supply-siders have done is to point out that the war between the proponents of incentives and the federal government's spending constituencies is not necessary. It is possible to attack at another point: to get tax rates down and stimulate growth sufficiently to pay for the current rate of social services, hence bypassing the question of whether social spending is too high.

Now, will these services be paid for out of tax revenues that have increased absolutely, while decreasing in terms of rates levied on individuals? Or will they be financed out of additonal savings generated by increased production? Or will we in fact find further deficits, albiet in the context of a policy that promises to get the country moving again rather than sinking under taxes and regulation? There are various answers to these questions, but in a broader sense, these questions are upstaged by the new awareness in the public debate of incentives—that there is supply as well as demand.

An example of this new awareness came in Mr. Carter's recently proposed tax package, which seems as if it were designed to catch attention as an alternative to Mr. Reagan's tax proposal. No one can deny the White House's exquisite sensitivity to currents abroad in the land—to style, if not to substance. When you look at President Carter's proposals in detail, you can see the extraordinary gains the supply-side offensive has made in the last two years—and also the stubborn and ferocious determination of the economic establishment to maintain and expand its power and that of the government, come what may. A recent H. C. Wainwright study by Paul Craig Roberts shows how President Carter's tax cut is really aimed at objectives other than tax reduction.

In the matter of a few short months over the summer, President Carter went from telling the American people that the $36 billion tax cut proposed by Governor Reagan would cause "fierce inflation" to proposing a $27.6 billion tax cut of his own, which he said would be "anti-inflationary." Following on the heels of the Senate Finance Committee's proposal for a $39 billion tax cut, it put to rest the argument that the Reagan-Kemp-Roth tax cut was bad politics. So we can now move to the merits of the proposals and determine which would provide the most incentives to increase production.

By comparison, the Kemp-Roth tax cut bill proposed by Governor Reagan is clearly a supply-side proposal, since it concentrates solely on reducing marginal tax rates. Measured by static revenue losses, it is more heavily weighted toward "individual" rather than "business" tax reductions. The Senate Finance Committee bill, although it wastes about $7 billion on enlarging the zero bracket amount, personal exemption, and earned income tax credit, is largely an application of incentive-oriented supply-side economics. It gives 56 percent of its cut to individuals and 44 percent to business. President Carter's proposal is more heavily weighted toward business, giving it 55 percent of the cut. But, although the Carter proposal is cloaked in supply-side rhetoric, a closer look shows that it is designed to achieve ends quite different from lowering marginal tax rates or increasing production incentives.

One example is the refundable investment tax credit. The purpose of the investment tax credit is to boost the incentive for investment in new equipment; there is no economic sense to excluding firms with no tax liability. It is often new and rapidly growing firms that have no tax liability against which to apply a non-refundable credit. But the main problem with the refundable investment tax credit is the precedent it establishes. How could we hope to avoid making, say, the child care tax credit refundable for poor people if big business has it? The child care tax credit is expensive—up to $800 per eligible return—and making it refundable would be a big step toward expansion of the federal welfare system.

The refundable investment tax credit would also expand the federal welfare concept to business. It would establish the concept of extending the dole to businesses that lose money. It would result in an institutionalized bail-out scheme instead of making the Congress consider it on a case-by-case basis. This is hardly the way to "make careful investments in American productivity"—Carter's way of differentiating his tax cut from Reagan's.

Another part of the President's proposal that will contribute to the growth of government intervention in the economy is the additional 10 percent refundable investment tax credit targeted to revitalize depressed areas. Firms that want to qualify must obtain certificates of necessity from the Commerce Department, but the criteria for determining eligible areas are not defined. This would give the government the ability to reward its friends and withhold the credit from the uncooperative. Even if the system could be kept free of political corruption, government allocation of resources will certainly reduce efficiency in the economy.

We should also note that President Carter is also suggesting that the Treasury Secretary be given the power to adjust depreciation rates at will. This is another expansion of the government's discretionary power. And it's likely that the accumulated effect of his proposed substitution of open-end for vintage accounting will tend to reduce the present value of the depreciation allowance for technical reasons. So the pro-business aspects of Mr. Carter's plan can be—and have been—exaggerated.

On the individual side of the Carter tax package, an income tax credit is used to partially offset the scheduled increase in the social security tax out of general revenue funds. Instead of reducing marginal tax rates, it is a scheme to redistribute income and turn social security into a welfare program by taking the first step into general revenue financing. If the President were really interested in avoiding the economic damage that will result from the social security tax increases, he could just postpone or repeal the scheduled increase. The only reason for the income tax credit approach is to attack the contributory nature of social security and plunge into general revenue financing. This type of tax cut is likely to guarantee continuing revenue losses and deficits. Although it has the smallest static revenue loss, it would probably be the most expensive, net of feedback, because of the negative supply-side effects.

On the whole, the Carter tax cut encompasses the welfare rather than the incentive approach to tax policy. Most of its provisions increase the discretionary power of the government to control the economy. It would divert resources from economic to political uses, and would lead to deficits and revenue losses that would prevent us from getting the incentive tax cuts the economy needs to grow.

Furthermore, the Democratic Platform contains 70 separate items that will result in federal government spending. Over the next five years, the platform would cost $608 billion in budget authority and $431 billion in outlays. In comparison to the Senate Budget Committee's second budget resolution for FY 1981, the Democratic Platform would add $74 billion in budget authority and $30 billion in outlays in FY 1981, and $566 billion in budget authority and $389 billion in outlays over the FY 1981 to 1985 period. If enacted into law, the Democratic Platform would cause federal outlays to increase to 24.7 percent of GNP in 1982, and this includes no additional outlays for interest on the public debt due to the higher deficits. Coupled with President Carter's tax cut, it would create a $261 billion deficit over the next five years as opposed to the $74 billion surplus Governor Reagan's plan would create.

I want to conclude tonight by commenting on the checkered fortunes of the tax revolt since it first materialized in California in 1978. Since then, it has been periodically proclaimed to have run out of steam. Certainly the lobbying groups arrayed on the side of increased spending still seem to be alive and dangerous; victory has been by no means as automatic as it first appeared it might be. But it might be remembered that we are fighting a momentum that has built up over a period of decades. The proponents of income redistribution, deficits and government intervention took years to perfect their appeal to the broad electorate, and to overcome the doubts, scruples and skepticism of the American people about charity, the expropriation of property, and the surrender of independence that the welfare state entails. It will take us years, too—although the success we have had in forcing our opponents to steal our rhetoric is evidence of some sort of progress. And in the end, our task will be easier. It is in the processes of liberty that we are fighting for, and they are intrinsic to the American tradition. After all, it was a dispute over taxation that triggered the American Revolution. It is not surprising—it is, indeed, highly appropriate— that we should have gathered here to think about tax policy in the consciousness that what we have been doing in reality is to contemplate at least the success and perhaps, ultimately, the survival of liberty itself.

13

The Economics and Politics of The Supply-Side View*

F. THOMAS JUSTER

Economic policy is, at least for the moment, set on a course which is distinctly different from the past. What are the prospects that the new policy will successfully produce the set of outcomes that its proponents hope to achieve—a reinvigorated economy with a smaller but more effective public sector; an incentive structure designed to produce more effort, saving, and investment; a business climate more conducive to innovation and productivity growth; and a sharply lower rate of inflation?

Seldom has an economic experiment been put in place with less conventional credentialing by professional economists. This is partly because supply-side policies represent a political statement at least as much as an economic perspective, partly because aspects of the supply-side view of economic life are not testable by assessing their consistency with the facts of economic life: supply-siders argue that many such facts are irrelevant because they come from a world where important expectational forces were substantially influenced by demand-side considerations.

What I judge to be the theoretical core of supply-side economics can be summed up in the following proposition:

1. Entitlement programs have eroded work incentives; cutting back on those programs will restore incentives and reduce the tax burden on the working and investing population.
2. The tax system is biased against effort, saving, and investment; reducing tax rates, especially marginal rates, will have a substantial effect on labor supply, saving, and investment.

*Reprinted with permission from *Economic Outlook USA*, Autumn, 1981.

3. Economic progress has been significantly impeded by an anti-business climate of regulation designed to protect consumer and employee groups against various risks: many of these regulations not only require large and unproductive investments, but have adverse cost/benefit ratios in terms of protection offered versus the costs of obtaining it.
4. The stubbornness of inflation forces is largely due to the expectational climate built up by the demand-side oriented fiscal and monetary policies followed by past administrations: modifying the expectations of decision makers will thus permit a much more rapid reduction in inflation rates, at less social cost, than would be predicted from past history.

In addition to the economic content of supply-side ideas, there is a strong political content as well. Supply-siders and their political allies are apt to believe that government in general is too big and inevitably inefficient, that an impersonal monetary policy is the only effective way to control the macroeconomy, that free markets are the only way to allocate resources efficiently under any and all circumstances, and that politicians of any persuasion are not to be trusted to carry out promises. Many of those who favor the current set of supply-side policies do not necessarily buy the economic underpinnings, or at least not all of them. Rather, they see supply-side theory and practice as a way to achieve other desirable objectives, and are willing to overlook its shaky intellectual foundations.

Whether or not supply-side policies will work depends ultimately on the adequacy of its economic underpinnings; from that perspective, the political content that is the basis for much of its support is largely irrelevant. Thus the basic question is: what can be said about the central analytical themes of supply-side economics?

ENTITLEMENTS AND INCENTIVES

There is a good bit of evidence to support the general thrust of the supply-side argument—that entitlement programs have sapped work incentives. Most economists would probably agree with the view that extended unemployment compensation benefits reduce people's willingness to seek work or to accept work that is less well paid than their previous occupation, and that the welfare system with its extremely high implicit marginal tax rates has discouraged people from entering or staying in the labor force, etc.[1]

The argument here is not whether such programs tend to reduce work incentives—they almost certainly do. Rather, it is a question of magnitude—is the incentive reduction aspect of the programs a major defect or a minor blemish? Moreover, is the incentive reducing effect sufficiently important to outweigh the income distribution aspects of the program? On the latter issue, economic analysis will not do much good, and value judgments are at issue.

The proposition that reducing marginal tax rates will have a significant effect on labor supply and effort for the working population is much more dubious. Here, there is quite a lot of evidence and general agreement among economists: the effect of reduced marginal tax rates on effort is quite minor, and much of the evidence suggests that there will be no effect at all. In fact, one can make a case that reducing marginal tax rates will actually cause less work effort rather than more—people may choose to work as many hours as needed to maintain a satisfactory consumption level, and increasing their after-tax income will make it possible to realize the consumption goal with fewer hours.

SAVING AND INVESTMENT INCENTIVES

It is true that the tax system is biased against saving and investment, relative to alternative tax systems that one could imagine. But that's a long way from saying that modification of the tax structure along the lines proposed by supply-siders will cause a great upswelling of saving and investment. There is a good bit of empirical evidence here, although much of it speaks only indirectly to the issue. On the whole, I would assess the potential impact of supply-side policies on saving decisions to be substantially weaker than the potential impact of such policies on investment decisions.[2]

On savings, there really is no persuasive evidence at all that personal or national saving rates would be impacted by modifications of the personal income tax structure, as argued by the supply-siders. Saving be-

---

[1] Incidentally, it is also true that some entitlement programs appear to have had major unintended effects on family structure—divorce, for example—which may be much more important than the labor supply effects.

[2] See F. Thomas Juster, "Saving, Economic Growth, and Economic Policy," in the Summer 1981 issue of *Economic Outlook USA*.

havior is influenced by a lot of factors, and after-tax rates of return do not loom large among such influences as best we can tell from the empirical evidence. In fact, as is true for labor supply responses, it is at least as plausible that increasing the after-tax rate of return on saving will cause people to save less rather than save more, and for the same reason— if people have wealth targets, they can reach them more easily with a higher rate of return on saving than with a lower one, and may therefore be induced to save less.

For investment, expected rates of return are crucial. But one needs a good deal more than a favorable tax structure to produce a favorable investment climate—business firms do not add to capacity without a robust forecast of higher sales, regardless of the tax climate for business profits, and the capital deepening that might result from a more favorable after-tax rate of return is a subtle and long-term effect that might or might not be importantly influenced by the tax structure.

REGULATORY CLIMATE

What may be potentially the strongest weapon in the supply-side arsenal is the impact of a change in the regulatory climate on private investment and on incentives to take risks. The evidence for the negative impact of present and prospective regulation on risk taking and investment decisions is not so overwhelmingly strong that one can confidently conclude that a change in the climate will produce a major impact on investment. However, the argument seems entirely plausible on theoretical grounds and has some empirical support. Business decision makers do seem to perceive the regulatory climate as one with a great many land mines, and tiptoeing through those mine fields does not seem conducive to bold investment strategies of the sort that we probably need in order to revitalize the economy. I would make the case by simply noting that bureaucracy generally stifles innovation, and whatever desirable social effects might be achieved by a vigorous regulatory climate, it is quite likely to create a distinct lack of enthusiasm for entrepreneurial adventure.

INFLATION AND EXPECTATIONS

An important underpinning to the supply-side view of life is the role given to expectations in influencing a variety of decisions. Much of our

recent economic history is consistent with the view that wringing inflation out of the U.S. economic system is likely to be a long and painful
process, involving very substantial losses in real income and output for a
very modest gain in lower inflation rates. Supply-siders argue that this
history is largely irrelevant, since it results from a widely held expectation that economic policy will be used to prevent a serious or prolonged
recession. And with an expectation that the government will bail the
system out of any temporary weakness, no one has any incentive to
modify behavior.

I am certainly not one to quarrel with the view that expectations
have a lot to do with behavior. On the other hand, I would feel a lot
more comfortable with the central focus given to expectational forces
by the supply-siders if they showed any interest in actually studying expectations, or how expectations change in response to events, or what
forces appear to influence expectations. But like most macroeconomists,
supply-siders seem quite content to infer the force of expectations from
observing consequences that could in theory be explained by expectational phenomena—a scientific procedure which has the great merit of
avoiding conflicts between theory and data, but the great demerit of
being untestable because it cannot discriminate among hypotheses.

Some of the expectational forces alleged to be important by supply-
siders seem to me quite plausible, others much less so. For example, I
think it is probably true that the stubbornness of inflationary forces in
the U.S. economy is a consequence of the widespread expectation that
policy will not tolerate extended periods of economic weakness. But it
remains to be seen whether changing those expectations will have a major
or only a minor impact on the cost of decelerating the inflation rate.

In other areas, the expectational views of supply-siders seem to me
simply implausible. For example, it is alleged on theoretical grounds
that the prospect of lower taxes on future income will shift labor supply
from the present, when income is taxed at a relatively high rate, to the
future, when income will be taxed at a lower rate. The notion that people
will buy more present leisure because they expect tax rates to decline
in the future is one that I find a little hard to relate to anything I think
I know about behavior.

One should be careful not to single out supply-siders for criticism on
this count. For example, most macroeconomists appear to believe that
people make saving, labor supply, and retirement decisions on the basis
of their expectations about social security entitlements in the distant
future. Thus they calculate a variable called "social security wealth"
and assume it represents a decision parameter in the household utility
function. Perhaps so, but I doubt it. People do have expectations of retirement income, and there is likely to be some influence on what they
do currently in terms of what they expect. But I doubt that the com-

puted actuarial value of future pension rights, properly discounted to
the present, is a very good representation of that expectational structure.
One indication of this problem is that pension rights, and even more so
changes in those rights, are pretty hard to calculate: for example, there
is an enormous advantage to continuing work between the ages of 62
and 65, in terms of the value of future social security benefits, but that
is not even realized by many of those who have written on social security
problems, let alone by the potential recipient.

Summing up the pluses and the minuses, it turns out that what many
see as the most important elements in supply-side economic policy—the
impact of changes in tax rates on labor supply and the flow of saving—
are the elements that are most in conflict with what we know about behavior, and the least likely to be effective. The other parts of the program—the effect on incentives of cutting entitlements, the effect on the
expectations of price and wage setters of changing the government's role
in setting limits to recession—seem more promising but represent views
supported by evidence that is shaky at best and often either casual or
impressionistic.

CURRENT POLICY ISSUES

Whether supply-side economics works or not will be determined over
the next several years—although there will doubtless be room for significant disagreement about why the economy does whatever it winds up
doing. But the current economic policy issue—should the budget be cut
by another $13 billion and taxes raised by about $3 billion, in order to
reduce the size of the prospective deficit in 1981-82—is not really a
supply-side issue at all. Rather, it seems to represent an attempt by the
administration to allay the concerns of the financial markets about the
impact of the massive tax cut on the present and prospective federal
deficits, in the face of an increase in the estimated current year deficit
that results largely from an economy whose behavior departs significantly
from the economic assumption built into the administration's original
projection. Thus the issues are: do deficits per se matter? And secondly,
are deficits per se important if the financial markets think they are important?

Few serious macroeconomists, supply-side or otherwise, regard deficits per se as an important target variable for economic policy, certainly
not in the short run. The only plausible case for targeting on deficits is
that they are symptomatic of an inability to make tough political decisions, and the only way to control the weakness of political decision

makers is to hold their feet to the fire, as it were, by imposing a balanced budget discipline.

Whatever merit that argument might or might not have as a long-run strategy for budget making, it certainly has little or no relevance to the situation currently facing the U.S. economy. We are, as the article by Victor Zarnowitz suggests, apparently slipping into recession: the most recent evidence suggests that the only question is how long and how deep will the recession be. In that environment, cutting back expenditures to bring the budget closer to balance is a prescription for foolishness.

Recessions represent a cumulative process of economic deterioration—economic weakness feeds on itself and spreads to sectors that were previously holding up, generating a cumulative sequence of weakening markets, deteriorating expectations, further weakening of markets, etc. In that environment, adding another $16 billion of weakness to an already soggy economy guarantees a worsening of whatever the cumulative deterioration might otherwise have been. The economy might even react to an additional nudge of this sort by weakening enough to produce the unpalatable outcome that the attempt to reduce the deficit is totally thwarted—the deterioration of incomes being sufficient to cause tax revenues to drop about as much as expenditures are cut. While that's an unlikely outcome—as is the supply-side scenario that cutting tax rates will stimulate enough activity to cause actual tax revenues to rise—it is not an impossible one.

To make matters even worse, the recommended cuts in expenditures will have a significant impact on areas that are crucially important to the long-term growth and development of the economy: virtually every major research and development activity supported from public funds has been earmarked for reductions in this "second round" of budget cuts. Thus not only would adoption of the administration's recommendations make a weak economy even weaker, but it would also result in cutting back on activities that are crucially important to the longer run growth of the system. It is hard to imagine a policy with less going for it, especially if its main purpose is to help Wall Street feel better about the president's overall program.

FISCAL EFFECTS OF
SUPPLY-SIDE ECONOMICS

Part III presents a bit more insight and depth into supply-side propositions. Moreover, it reveals some of the doubts and weaknesses of supply-side proposals.

14

Supply-Side Tax Policy: Reviewing the Evidence*

ROBERT E. KELEHER

"Supply-side economics" has come to mean different things to different people. A variety of proposals now are identified with the "supply-side" label. More importantly, there is a good deal of disagreement about the evidence relating to supply-side tax policies.

WHAT ARE SUPPLY-SIDE TAX CUTS?

Supply-side tax policies constitute more than a mere recognition that tax changes affect the supply of goods and services. What distinguishes supply-side policies from other policies is the manner in which tax changes affect factors of production (labor and capital, for example) and, hence, aggregate supply. Tax changes which are especially relevant to aggregate supply are changes in tax *rates*—(the rate at which the additional increment of activity is taxed). It is tax rates at the margin (not average tax levels) which affect behavior and incentives. Proponents of supply-side tax cuts indicate that there is an important distinction between tax rates and tax revenues. They emphasize that changes in such tax rates are changes in relative prices and thus affect choice, allocation of resources, and, hence, real economic activity. Thus, tax rate changes should be thought of as *relative price* changes and not as revenue or income changes; it is the change in relative prices and not the change in income or spending that matters for aggregate supply. Proponents of supply-side economics, therefore, do *not* see tax cuts as injections of purchasing power or spending.

*Reprinted from *The Economic Review*, April 1981, The Federal Reserve Bank of Atlanta.

A BRIEF REVIEW OF SOME EMPIRICAL EVIDENCE

Tax Cuts and the Supply of Labor: Several empirical studies have examined the effects of tax cuts on the supply of labor. The bulk of the evidence indicates that income tax reductions have only a limited effect on the overall supply of labor (usually measured by hours of work). Workers do not markedly increase or decrease hours of work, in other words, in response to changes in after-tax wage rates. (The elasticity of aggregate labor with respect to wages is low.) A 10-percent income tax reduction, for example, might increase hours of work for various groups of workers by anywhere from about 1 to as much as 10 percent, depending on the relevant groups considered.[1]

These responses are especially low for prime age male workers. A 10-percent income tax reduction, for example, might increase labor supplied by such workers by about 1 percent.[2] This evidence, then, indicates the tax cuts would have little effect on hours worked by prime age males. Secondary workers (mostly married women) together with younger and older workers make up about one-half of the total work force. Those groups have been found to be much more responsive to changes in after-tax wage rates.[3]

Tax Cuts and Savings: Although few studies have carefully examined this issue, most studies have found that saving is not responsive to changes in interest rates. The conventional view holds that tax cuts which would increase the after-tax rate of return to saving would have little or no effect on increasing the supply of saving. Because of this, some large econometric models do not include mechanisms representing the effect of taxes on personal savings.

Recently, however, some evidence has been provided which contradicts this accepted doctrine. Michael Boskin, employing more relevant measurements of interest rates, found a substantial interest elasticity of saving (about 0.4). While this is not an enormous elasticity by conventional standards, it is substantially larger than virtually all previous

---

[1]See, for example, Harvey Rosen, "What is Labor Supply and Do Taxes Affect It?", *American Economic Review,* May 1980; Don Fullarton, "On the Possibility of an Inverse Relationship Between Tax Rates and Government Revenues," Working Paper Series, National Bureau of Economic Research, No. 467; and Jerry Hausman, "Income and Payroll Tax Policy and Labor Supply," paper prepared for a conference on "The Supply-Side Effects of Economic Policy," Washington University and the Federal Reserve Bank of St. Louis, October 24-26, 1980. The labor studies referred to here are cross-section studies and, hence, are not associated with a time dimension. Consequently, they provide no information as to the timing of the response.

[2]See, for example, Hausman, *op. cit.*, p. 25.

[3]See Rosen, *op. cit.*, p. 171. (Elasticities for married women workers, for example, have been estimated to be as high as 1.0.)

estimates and the conventional wisdom.[4] Results indicating a substantial interest elasticity of saving have also been recently found by Evans, Ture, and especially King, Summers, and Boskin and Lau.[5] This recent evidence tends to indicate that the interest elasticity of saving is larger than conventionally believed. (Some of these recent estimates have been as high as 2.0 or 2.5!)[6] The implication is that tax cuts which increase the real after-tax return to saving would work to induce an important increase in saving.

Tax Cuts and Investments: Whereas the conventional doctrine holds that tax cuts have relatively small effects on the supply of saving and labor, it accepts the idea that tax changes can importantly affect investment. This view suggests that tax cuts directed at investment may be the most potent area to stimulate aggregate supply via their effect in increasing the capital stock. Otto Eckstein, for example, suggests that tax cuts for investment are the best way to boost real GNP. The effect on investment and the capital stock, of course, depends on the size and type of the tax cut. A study by Eckstein indicates that the elasticities of investment with respect to taxes (over the 1982-85 period) for various tax policies are the following:[7]

corporate income tax rate	−0.3
depreciation allowances	−1.1
investment tax credit	−0.9

As an illustration of the potency of depreciation allowances, Eckstein studied the so-called 10-5-3 proposal and concluded that if this proposal had been enacted in 1980, real business fixed investment would have

---

[4]Michael J. Boskin, "Taxation, Saving, and the Rate of Interest," *Journal of Political Economy*, Vol. 86, No. 2, Part 2, April 1978, p. 54. Boskin's study employs annual time series data. His results, then, imply that a 10-percent increase in the after-tax rate of return would increase saving by 4 percent per year. The other studies mentioned can be interpreted similarly.

[5]Michael K. Evans, "An Econometric Model Incorporating the Supply-Side Effects of Economic Policy," paper prepared for a conference on "The Supply-Side Effects of Economic Policy," October 24-25, 1980; Norman Ture, testimony before the Joint Economic Committee, *Forecasting the Supply Side of the Economy*, Ninety-Sixth Congress, Second Session, May 21, 1980; M. King, "Savings and Taxation," G. A. Hughes and G. M. Heal, eds., *Essays in Public Policy* (London, 1980); L. H. Summers, "Tax Policy in a Life Cycle Model," National Bureau of Economic Research Working Paper No. 302, 1978; and Michael Boskin and L. J. Lau, *Taxation, Social Security and Aggregate Factor Supply in the United States*, Washington, 1978.

[6]See, for example, Summers, *op. cit.*, King, *op. cit.*, and Lawrence H. Summers, "Tax Policy and Corporate Investment," paper presented at the St. Louis Conference on "Supply-Side Effects of Economic Policy," October 24, 1980, p. 32.

[7]Otto Eckstein, "A Time for Supply Economics," testimony submitted to the Joint Economic Committee, 96 Cong., 2 Sess., May 21, 1980.

been $20.9 billion higher in 1984. (Moreover, during the phase-in period before 1984, additional investment would have averaged $10 billion a year.)[8] Several authors have contended that if judiciously chosen, tax cuts in the investment area could lead to a substantial increase in investment without any large revenue loss to the government. They have indicated that it is possible for certain of these business tax cuts to be self-financing.[9]

Tax Cuts and Aggregate Supply: What does all this mean for aggregate supply? The conventional view holds that tax cuts do—to some extent—increase the supply of labor, saving, investment, and, hence, aggregate supply. But the conventional view holds that these effects will not be very large.

Eckstein, for example, simulated Kemp-Roth type income tax cuts on the DRI model.[10] He concluded that if Kemp-Roth had been introduced in 1980, by 1985, real GNP would have increased by 2.6 percent and potential GNP would have increased by 1.9 percent. (The elasticity of potential output with respect to personal income taxes is small, i.e., −0.05.) Thus, according to Eckstein, personal income tax cuts have little effect on aggregate supply. He indicates that the 50-percent increase in the personal income tax rate over the last 15 years has reduced potential GNP by only 2½ percent. Of course, this consensus view of the effect of Kemp-Roth type tax cuts is premised on little or no response of either labor or capital to a reduction in personal income tax rates. Most large econometric models, it should be remembered, are essentially demand-oriented, income-expenditure models with little or no supply-side constructs built into them.

Supply-side models, on the other hand, have been built by Laffer-Ranson, Evans, Ture, and others. The Evans model includes larger responses of savings and labor to a cut in taxes. As a consequence, Evans indicates that you get important supply-side effects in three to five years with a Kemp-Roth type tax cut. Unemployment will be reduced by 2.4 percent by 1985 if the tax cuts are not offset by government spending decreases and by 1.8 percent if they are offset. (Inflation is slightly worsened—up by 1.8 percent in 1985—with these tax cuts if they are not offset by government spending cuts, but it is substantially improved—down by 5 percent—if these tax cuts are accompanied by spending limits.)[11]

---

[8] Otto Eckstein, "Tax Policy and Core Inflation," a study prepared for the use of the Joint Economic Committee, 96 Cong., 2 Sess., April 10, 1980.

[9] See, for example, Lawrence H. Summers, "Tax Policy and Corporate Investment," paper presented at the St. Louis conference on "Supply-Side Effects of Economic Policy," October 24, 1980.

[10] See Eckstein, "A Time for Supply Economics," *op. cit.*

[11] See Evans, *op. cit.*

Tax Cuts and Tax Revenues: There is little empirical evidence relating to the so-called Laffer curve (according to which higher tax rates eventually lead to lower tax revenues). Conventional opinion often tends to equate tax rate cuts with tax revenue cuts so that both tax rates and tax revenue are often presumed to fall in the same proportion. However, since the conventional view concedes that Kemp-Roth type tax cuts induce some small increases in aggregate supply, it is forced to concede that feedback effects do exist and, consequently, tax revenues will proportionally fall by less than will tax rates. Hausman, for example, estimates that a 10-percent cut in tax rates will result in a fall of tax revenues by 6.1 percent.[12] However, this conventional view emphasizes that Kemp-Roth type tax cuts are not self-financing (especially in the short run).

Some evidence exists which indicates that tax cuts aimed at specific sectors (i.e., investment) specific groups (i.e., high income groups), or specific localities may be self-financing. In other words, the Laffer effect (of self-financing tax cuts) is more likely to exist for narrowly based taxes than for broadly based taxes. The only empirical study of the Laffer curve (for labor) at the macro level—by Fullarton—indicates that the U.S. could conceivably be operating in the area where tax rate cuts lead to tax revenue increases. For this to be the case, however, labor supply elasticity would have to be higher than most estimates now suggest.[13]

The supply-side models of both Evans and Laffer-Ranson indicate that Kemp-Roth tax cuts are self-financing in a longer run time frame. The Evans' model, for example, indicates that such tax cuts would bring about a surplus of $78 billion by 1985, even if government spending continued to grow at a 10-percent rate. The Laffer-Ranson model indicates that, by the fifth year after passage, Kemp-Roth would increase total aggregate tax revenue above what it would have been in the absence of a tax cut.[14]

SOME CRITICISMS OF THE EVIDENCE

Why hasn't the supply-side theory received more empirical support? Is the theory wrong? Are the appropriate data not available? Is

---

[12] See Hausman, *op. cit.* This study is based on cross-section data. See footnote 1.

[13] Fullarton's research, for example, indicates that high elasticities of labor supply with respect to tax rates—elasticities at least as high as 1.0 (together with a tax rate of at least 30 percent)—would make the Laffer effect plausible. It should be remembered that Fullarton's paper applies only to labor, whereas the Laffer curve applies to all factors of production.

[14] See Evans, *op. cit.,* and Arthur Laffer and David Ranson, *"The 'Prototype Wedge Model':* *A Tool for Supply-Side Economics* (H. C. Wainwright & Co., Economics, September 14, 1979).

the theory difficult to test? There are various reasons to believe that a good deal of the conventional evidence may be misleading.

Measurement Problems: One problem with much of the evidence relates to measurement. The critical tax variable for supply-side economists is the marginal tax rate. Marginal tax rates differ across individuals and sectors of the economy. Moreover, because of inflation and economic growth, they change over time. Hence, there are many conceptual difficulties associated with measuring an aggregate marginal tax rate. Consequently, average tax rates and even levels of tax revenue are often employed as proxies for marginal tax rates in various empirical studies. These variables can obscure the effects that rising marginal tax rates may have on economic activity. In short, many of the studies purporting to test supply-side propositions have employed the wrong tax variable.

Much of the labor supply evidence uses hours worked as a proxy for labor supply. Because of the institution of a 40-hour workweek, this variable would not be expected to be responsive to tax changes for some of the labor force. However, other variables relating to the supply of labor may still respond to tax incentives. Variables, such as motivation, entrepreneurship, work intensity, the quality of work, innovation, managerial skills, and ambition, although difficult to measure, may respond to tax incentives and be very important for the supply of labor. Tax cuts may also result in less absenteeism, later retirement, and shorter periods of unemployment. They may encourage people to assume more responsibility and accumulate more human capital. These effects are not measured in the conventional empirical work. If they were included, the response of the labor supply with respect to tax changes would undoubtedly be greater than is normally believed to be the case.

Finally, these studies do not recognize the effect of the so-called underground economy. The supply of labor to the market might be found to be more responsive to tax changes if this could be measured. Virtually all economists recognize that the Laffer curve works better for narrowly based taxes than for broadly based taxes. The existence of the underground economy (plus various tax loop-holes) implies that personal income tax is much more narrowly based (and is becoming more so) than is commonly believed. Laffer effects, then, may be more likely to occur than is conventionally believed.

Some Criticisms of the Large Econometric Models: There are several reasons to believe that the large macroeconometric models often used to simulate tax policies such as Kemp-Roth will not detect supply-side effects of tax cuts. In general, these models are demand-oriented, income-expenditure models with underdeveloped supply-side constructs. Being income-expenditure models, they emphasize spending flows rather than relative prices. Consequently, they are unlikely to detect supply-side effects of changes in marginal tax rates. As a result, they exaggerate revenue losses.

Secondly, taxation is often assumed to have no independent effect on saving in most models. As Evans has indicated, changes in saving do not translate into changes in investment in many of these models. Instead, saving retards demand whereas investment increases it.

Thirdly, many *general* effects of tax rate reductions are not captured in many of these studies. For example, the common notion implicit in many studies of Kemp-Roth that taxes on individuals only affect labor income is simply not correct. The individual income tax affects small businesses as well as income from interest, dividends, and capital gains. Personal income taxation, then, is hardly irrelevant to capital formation.[15] A reduction in income tax rates, in fact, affects at least four relative prices at the same time:

1. The price of leisure *vis-a-vis* work. Leisure becomes more expensive in terms of foregone income. (At the margin, then, such a tax rate reduction lessens the attractiveness of tax-free unemployment and welfare benefits relative to work.)
2. The price of current consumption *vis-a-vis* future consumption, i.e., saving and investment. Current consumption becomes more expensive in terms of future income foregone by not saving or investing.
3. The return to work in the market economy *vis-a-vis* work in the nonmarket (underground) economy.
4. The return on investment in the taxable sector *vis-a-vis* the return on investment in tax shelters.

Consequently, at the margin, resources will shift from leisure to work, from consumption to saving and investing, from the underground economy to the market economy, and from investments in tax shelters to more productive taxable investment.

None of the studies of Kemp-Roth or econometric models contain all of these relative price changes and capture all of these resource shifts into saving and investment as well as into market labor. If they did, the response of aggregate supply to reduction in tax rates would undoubtedly be larger than is commonly supposed.

Time Frames: Finally, supply-side economics relates to the long run. Many of the studies, as well as the large macroeconometric models,

---

[15] Alan Reynolds, "Individuals and the Tax Question," *Wall Street Journal,* October 24, 1980; see also *World Report,* First Chicago Corporation, July-August 1980.

focus on a relatively short-term time frame. Alice Rivlin, in her testimony before the Joint Economic Committee on supply-side economics, for example, pointed out the inadequacies of macroeconometric models in dealing with issues relating to long-run economic growth.[16] These large macroeconometric models were essentially built to analyze short-term stabilization policies, not policies relating to long-run growth. All economists recognize that elasticities become larger the longer the time frame under consideration. Hence, supply-side economics becomes more relevant the longer the time frame. Supply-side economics, then, has nothing to do with stabilization policy; it pertains to long-run economic growth.

SOME BROADER HISTORICAL EVIDENCE

Because much of the econometric evidence may be inadequate, we should consider other sources of information about supply-side tax policy. A great deal of "casual evidence" shows that in various historical episodes, tax rate cuts were associated with tax revenue increases—particularly for narrowly based taxes (such as tariffs).[17] During the Gladstone era in England, for example, various tax rates were reduced and economic growth and tax revenues increased.[18] Historical examples of cuts in income taxes are not as numerous. The U.S., for example, has had very little historical experience with significant reductions in federal income tax rates. The Mellon tax cuts in the 1920s and the Kennedy tax cuts in the early 1960s provide probably the only good examples. Although no extensive empirical work has been done on the Mellon tax cut episode, the casual evidence seems to support the supply-side position. Specifically, the tax cuts—which lowered *marginal* rates of taxation—were associated with both rapid economic growth and increases in tax revenues.[19]

Marginal income tax rates were also reduced in the early 1960s. Although there are always important differences between various histori-

---

[16] Alice Rivlin, *Forecasting the Supply Side of the Economy,* op. cit., pp. 6, 7.

[17] See, for example, Robert E. Keleher and William P. Orzechowski, "Supply-Side Effects of Fiscal Policy: Some Historical Perspectives," Working Paper Series, Federal Reserve Bank of Atlanta, August 1980.

[18] *Ibid.*

[19] See, for example, *ibid;* Andrew W. Mellon, *Taxation: The People's Business* (MacMillan & Company, 1924); Jude Wanniski, *The Way the World Works* (Basic Books, 1978); and Jack Kemp, "Kemp on Stein: Are We All Supply-Siders Now?", letter to *Wall Street Journal,* April 4, 1980.

cal periods, the Kennedy tax cuts provide a useful example of the type of impact that a Kemp-Roth tax cut might have. Specifically, in 1964, marginal tax rates were cut across the board from 91 percent to 70 percent at the top and from 20 percent to 14 percent at the bottom.

Evidence indicates that the Kennedy tax cuts worked, but not for reasons the Keynesians who designed them have stated. Specifically, Denison's estimate of the gap between actual and potential GNP for 1962 and 1963 indicates that this gap may have been too small for demand-side policies to have created the growth in real GNP that actually ensued.[20] Something else had to have caused aggregate supply to increase. What happened appears to be fully consistent with an increase in aggregate supply in response to the various tax incentives which were created. This assertion is fully supported by two recent empirical studies by Canto, Joines, and Webb (1979 and 1980).[21]

The evidence with respect to tax revenues also seems to support the supply-side view. Specifically, the work by Canto, Joines, and Webb indicates that the Kennedy tax cuts caused only a small loss of revenues from the individual income tax by 1966—a loss which was largely offset by gains in corporate and other tax receipts from the increased real economic growth.

CONCLUSIONS

- A supply-side cut in income and business taxes will probably result in some increase in the supply of labor, saving, investment, and, hence, in aggregate supply.
- Because of this additional real growth, the tax base will increase and, hence, revenues will not fall in proportion to tax rates. In short, the deficit will not be as large as many have predicted because of these feedback effects. Moreover, with increased real economic growth, some government spending (such as transfers) may decline, futher minimizing the deficit.

[20] See Paul Craig Roberts, "The Economic Case for Kemp-Roth," *The Economics of the Tax Revolt,* Arthur B. Laffer and Jan P. Seymour, eds. (Harcourt Brace Jovanovich, 1979), p. 61; Denison's estimates are published in E. F. Denison, *Accounting for Slower Economic Growth* (Brookings Institute, 1979).

[21] Victor A. Canto, Douglas H. Joines, and Robert I. Webb, "Empirical Evidence on the Effects of Tax Rates on Economic Activity," unpublished manuscript, University of Southern California, September 1979, and Victor A. Canto, Douglas H. Joines, and Robert I. Webb, "The Revenue Effects of the Kennedy Tax Cuts," unpublished manuscript, University of Southern California, November 1980.

- Despite the increase in aggregate supply, the tax cuts will produce
  an increase in the deficit, at least in the short run. However, to the
  extent that the tax cuts create an increase in saving, the deficit
  may be, in part, financed without increasing the money supply.
- In the long run, the supply-side effects should be more potent and
  the deficit should be less worrisome. Supply-side economics pertains to long-run economic growth policy rather than short-run
  stabilization policy. If lower tax rates increase deficits for two to
  three years but result in a stronger economy after that, in the long
  run, future taxpayers may inherit both a stronger economy and a
  smaller debt burden.

In assessing the effects of such tax cuts, several other factors should
also be mentioned. First, there is a large amount of evidence which indicates that tax rates for individuals, as well as for businesses, have increased substantially in recent years. As classical economists repeatedly
and forcefully indicated, when people spend a significant amount of
time and resources in order to circumvent or avoid taxes, tax rates
probably are too high. (The underground economy may be telling us
something.) In addition to being too high, tax rates on labor, saving,
and investment are increasing every day due to inflation. In addition to
increases due to inflation, Social Security tax increases, as well as increases in windfall oil profits taxes, are already scheduled. In short, tax
rates are not only too high but are increasing every day and scheduled
to increase even further in the future. Thus, to some extent, a Kemp-
Roth type tax cut will simply be offsetting these past, present, and future
increases in tax rates.

In addition, although a few supply-side proponents still contend that
tax cuts can be made without regard to government spending, many
supply-side economists assert that government spending restraints should
accompany the tax cuts wherever possible. If such restraints do accompany tax cuts, the deficit will be smaller and less worrisome.

15

The Uncertainties of the Laffer Effect*

PRESTON J. MILLER & ALLAN STRUTHERS, JR.

The one hope that a cut in tax rates will increase tax revenues is the "Laffer effect," but this is a slim hope at best. It depends on the assumption that people will work significantly more when their after-tax wages rise or that they will invest significantly more when their after-tax profit or rate of return rises.

The presumed relationship of tax rates and tax revenues for a particular tax, like the payroll tax or the business tax, is shown in the chart. As this chart indicates, when tax rates fall to zero, revenue falls to zero. When tax rates rise to 100 percent, revenue also falls to zero, because people have no incentive to work. Between these two extremes lies the tax rate that will produce the maximum revenue for this particular tax, rate C. No one knows what this rate is. It could be close to the middle or close to one of the extremes. Furthermore, no one knows the shape of the curve. It could have irregularities that do not appear on this simple chart.

The Laffer effect depends on two conditions which are highly uncertain and unlikely. First, for any given tax, the current tax rate must be beyond the point of maximum revenue—that is, the tax rate must be higher than rate C. If tax rates were cut from E to D, for instance, revenues would rise. However, since no one knows where the point of maximum revenue is, no one can be sure that the Laffer effect will occur. If the tax rate were below rate C, a cut in rates would not raise revenues. If rates were cut from B to A, for example, tax revenues would fall.

The second crucial condition that must be met for the Laffer effect

*Reprinted from *Federal Reserve Bank of Minneapolis 1979 Annual Report,* Federal Reserve Bank of Minneapolis.

The Laffer curve

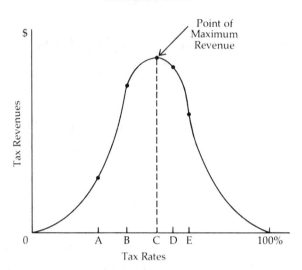

to work is that the tax cut must not be too large. Even if we assume that the tax rate is above rate C, the Laffer effect won't work unless it is cut just enough to bring revenues closer to the point of maximum revenue, but not much beyond it. Lowering tax rates from E to D or from D to C, for example, would increase revenues. But lowering them from D to B would make revenues fall. Since no one knows the shape of the curve or the location of the point of maximum revenue, it would be very difficult to cut tax rates correctly. Perhaps just a small change in rates would carry us all the way from E to A.

If the tax rate is now higher than the point of maximum revenue and if the rate were cut just the right amount, the Laffer effect would work— lower tax rates would produce higher tax revenues. Both conditions, though, are extremely uncertain.

Worse, they seem very unlikely, judging from what little evidence is available. For the payroll tax cut to succeed, people must work significantly more when their real after-tax wages rise, because only then could a cut in tax rates fail to reduce tax revenues. If payroll taxes were assessed at a lower rate and people worked the same amount or less, tax revenues obviously would fall. Recent data, in fact, suggest that people do *not* work less and enjoy more leisure when their real wages rise. In recent years, at least, when real wages have gone up, people have worked less.

Similarly, for the business tax cut to raise tax revenues, firms must invest significantly more when their real after-tax return rises and output must increase significantly in response to the added investment.

Output must increase enough so that the initial decrease in taxes is off-set. For example, if a tax on business output is lowered from 50 to 45 percent, then output would have to increase more than 10 percent to make up for lost tax revenues. But even the proponents of the business tax cut concede that an increase in tax revenues is highly unlikely. They admit that tax revenues would probably drop.

Since there is a good chance that a cut in tax rates would ultimately lower tax revenues, experimenting with such a cut would be to risk making our high inflation rates even higher and our large budget deficits even larger. The uncertainties of the Laffer effect seem far too great to justify such a risk.

16

The Capital Cost Recovery Act: Its Effect on Revenues*

AMERICAN ENTERPRISE INSTITUTE

The proposed Capital Cost Recovery Act (CCRA), commonly referred to as the 10-5-3 plan, would effect a major change in current tax law by grouping many assets having differing asset lives under the current system into three broad classes of assets: Class 1 includes buildings and structural components; Class 3 comprises automobiles, taxis, and light-duty trucks; and Class 2 includes all other eligible property that is "used in business or held for the production of income." Equipment is the major component of Class 2. Ineligible property consists mainly of residential rental property, inventories, and land.

Once the CCRA system becomes fully effective, Class 1 assets would be depreciated over a period of ten years and would be allowed a 10 percent ITC, Class 2 assets would be depreciated over five years and allowed the same 10 percent credit, while Class 3 assets would be depreciated over three years and would have a 6 percent ITC with a $100,000 limit on the amount depreciable in the first year. The CCRA treats the amount of a Class 3 asset in excess of $100,000 as a Class 2 asset. The percentages to be depreciated in each year, after a transition period, for the three classes are as given in table 1.

The half-year convention that is used assumes that assets acquired any time during a year are placed in service halfway through the year. The application of this convention reduces by half the maximum amount of assets depreciable in the first year. Taxpayers may deduct all or any part of the amount allowed by the CCRA and may carry forward the remaining amount into any future year.

*Reprinted from *American Enterprise Institute Legislative Analysis No. 17*, May 1980; American Enterprise Institute, Washington, D.C.

Table 1 Depreciation Allowable Under Capital Cost Recovery Act
(percentage)

Ownership Year	Class 1	Class 2	Class 3
1	10	20	33
2	18	32	45
3	16	24	22
4	14	16	0
5	12	8	0
6	10	0	0
7	8	0	0
8	6	0	0
9	4	0	0
10	2	0	0
	100	100	100

The system would be phased into use by basing the Class 1 asset lives on eighteen years in 1980, sixteen in 1981, fourteen in 1982, twelve in 1983, and ten years thereafter.[1] Class 2 assets having current asset depreciation range lives of ten years or longer are given nine-year asset lives in 1980, eight in 1981, seven in 1982, six in 1983, and five years thereafter. During the phase-in the asset lives of Class 2 assets having ADR lives between five and ten years are reduced by one year for each year of the phase-in until they reach a five-year life. The depreciation rates shown in table 1 would apply to Class 2 assets having ADR lives of five years or less and Class 3 assets without a phase-in period.

Any gain from the sale of assets before they are fully depreciated, up to the maximum deduction allowable, would be taxed as ordinary income. Similarly, salvage value is not figured into an asset's depreciable base but is taxed as it is realized. The Treasury could recover the ITC if an asset is sold before it is fully depreciated. The amount of the ITC recoverable is indicated in table 2.

The principal change that would be made by CCRA is that most assets would be depreciated in a considerably shorter time than is currently allowed. This would benefit businesses since the more they can depreciate in the early years of assets' lives, the higher the value of the "interest-free loan." The CCRA would extend the investment tax credit to assets other than equipment.

The principal objectives of the CCRA are to increase investment—

[1] This assumes enactment of the bill in 1979.

Table 2   Amount of Investment Tax Credit Recoverable Under the
Capital Cost Recovery Act (percentage)

Taxable Year of Ownership in which Asset is Sold	Classes 1 and 2 Assets	Class 3 Assets
1	100	100
2	80	66
3	60	33
4	40	0
5	20	0

SOURCE: H.R. 4646, p. 19.

thus stimulating productivity, employment, and economic growth and enhancing the position of the United States relative to foreign competition in industrial production—and to offset depreciation losses due to inflation. Another objective of CCRA is to combat inflation by the forecasted increase in productivity.

EFFECT ON THE ECONOMY

One of the main goals of the Capital Cost Recovery Act is to increase investment over the long run with a view to increasing the productivity of labor. All things being equal, improved productivity would increase output in the economy and would lower the price level. Business investment is said to play a dual role in the economic system by directly creating jobs and income in the capital goods industries and in the businesses that supply them, and by adding to the overall demand for goods and services. As it adds to demand, new investment also increases supply. Because business investment affects both demand and supply it is said to play a crucial role in the achievement of the nation's economic goals.[2] President Nixon's Task Force on Business Taxation, established in 1969, recommended a capital cost recovery system to help modernize and expand the nation's productive system by increasing the ability of business to finance additions to its facilities. It is believed that the Capital Cost Recovery Act, by accelerating the rate at which depreciation may be taken, will stimulate investment more than a general cut in corporate

[2]*Hearings on Economic Growth,* prepared statement of Gramley, p. 2.

taxes, for example, because of the close linkage between depreciation and investment in productive facilities and a loose linkage between a general tax cut and investment. After-tax funds are made available for investment sooner through CCRA, and it is argued that companies that have difficulty raising long-term capital would benefit. Such companies could use five-year writeoffs for machinery and could finance machinery purchases with bank loans that would be repaid out of cash flow enhanced by tax deferral. The need for additional capital investment is said to be demonstrated by the fact that the United States spends only 9 percent of its national income on such investment while West Germany spends 15 percent and Japan 20 percent.[3]

Critics of CCRA argue that its effect on capital investment is overestimated. Investment, it is claimed, is close to its historical highs, even after adjustment for the cost of pollution-control equipment, and additional real incentives to invest can come only from the expectation of growing markets, not from lowering the cost to business of investment in capital assets. (Proponents counter that it is net investment that determines the growth of the capital stock and net investment is below its historical highs.) Critics claim that CCRA would do little for the major steel companies, for example, because they now pay little in income taxes because of depletion allowances on iron ore and coal and because of weak sales revenues. Capital formation, some claim, is not primarily a tax issue. Rather, more fundamental reasons will explain why the rate of capital investment is not higher. Some claim that just because a business might have added funds available through CCRA would not guarantee that these funds would be expended for capital investment.[4]

On the other hand, a Data Resources Inc. (DRI) study commissioned by the Committee for Effective Capital Recovery found that in the first year CCRA would be fully effective, 1984, real business fixed investment would be $20.9 billion higher than under current policy and that over the phase-in period before 1984 it would be $10 billion a year higher on average, which represents an increase of about 5 percent.[5]

How capital investment can be most effectively increased is one of the most disputed questions in recent economic study. Pioneering work in 1967 by Dale Jorgenson and Robert Hall employed the following investment model: increasing the tax benefits to capital decreases its cost; this cost reduction will induce businesses to increase desired capital stocks, and greater investment will follow.

[3] *Hearings on Federal Finance*, pp. 39-42, statement of Summa who served on the task force; Terborgh, *Realistic Depreciation Policy*, p. 4; Hughey, "10-5-3 or Fight," p. 37; "Pressing a Capital Idea," *Time*, vol. 113 (June 4, 1979), p. 40.

[4] "The Huge Stakes in 10-5-3 Depreciation," p. 129; *Hearings on Economic Growth*, statement of the late Laurence N. Woodworth, assistant secretary of the treasury for tax policy, p. 1.

[5] "The Huge Stakes in 10-5-3 Depreciation," pp. 124-25.

In examining the effects of the tax incentives for investment in the 1950s and 1960s, Hall and Jorgenson found that "[t]he effects of accelerated depreciation are very substantial, especially for investment in structures. The effects of [shortened asset lives] are significant, but these effects are confined to investment in equipment. The effects of the investment tax credit of 1962 are quite dramatic and leave little doubt about the efficacy of tax policy in influencing investment behavior."[6] Since these three tax incentives are all incorporated in the CCRA, such prior results suggest that 10-5-3 could be very effective in increasing investment.

The Hall-Jorgenson analysis has come under attack, however, by critics claiming that their model was structured in a manner that overstates the impact of tax policy on investment. One problem is that the model assumes that all other variables stay constant. This may be an untenable assumption for two variables in particular—the interest rate and the price of the output. The interest rate under most circumstances will rise in response to investment incentives because more investment creates more competition for funds. If the federal government finances any part of the revenue loss by increased borrowing, then this will put upward pressure on interest rates. A higher interest rate will inhibit investment so that the net investment will be less than otherwise predicted. The precise amount of this reduction cannot be readily estimated, however, since it depends very much on the actions of both business and government.

The assumption that the price of the output of firms receiving the tax incentive will stay constant may also be unsound, for if firms in a given industry do increase their capital stock as predicted by the Hall-Jorgenson model, then they will also increase their output. With a greater market supply of the good and no corresponding change in its demand, the price will fall in almost any market. A lower selling price will discourage production and dampen the incentive of businesses to increase the capital stock in the industry. This in turn will diminish the volume of new investment somewhat.

Another problem with estimating how much investment will be affected by changes like the CCRA lies in the technical relationship between the factors of production. At any given time, a firm will have a certain capital-labor ratio that maximizes its profits. If the cost of capital falls, this optimal ratio will shift (more capital relative to labor will be desired). However, the degree and speed with which the firm adjusts to the new optimal ratio is crucial to the amount and timing of the increase in investment. For instance, if the firm can easily and quickly

[6] Robert E. Hall and Dale W. Jorgenson, "Tax Policy and Investment Behavior," *American Economic Review,* vol. 57 (June 1967), p. 414; and see Robert E. Hall and Dale W. Jorgenson, "Application of the Theory of Optimum Capital Accumulation," in Gary Fromm, ed., *Tax Incentives and Capital Spending* (Washington, D.C.: The Brookings Institution, 1971), p. 9.

substitute labor and capital for each other, then a strong and rapid change in investment will occur. If, on the other hand, capital and labor are most readily used in fixed proportions, then the change will be much smaller and slower.

Economists disagree on the extent of substitutability between the factors of labor and capital in the economy as a whole. Hall and Jorgenson believe that these factors can be more readily substituted one for the other than do many other economists, and their analysis has been criticized on the ground that this biases upward their estimate of increased investment attributable to tax incentives. One critic, Charles Bischoff, using different assumptions about the substitutability of factors, the interest rate, and output prices, nonetheless concluded, as did Hall and Jorgenson, that "The investment tax credit adopted in 1962 has probably directly stimulated more investment spending than the policy has cost the government in taxes."[7] He also found, however, that "in this model, the data give no support to the hypothesis that accelerated depreciation has any effect at all on investment! Of course the data do not deny the hypothesis either; they simply shed no light."[8]

Bischoff's estimate of the effect of accelerated depreciation in the 1960s may not be entirely relevant to the proposed CCRA for the effect of increases in the speed of depreciation may be more significant per dollar of tax revenue loss than it initially appears to be. More rapid depreciation acts as an interest-free loan, the value of which is much lower than the ITC, which is a subsidy. Therefore, for the same ultimate tax revenue loss, the depreciation liberalization would have to be much greater than the ITC increase. This was not the case in the 1962 investment incentives, but it is true of the CCRA.

Rates of return to capital and relative prices form the basis of a major alternative to the Hall-Jorgenson model in which investment is more influenced by output. The basic tenet behind this model is that investment decisions are based primarily on expectations of future sales, and less on the cost of capital. Similarly, a recent study by Peter Clark following earlier works by Robert Eisner notes that in the short run output is the most accurate predictor of nonresidential fixed investment and that the cost of capital is a poor predictor. Clark writes that in the long run a drop in the cost of capital will certainly induce additional investment, but its effects will be of uncertain magnitude and will be much more gradual.[9]

[7] Charles W. Bischoff, "The Effect of Alternative Lag Distributions," ibid., p. 125.

[8] Ibid., pp. 123-24.

[9] Peter K. Clark, "Investment in the 1970s: Theory, Performance and Prediction," Brookings Papers on Economic Activity, No. 1 (Washington, D.C.: The Brookings Institution, 1979). Incentives for investment, such as the investment tax credit, may have much less impact on business behavior than the normal cyclical forces in the overall economy. "The Huge Stakes in 10-5-3 Depreciation," p. 129, quoting Clark.

The time considerations introduced by Bischoff and Clark may be irrelevant. Since the CCRA is intended to be a long-term incentive to investment, it may only be of little importance that its effects might take several years to manifest themselves. Another concern, however, is the effect of possibly large losses in revenue. If there are no major net additions to federal revenues, Keynesian theory would say that a tax cut of the magnitude of the CCRA could, in the short term, stimulate demand markedly. And if there were no quick expansion of productive capacity from 10-5-3 to mitigate this effect, the short-run effect of the bill could be inflationary. As the effects of the decreased cost of capital worked their way through the system, inflation would be reduced in the long run, but a trade-off would have to be made between a decreased long-run inflation rate and an increased short-run inflation rate. Moreover, Clark warns of the danger that "if rising prices and high interest rates put the economy into a tailspin, the percentage of nonresidential fixed investment in total output will fall, with adverse consequences for future productivity and inflation."[10] But this possible series of events assumes the worst about trends in output and also assumes that output is a more important factor in determining investment than are relative prices.

The conclusions that can be drawn from the foregoing analysis are relatively weak considering the amount of work that has been done. Measures like the CCRA that change the cost of capital assets do stimulate investment, but the extent of stimulation is uncertain, as are the time lags involved. Furthermore, the particular measures that affect capital cost—the ITC, accelerated depreciation, and corporate tax cuts—do so in different degrees. Nonetheless, a consensus can be reached on the desirability of achieving a permanency in policy. Business investment is probably most closely related to business confidence, which can be quickly eroded by uncertainty, be it of future sales or future capital costs. Thus a firmly set tax treatment of depreciable assets and steady demand for producers' goods can, over time, provide for strong investment.

EFFECT ON TAX REVENUES

Preceding sections have examined the effectiveness of CCRA in achieving goals such as increasing investment and improving the economy of the nation. This section will examine the possible costs of CCRA in terms of foregone revenues and the extent to which these revenue losses may be offset by taxes collected on additional business activity stimu-

[10] Clark, "Investment in the 1970s," p. 107.

lated by adoption of the proposal. Table 3 estimates the near-term revenue losses as seen by various sources. Since CCRA would be phased in, 1984 would be the first year in which CCRA would be fully effective. Estimates of revenue losses vary because such estimates depend on projections of the amount of qualified investment that will be made in the future and the extent to which businesses will take advantage of the more liberal depreciation provisions.

The 10-5-3 plan is phased in over five years so that the revenue loss can be planned for within the constraints of the budget. The phase-in provisions would make the CCRA more complicated in its initial stages, however, since a new depreciation schedule would be instituted every year for the first five years of the bill. In addition, Treasury Secretary G. William Miller criticized the phase-in rules claiming that they would "create a perverse incentive effect that postponement of investment until the following year will increase the rate of capital recovery allowances."[11] This, it is argued, could create inefficiencies as well as postponing the benefits of increased investment. On the other hand, instituting the CCRA without a phase-in could decrease revenues too quickly for effective budgetary planning.

The revenue losses projected by various sources in table 3 do not make allowance for offsetting feedback in the form of increased taxes

Table 3   Static Revenue Loss of the CCRA
(billions of dollars)

Source	1980	1981	1982	1983	1984	1987	1988
Data Resources Inc.[a]	5.5	14.8	22.9	31.7	40.3		
Congressional Budget Office	4.0	11.5	18.9	30.3	41.4		
Congressional Research Service					50–60	75–85	
Department of the Treasury	4.0				50.0+		85+
Robert Eisner	4.0				52.0		86.0

NOTE: Years are calendar years and assume that the bill was enacted in 1979.

a The Data Resources Inc. figures are derived from their estimates based on the assumption that Class 1 assets are phased in over ten years instead of the figures provided for in the bill. To adjust these figures, Class 1 revenue loss is doubled for all years (see footnote 7 in DRI report).

SOURCES: Allen Sinai (DRI), "Economic Impacts of Accelerated Capital Cost Recovery," Bureau of National Affairs, Inc., September 13, 1979, pp. J1-J10; Peter Karpoff, memo, Congressional Budget Office; Gravelle, "The Capital Cost," p. 9; prepared statement of the Honorable G. William Miller, secretary of the treasury, before the Subcommittee on Taxation and Debt Management of the Senate Finance Committee, October 22, 1979, p. 3; Robert Eisner, National Journal Conference.

[11] *Hearings on Capital Cost Recovery,* statement of G. William Miller, p. 12.

that would result from increased revenues generated by increased output, which would be created as the effect of the tax cut provided by CCRA works its way through the economy. The extent of the static (before feedback) losses in revenues is placed in perspective by DRI, whose figures on revenue loss are in the lower range of the estimates, by the statement of its representative that "in ex-ante, or static terms, the expected revenue losses over the five year period make this tax policy one of the most expensive in the postwar period."[12] In addition, Robert Eisner has estimated that his predicted $86 billion in losses in 1988 will equal half of what the total corporate income tax liabilities would be in 1987 if the bill were not enacted.[13]

The extent of increased investment generated by more generous depreciation allowances is difficult to project. On the basis of models formulated to determine the effect of tax incentives adopted from 1954 through 1964 on the capital expenditures of manufacturers, Robert M. Coen concluded that changes that produced tax savings to manufacturers of $13.7 billion through the third quarter of 1966 only added $4.8 billion to capital expenditures.[14] Norman B. Ture concluded that corporate tax liabilities in 1959 were $1.265 billion lower than they would have been without accelerated depreciation allowances, but that outlays for depreciable facilities in 1959 were no less than $1.3 billion more and may have been as much as $5.7 billion more than they would have been in the absence of accelerated depreciation.[15] DRI found that in 1984 CCRA would increase real business fixed investment by $20.9 billion and during the phase-in period such investment would be $10 billion a year higher on average or an increase of about 5 percent.

The amount of additional revenues that may be generated as a result of additional capital investment stimulated by accelerated depreciation—the so-called "feedback" effect—is even more difficult to determine. The Treasury Department estimates that these additions to revenue will amount to about 30 percent of the cost of the bill.[16] DRI, however, estimates that these "feedback" effects will amount to an average of 40

[12] Allen Sinai, *Economic Impacts of Accelerated Capital Cost Recovery* (Washington, D.C.: Bureau of National Affairs, Inc., 1979), p. J-4, fn. 7. Estimated tax expenditures for the existing asset depreciation range are $2.88 billion for 1980 and $4.33 billion for 1983. *Estimates of Federal Tax Expenditures 1980-1985*, prepared for the House Ways and Means Committee and the Senate Finance Committee by the staff of the Joint Committee on Taxation, March 6, 1980.

[13] Eisner, "New Directions."

[14] Robert M. Coen, "The Effect of Cash Flow on Speed of Adjustment," in Fromm, ed., *Tax Incentives and Capital Spending*, p. 179.

[15] Ture, *Accelerated Depreciation in the United States 1954-1960*, p. 100. Hall and Jorgenson estimated that 17.5 percent of net investment in manufacturing equipment from 1954 through 1970 can be attributed to the change in methods of calculating depreciation. Hall and Jorgenson, "Application of the Theory of Optimum Capital Accumulation," p. 49.

[16] *Hearings on Capital Cost Recovery*, statement of G. William Miller, p. 4.

percent over the five years after enactment.[17] Their exact magnitude will depend on the state of the economy in the years after the bill takes effect, and the extent to which investment has stimulated growth. Allen Sinai of DRI is quoted as saying that the higher output generated by the additional investment from 10-5-3 would produce new personal and corporate income tax revenues that would reduce the net cost to the Treasury of this proposal to $19.7 billion by 1984.[18] Some proponents of CCRA contend that it will provide other benefits that should be weighed against costs—for example, improved environmental and better worker health and safety—because businesses will acquire safer new equipment that is frequently designed with new environmental standards in mind.[19]

---

[17] Sinai, *Economic Impacts of Accelerated Capital Cost Recovery*, p. J-7.

[18] "Huge Stakes in 10-5-3 Depreciation," p. 125, quoting Sinai; see also *Hearings on Federal Finance*, p. 109; and Terborgh, *Realistic Depreciation Policy*, p. 165. The figure of $19.7 billion is adjusted by applying the feedback percentage used by Sinai to the 1984 adjusted DRI figure in table 6.

[19] Hughey, "10-5-3 or Fight," p. 38.

17

Lessons of the Tax Cuts of Yesteryear*

JOHN MUELLER

Significant across-the-board cuts in marginal income tax rates, of the sort proposed by President Reagan, have occurred twice: in 1922-25 and 1964-65. In both cases, claims of eventual revenue increases played a significant part in congressional debate. An analysis of IRS revenue statistics for the two periods should encourage the Reagan administration.

In 1913, marginal income tax rates ranged from 1% to 7%. Because of World War I, they stood at 4%-73% by 1921. These rates comprised a 4%-8% "normal rate" on all net income and a "surtax rate" on incomes over $6,000 of up to 65%. President Harding described his "return to normalcy," in part, as "to lift the burdens of war taxation." At his urging, Congress cut the surtax rates for 1922 from a 65% to a 50% maximum, lowering the top rate from 73% to 58%. It also repealed the wartime "excess profits tax" and instituted preferential treatment for capital gains.

When 1922 income-tax receipts exceeded expectations, Treasury Secretary Andrew Mellon began pushing for a further halving of surtax rates. Reported Time: "He asserts that such readjustment would yield as large or larger revenues. The reason for his belief is that high surtaxes drive wealthy men to invest their money in tax-free securities and nonproductive enterprises and to seek every permissible means of avoiding the realization of taxable income. The result is an unsound industrial condition and actually a decrease in revenue."

"SOAK THE RICH!"

The political prospects were poor. Harding died suddenly, the Democrats cried "Soak the rich!" and Mellon's own party followed Senator

*Reprinted by permission of *The Wall Street Journal*, © Dow Jones & Company, Inc. 1981. All rights reserved. John Mueller is Economic Counsel to the House Republican Conference.

Smoot, heir-apparent to the Finance Committee chairmanship, who declared that as sure as God lives and the sun rises in the morning, Congress would enact a veterans' bonus, not a tax cut.

In December 1923, Mellon proposed to Congress a cut in normal rates, a halving of surtax rates to a 25% maximum, an increase in personal and surtax exemptions and a 25% credit for all earned income. Mellon told Congress that "in all probability the revenue from the reduced (surtax) rates will soon equal or exceed what would accrue at the present rates"; but as he later wrote, it was thought that the other changes "would result in considerable loss of revenue."

President Coolidge argued: "Taken altogether, I think it is easy enough to see that I wish to include in the program a reduction in the high surtax rates, not that small incomes may be required to pay more and large incomes required to pay less, but that more revenue may be secured from large incomes and taxes on small incomes may be reduced."

Congress responded, whether convinced by the administration's arguments or by other factors ("Secretary Mellon gained more applause for his tax proposal than John Barrymore in 'Hamlet.' It was a tremendous surprise to the professional politicians," Time reported). In 1924, Congress retroactively refunded 25% of taxes for 1923, cut normal and surtax rates for 1924 to a 2%-46% range, and enacted the 25% earned income credit.

In a final round of tax-cutting, effective with 1925, Congress enacted increases in the personal and surtax exemptions and cut marginal rates to a 1.5%–25% range.

IRS statistics show that for every year in which marginal tax rates were cut, there was a level of net income, below which revenue dropped in all classes and above which revenue increased in all classes. This "break-even" point was $20,000 in 1922, $30,000 in 1924 and $20,000 in 1925. (A $20,000 net income typically faced a marginal tax-rate of 18% in 1921, before the tax-rate cuts.)

These revenue changes became progressively larger toward the top and bottom of the income scale. From 1921 to 1925, income tax paid in the $0-$5,000 class dropped by 85%; in the $5,000-$10,000 class, by 72%; in the $10,000-$15,000 class, by 57%; and in the $15,000-$20,000 class, by 39%. Income tax paid in the $20,000-$50,000 class was virtually unchanged. In the $50,000-$100,000 class, revenue increased by 28%; in the $100,000-$500,000 class, by 64%; in the $500,000-$1 million class, by 114%; and in the over $1 million class, by 113%.

The result was a revolution in the distribution of the income tax burden. In 1925, 44% of the taxpayers were removed from the rolls by the increase in personal exemptions. From 1921 to 1925, the share paid by the under-$10,000 class fell from 22% to 4%; by the under-$20,000 class, from 35% to 11%. The share of tax paid by the over-$100,000 class rose from 28% to 49%; by 1928, this class paid 61% of the tax burden, or $714 million, which exceeded total income tax revenue for 1923 or 1924.

The net effect was a revenue increase in every year except 1923, for which Congress had retroactively refunded 25% of taxes without changing marginal rates (revenue declined 23%). Revenues were $719 million in 1921, $861 million in 1922, $664 million in 1923, $704 million in 1924, and $735 million in 1925, a net increase of 2% over 1921. Revenue rose another 59%, to $1.16 billion, by 1928. Since prices were declining, the real increases were somewhat larger.

The circumstances of the Kennedy tax cuts need less description. In 1962, the Treasury accelerated depreciation rules and Congress enacted a 7% investment tax credit. In January 1963, Kennedy asked Congress to cut the World War II-vintage 20%-91% personal rates over three years to 14%-65%, an average of 23%. He also asked for offsetting "structural changes" amounting to a 5% tax increase and a cut in the corporate rate from 52% to 47%.

In February 1964, Congress enacted a 14% to 70% personal rate schedule—a 20% average cut, two-thirds effective in 1964 and the rest in 1965. Most of the "structural changes" were jettisoned. Congress increased the capital gains exclusion and cut the corporate rate to 48%. About two million lower-income taxpayers were dropped from the rolls in 1964 by the new minimum standard deduction.

The Kennedy administration argued that the tax cuts would ultimately result in increased revenues but did not spell out whether these increases were expected in any particular income classes or tax brackets. The Treasury's static estimates, derived by applying the proposed rates to a sample of actual returns from an earlier year, predicted revenue losses in all income classes. Since such estimates are still the basis of official revenue predictions, it is interesting to compare the static estimates with the actual revenue change by adjusted gross income class from 1963 to 1965.

In the $0-$5,000 class, the predicted revenue loss was 30% and revenue declined 27%. In the $5,000-$10,000 class, the predicted decline was 21%, and revenue declined 11%. In the $10,000-$20,000 class, the predicted decline was 17% and revenue increased 15%. In the $20,000-$50,000 class, the predicted decline was 16% and revenue increased 11%. In the over $50,000 classes, the predicted decline was 13%, and revenue increased 38%. The 38% increase included a 25% increase in the $50,000-$100,000 class, a 46% increase in the $100,000-$500,000 class, a 68% increase in the $500,000-$1 million class, and an 85% increase in the over $1 million class.

Revenue increased in tax brackets as low as the 26% marginal rate, which was cut to 22%. It is not possible to say with certainty that revenue increased in every taxable income bracket of 26% or above, however, because of a discontinuity of the data; beginning in 1964, a $2 billion chunk of revenue, representing special computations such as income averaging, is not broken down by marginal tax rate. The effective or average tax rate for this revenue is almost twice the rate for all revenue, which means it belongs largely in the upper brackets. It can be said that in both 1964 and 1965 revenue increased in all adjusted gross income classes above $10,000. By 1966, the revenue increases ranged from 30% to 88%.

The net result was that total individual income tax revenue declined from $48.2 billion in 1963 to $47.2 billion in 1964, or by 2%, though there was no absolute decline on a fiscal-year basis. Revenue rose to $49.5 billion in 1965 (3% above 1963), $56.1 billion in 1966 (16% above 1963), and $62.9 billion in 1967 (31% above 1963), the last year before the Vietnam surtax. Inflation averaged 2% a year.

LESSONS FOR REAGAN PLAN

President Reagan's three-year 30% cut in marginal income tax rates would take four tax-filing years because of its July 1 effective date. The 15% cut of the first two years approximates the first year of the Kennedy cuts, and the whole plan is half the percentage size of the Mellon cuts. What are the lessons for the Reagan plan?

1. Paring down the upper-bracket marginal rate reductions to "save revenue" or "tax the rich" would almost certainly have the opposite result. Especially in the short run, cuts in higher marginal rates help finance cuts in lower rates and non-marginal tax cuts, which have no incentive effect.

2. The initial "break-even" level may be much lower than even some advocates of the Reagan plan seem to think. For example, the 26% tax-bracket (the apparent break-even point for the Kennedy cuts) is reached or exceeded today at an adjusted gross income of $16,200 for a single person and $24,200 for a family of four, using the standard deduction. Because of inflation, the portion of taxpayers in tax brackets of 25% or above was almost three times as high in 1977 as in 1963, and is probably much larger today.

Finally, the historical evidence should prod those who think of tax policy in terms of aggregates—disposable income and multipliers or average tax rates and supply elasticity—to think instead about marginal tax rates: those which confront real, live people.

18

Supply-Side Economics: What Is It? Will it Work?*

JAMES TOBIN

Revolutions and revelations in economics are rare. They have generally occurred at intervals of 30-60 years and have taken decades to influence public opinion and policy. The Keynesian revolution, initiated by a forbidding theoretical book in 1935, made its way only gradually through academe to lay intellectuals, media pundits, business and labor leaders, bureaucrats and politicians. When, after considerable resistance and revision, J.M. Keynes's ideas became explicit rationales for American macroeconomic strategy in 1961-65, the press hailed them as the "New" Economics.

RECENT ECONOMIC COUNTER-REVOLUTIONS

Has the pace of innovation quickened? Since 1965 three counter-revolutions swept through the economics profession, received lavish attention in the media, and powerfully affected influential opinion and the making of public policy. One was Monetarism, an ancient doctrine modernized and persuasively propagated by Milton Friedman beginning in the 1950s. When the New Economics appeared unable to explain or control the inflation of the late 1960s and the 1970s, Friedman's alternative attracted hordes of disciples. A second and related counter-revolution was the so-called New Classical Macroeconomics, based on the elegant and appealing theory of rational expectations. In the 1970s under the leadership of Robert Lucas and others, this movement made

*James Tobin is Sterling Professor of Economics at Yale University. Reprinted from *Economic Outlook USA*, Summer 1981, published by the Survey Research Center, University of Michigan.

many theorists and practitioners skeptical of Keynesian hopes that fiscal and monetary policies can smooth out business fluctuations.[1]

The third is Supply-Side Economics, which in just a few years has become not only an obligatory slogan but the philosophy of the federal government. Though the three counter-revolutions differ, they have in common conservative messages popular in today's political climate: Government interventions, however well-intentioned, do harm, not good. They have led to inflation, instability, inefficiency, and declining productivity. Keynesian policies have failed, and the theories that supported them are discredited.

Supply-Side Economics, currently the most popular counter-revolution, is also the most amorphous. Without a Keynes or Friedman or Lucas, it lacks a sacred text expounding its theoretical foundations. It is more spirit, attitude, and ideology than coherent doctrine, and its enthusiasts are of many minds. They generally share the view that for forty years, under the malign spell of Keynesian concentration on demand, economic analysis and policy went wrong by neglecting supply. The most common theme is the sensitivity of work, productivity, saving, investment, and enterprise to after-tax rewards. The more exuberant supply-siders, economist Arthur Laffer and Congressman Kemp, expect cuts of tax rates to generate miracles of production and growth. While the more sober architects of Reagan administration policy do not promise that their tax cuts will pay for themselves in federal revenues, they do predict radical and durable renewal of the vitality of the United States economy.

SUPPLY, DEMAND, AND EQUILIBRIUM

All economics balances supplies and demands, *ad nauseam* of generations of students. Keynesian economics is no exception. Choosing up sides would be a laughable and harmless media diversion were it not taken so seriously. Clearly production and consumption are limited by supplies of labor, capital equipment, and other productive resources, and by technical know-how. Almost all economists, Keynesian or classical or eclectic, agree that in the long run these supply factors call the tune and demand adapts. They used to agree also that short-run business cycles are principally fluctuations of demand, economy-wide capacity to produce changes slowly and smoothly. Keynes pointed out that when labor and other resources are under-utilized, supply responds to

[1] For exposition and critique of this counter-revolution see *Rational Expectations,* a Seminar sponsored by the American Enterprise Institute for Public Policy Research, *Journal of Money, Credit and Banking,* November 1980 Part 2, especially the papers by B.T. McCallum, R.C. Lucas, Jr., J. Tobin, and A.M. Okun.

demand. The New Economics of the 1960s stressed both demand policies to restore and maintain full employment, and supply measures to accelerate long-run growth. Among the latter were the investment tax credit, accelerated depreciation, and manpower training and retraining.

A serious intellectual challenge to the neo-classical-Keynesian synthesis just sketched is the New Classical view that a competitive market economy, to which the United States is taken to be a reasonable approximation, is continuously in demand-equals-supply equilibrium. Unemployment and idle capacity then appear not as pathologies but as voluntary choices at prevailing prices and taxes. The remedies, if any are needed, are not Keynesian demand stimuli but improvements of incentives, e.g., less generous unemployment insurance, more take-home pay for workers, businessmen, and investors. Forget about fine tuning, counter-cyclical fiscal and monetary policy. Set up a good stable framework of incentives and price signals and the market, preferable deregulated, will take care of both short-run stabilization and long-run growth. In this spirit a sophisticated economist like Rudolph Penner defines Supply-Side Economics as simply good microeconomics.[2] That involves minimizing or countering the distortions that taxes, subsidies, and regulations inject into market choices—work is taxed but leisure is not, income saved is taxed twice but income consumed only once, etc.—and then accepting whatever short- and long-run outcomes occur.

INCOME AND SUBSTITUTION EFFECTS

As economics students know, those results are not theoretically predictable, even as to direction. Price and tax changes have both income effects and substitution (incentive) effects, and the two often conflict. An increase in real take-home pay is an inducement to work more hours per year, but since it makes workers better off anyway it may encourage them to take more time off. An increase in real after-tax returns is an incentive to save an extra dollar, but the enrichment of wealth-owners may dispose them to consume more both now and in the future. Standard microeconomic theory provides no license for assuming that substitution effects dominate, and certainly none for declaring income effects null and void, as Under-Secretary of Treasury Norman Ture is bold to do.[3]

Whether supply-side budget cuts, tax cuts, and other measures will,

---

[2] "Policies Affecting Saving and Investment," paper presented at the Colloquium on Alternatives for Economic Policy, Washington, D.C., June 10-12, 1981, forthcoming in Proceedings to be published by the Conference Board, New York City.

[3] "Supply-Side Analysis and Public Policy," unpublished paper presented to the Economic Policy Round Table, the Lehrman Institute, November 12, 1980.

as advertised, lift the American economy from stagflation to a new era of prosperity, productivity and growth depends on empiricial magnitudes of income and substitution effects that are not very well established. Supply-siders' diagnoses of our economic ills do not fit the facts.

THE GOVERNMENT BITE

One allegation is that government has been taking too much of the national product for its own use, leaving too little for private disposition. Actually federal absorption of GNP declined during the 1970s; it was 7½ percent in 1980, compared to takes of 10 to 11 percent in the 1950s and 1960s. The reason was the decline in defense spending relative to GNP, a trend the administration now is reversing. State and local civilian purchases, aided by federal transfers, filled the gap, but all-governments absorption was the same fraction of GNP, 20 percent, in 1980 as in the pre-Vietnam year of 1965. When correction is made for the increasing relative cost of public goods, which are comparatively labor-intensive, government purchases are now smaller relative to private purchases than in the 1950s and 1960s.[4]

What did happen since 1965, thanks to LBJ's Great Society as extended by presidents of both parties and Democratic Congresses in the 1970s, was an explosion of transfer payments, largely for retirement and disability insurance, Medicare, and Medicaid. Even so the federal tax burden is lower than in 1969 and only two percentage points higher than in 1956 and 1965. The all-government tax take is the same as in 1969 but because of increases in state and local taxes 4-5 points higher than in 1956 and 1965. Compared to other advanced capitalist democracies, United States taxes are on the low side.[4]

TAXES AND LABOR SUPPLY

Supply-siders deplore particularly the increase in the marginal federal personal income tax rates arising from the interaction of inflation and

---

[4]On the figures and analyses of these two paragraphs see my paper, "Reflections Inspired by Proposed Constitutional Restrictions on Fiscal Policy," forthcoming in Kenneth D. Boyer and William G. Shepherd, editors, *Economic Regulation, Papers in Honor of James R. Nelson,* East Lansing: Michigan State University Press, 1981. Extension of the tables there compiled to 1980 does not significantly alter the story.

progressive rate structure. This has indeed happened faster than Congress has reduced rates, especially since 1977. According to calculations from the Brookings Institution tax file, the average rate of federal income plus payroll tax on an extra dollar of income for a breadwinner with spouse and two children was 18.0 percent in 1960, 15.9 percent in 1965, 18.2 percent in 1970, 18.0 percent in 1975, and 21.6 percent in 1980.[5] Whatever one may think of the specifics of the personal income tax cuts now before the Congress, it is high time for another tax reduction to arrest bracket creep and fiscal drag.

Nonetheless it is hard to detect evidence of weakened propensity to supply labor. Figures on labor force participation, overtime hours, multiple jobholding, weekly hours of work corrected for industry mix—all are in line with trends and cyclical effects dating from earlier decades. Econometricians have a hard time finding significant effects of real after-tax pay on labor supply.[6] Those they do find are mainly for secondary workers from low-income families, whose incentives will actually be diminished by proposed tax and transfer cuts in combination.

TAXES AND SAVING & INVESTMENT

Supply-siders also blame high taxes, their bite sharpened by inflation, for low rates of saving and capital investment in the United States. Public discussion of the effects on national saving of general income tax reduction have been confused and confusing. Taxpayers will both spend more and save more. The spending effect will be somewhat mitigated in the administration proposal, which distributes gains in disposable income disproportionately to wealthy taxpayers with higher than average marginal propensities to save the proceeds. But it will not be reversed. From given GNP household saving will be greater by some fraction of the tax cut but government dissaving will be greater by the full amount. Thus the tax cut *by itself* diminishes the national—government plus private—propensity to save. However, in the Reagan economic program, the tax reductions are roughly balanced by budget reductions and implicit tax increases due to inflation and economic growth. The net effect of the program as a whole is a small increase in national saving for given GNP.

As in the case of labor supply, econometric evidence for incentive ef-

[5] I am grateful to Joseph A. Pechman for these calculations.

[6] See Jerry A. Hausman, "Labor Supply," in Henry Aaron and Joseph A. Pechman, editors, *How Taxes Affect Economic Behavior*, Washington, Brookings Institution, 1981, 27-84.

fects on household saving is weak.[7] Proposed tax concessions to stimulate saving suffer not only from the usual income effects favoring consumption but also from their restriction to specific kinds and amounts of saving. Most taxpayers will simply shift other savings into the favored vehicles. This has already occurred as Congress has multiplied tax-free or tax-deferred ways of saving for retirement, home ownership, and posterity, a fact that itself limits the credence of the high-tax explanation of declining household saving.

Business non-residential investment held up much better in the 1970s than the spate of solicitous rhetoric suggests. For its weakness through much of the decade, 1970-72 and 1975-78 recessions, tight money, and energy shocks are sufficient explanation. At 11.6 percent of GNP in 1979, plant and equipment investment surpassed previous post-war cyclical peaks. However, for various reasons, some economic and some tax-accounting, investment net of replacement is estimated lower than at previous peaks.

MISGUIDED POLICY PROPOSALS

Spurred by supply-side ideology, the administration and both parties in Congress are vying to bestow on business and on wealthy individuals tax cuts and subsidies rationalized as investment incentives. These are half-baked proposals, which will introduce more distortions of efficiency and equity than they correct. Reform to diminish tax-cum-inflation distortions is overdue. But neither the Reagan depreciation plan nor the Democratic alternative is the specific remedy, which would be indexing of depreciation and debt. Both propose costly giveaways, subsidies that will still be there if and when inflation subsides. While inflation erodes the real value of tax deductions linked to historical cost depreciation, it also enhances the real value of tax deductions for debt interest. The latter is partially offset by personal income taxation of the same nominal interest payments, but much such income never appears on taxable returns.[8] The proposals distort choices among different types and durabilities of investment projects, and they waste revenue by granting tax relief to income from existing capital and from investment that will occur anyway. The results are likely to fall short of the administration's goal of increasing the business investment share of GNP by two or three

[7] See George M. von Fustenberg, "Saving," in Aaron and Pechman, *op. cit.*, 327-402.

[8] See Eugene Steuerle, "Is Income from Capital Subject to Individual Income Taxation?," U.S. Department of the Treasury, Office of Tax Analysis Paper 42, October 1980.

percentage points. One reason is that the supply-side incentives will be bucking an inclement macroeconomic climate, dominated by restrictive monetary policy.

The anti-inflation strategy is to slow down the growth of money stocks while the new incentives expand the supplies of goods the money is chasing. Confidence that this scenario will bring disinflation together with prosperity rather than recession and stagflation is borrowed from the other two counter-revolutions, monetarist and new classical. Keynesians, eclectics, and traditional conservatives are skeptical that entrenched patterns of inflation will melt away so painlessly. Lucky breaks on oil, food, and exchange rates make the price indexes look good for a while, but there cannot be permanent improvement unless and until wage and cost trends give way.[9]

THE ESSENTIAL MESSAGE OF THE
SUPPLY-SIDE REVOLUTION

The only sure results of supply-side policies are redistributions of income, wealth, and power—from government to private enterprises, from workers to capitalists, from poor to rich. A revolution is in process all right, social and political more than economic. A capsule symbol is the nearly universal enthusiasm in Washington to rid the federal tax system of all semblance of taxation of intergenerational transfers of wealth. This capitalist democracy was never committed to equality of opportunity. and for more than forty years we have shown that an essentially capitalist economy can prosper and grow while the society collectively moderates extremes of wealth and poverty, privilege and deprivation, power and insecurity, boom and depression. Keynes and a generation of economists he influenced believed that capitalism was robust enough to flouirsh under these compromises with democracy and equality. Both Marxist critics on the extreme Left and conservatives of the exteme Right have always doubted it, and theirs is the essential message of the supply-side counter-revolution.

---

[9] For discussion of the Reagan administration's macroeconomic and anti-inflation strategy see my article "The Reagan Economic Program: Budget, Money, and the Supply Side," May 1981, forthcoming in *Federal Reserve Bank of San Francisco Quarterly Review.*

19

Supply-Side Effects of Fiscal Policy: Some Historical Perspectives*

ROBERT E. KELEHER
WILLIAM P. ORZECHOWSKI

A fundamental premise of "supply-side" economics is that changes in fiscal policy, and especially changes in tax rates, have important effects on incentives, aggregate supply, and economic growth. While the supply-side approach is having a significant impact on current policy discussion, it has nevertheless been seen by many economists as a new, untested idea or as a temporary fad. In this lengthy Working Paper, Robert E. Keleher, Senior Financial Economist, Federal Reserve Bank of Atlanta, and William P. Orzechowski, Assistant Professor of Economics, George Mason University, show through an extensive review of economic doctrine that the supply-side view is neither novel nor a fad. The authors demonstrate, in fact, that supply-side economics is essentially a return to the fiscal orthodoxy of the nineteenth century. Supply-side principles, which originated with the attacks of the physiocrats, Hume, Smith and other economists on mercantilism, were explicitly endorsed and utilized by most important public finance scholars for over a century before the Great Depression.

In contrast to much conventional macroeconomic analysis, which focuses primarily on the aggregate demand impacts of changes in fiscal policy, supply-side proponents emphasize that tax rate changes have important repercussions on the incentives of individuals to supply labor and capital to the market. Keleher and others have described the fundamental assumptions of the supply-side view in previous Working Papers; in this study, the authors focus on the historical development of that view.

The supply-side view originated in the eighteenth century with the attacks of the French physiocrats against mercantilism. The mercantilists, whose principal goal was a strong nation state (including, in their view,

*Reprinted from *Economic Review,* February 1981, the Federal Reserve Bank of Atlanta.

a large stock of precious metals), endorsed policies to effect a trade surplus. They subsidized exports, for example, and taxed imports. They also believed that higher tax rates, by lowering (after tax) wages, would stimulate work effort and consequently contribute to the production of exports and hence a trade surplus. High tax rates, then, were not at all inimical to the mercantilist view.

Although both the physiocrats and David Hume identified important elements of the supply-side view, neither developed a complete, fully consistent set of supply-side principles. Adam Smith, writing in 1776, was the first to articulate a supply-side theory fully removed from vestiges of mercantilist thought. To increase wealth, Smith believed, a country must emphasize production, aggregate supply and growth, not the money supply or aggregate demand. Accordingly, Smith advocated positive incentives (including tax policies) to stimulate the supply of capital and labor into the production process. Smith called high direct taxes on wages "absurd and destructive," since they led to decreased employment and decreased production.

The authors show that Smith also recognized that as tax rates rise from low levels, output initially increases because efficiency gains stemming from the provision of public goods outweigh the adverse effects of these tax rate increases. As tax rates continue to increase, however, the balance shifts in favor of the disincentive effects of high tax rates, and output begins to decline. Moreover, because of Smith's subsequent influence, his supply-side fiscal principles became the orthodox view for nineteenth century economists and, as such, can scarcely be accused today of being radical or novel.

Builidng on and refining the arguments of the physiocrats, Smith, and others, J. B. Say and James Mill developed Say's Law, which, as J. J. Spengler notes, "dominated economic thinking until . . . World War I." A central theme of Say's Law is that it is production and aggregate supply (not the growth of the money supply) that create wealth and economic growth. Thus, the Law places emphasis on the stimulation of production and aggregate supply and on the encouragement of factor supplies—not on stimulating demand or consumption. Some of the most significant implications of Say's Law relate to governmental fiscal and especially tax policy. Given that Say's Law indicates that it is production and aggregate supply rather than demand and expenditure that create growth and wealth, the tax (and expenditure) policies in harmony with the law are those which foster aggregate supply (rather than aggregate demand). If taxes adversely affect aggregate supply or factor inputs, for example, supporters of Say's Law indicate that these taxes should be either eliminated or minimized. Since advocates of Say's Law recognized that high tax rates would work to destroy the incentives to work, save, and invest, and hence would adversely affect supplies of factors of production, they often recommend a lowering of these tax rates. Such a lowering of tax rates was often identified with increases in aggregate production and increases in tax revenues.

After identifying Say's Law as a cornerstone of the supply-side view, Keleher and Orzechowski discuss the contributions to supply-side thinking of some later economists, including John Stuart Mill, J. R. McCulloch, and Sir Henry Parnell. These nineteenth century writers, for example, documented many historical cases where tax rate increases were associated with tax revenue decreases. Interestingly, McCulloch suggested that one sure way to recognize when tax rates are excessive is to identify when a great deal of circumvention activities (smuggling, evasion, fraud) is taking place. (Today, this activity is associated with the growth of the so-called underground economy.)

Although supply-side principles were often stated in the literature, politicians normally did not embrace these concepts. The administration of William Gladstone in Great Britain (from the 1840s to the 1890s), however, was an exception. This administration was one of the first examples of the formal application of supply-side principles. Gladstone's program was successful; it included large reductions in tax rates, rapid economic growth, and the elimination of budget deficits. Not only were these principles implemented as early as the mid-nineteenth century, but they were recognized (as the authors show) as the dominant view of fiscal policy in economics textbooks in the late nineteenth and early twentieth centuries.

Events in the interwar period disrupted the century-long dominance of the supply-side view. The collapse of aggregate demand in America in the 1930s led many economists to reject Say's Law and to adopt positions "which classical economists would have labeled as mercantilist." The Keynesian Revolution encompassed a dramatic shift from encouraging supply to stimulating demand, and from long-run economic growth to short-run stabilization of the business cycle. Taxation was seen, not as a means of funding government spending, but as a method of ensuring general economic and monetary stability. "What would appear as heresy in 1910," the authors conclude, "had become orthodoxy and was embraced by the new economics."

An example of the subordination of supply-side principles appears in the "modern" discussion of saving. Since proponents of the "new economics" considered saving a leakage to the income-expenditure flow, they (like the mercantilists centuries earlier) came to view savings as adversely affecting the level of economic activity. Consequently, they often endorsed government policies which were oriented toward the stimulation of consumption and discouragement of saving.

In their concluding section, Keleher and Orzechowski point out the similarities of the 1970s to those conditions of the mercantilist era which led classical economists to reject the demand-oriented framework of mercantilist writers. Both periods saw high and increasing tax rates, government regulation and intervention into the economy, a growing underground sector, and low rates of productivity and growth. The result has been the revival of the long dormant supply-side view. In order to foster growth, its proponents argue, work, saving, investment, and honesty should be encouraged instead of nonwork, consumption, and tax avoidance. Hardly a new approach or an untested fad, the supply-side view is well-rooted in classical macroeconomic analysis. In fact, the authors show that it actually represents a return to the classical principles of public finance.

IV

THE SUPPLY-SIDE AND INFLATION

Part IV contains a series of articles about supply-side economics and its ability or inability to solve inflation and/or stagflation, which has been our most serious economic issue for the past decade and one-half.

20

Supply-Side Economics: Its Role in Curbing Inflation*

LYLE E. GRAMLEY

During the past several years, a profound revolution has been occurring in the thinking of many of our nation's leaders concerning the proper role of fiscal policy in helping to maintain the health of our economy. For more than 30 years, our Government tried to use fiscal policy as a means of smoothing out fluctuations in business activity. Tax rates were cut, and expenditures increased, when recessionary forces were pervasive. Growth in expenditures was restrained—and on one occasion, tax rates were increased—to cool off inflation.

Deep disillusionment has set in regarding the results of those efforts. As the prestigious Joint Economic Committee stated in its recent Mid-year Report on the economy, a review of the postwar period shows that "government attempts to shorten the duration or reduce the intensity of recessions . . . have been ineffective." Economic policy for the future, the JEC argues, "must focus on the supply side of the economy, on the long-term capacity to produce. . . ."

Supply-side economics is an exciting doctrine. Its central tenets are not entirely new, but they certainly are relevant. Our principal economic problem today is inflation. A long-term strategy is needed to deal with it.

Supply-side economics in fiscal policy is a logical complement to the way in which monetary policy is currently being conducted. Last October the Federal Reserve announced that it was changing its methods of implementing monetary policy in ways that would improve its control over the expansion of money and credit. Under this new monetary policy strategy, prospects have been enhanced that growth of money and credit will slow over the long run to rates that are consistent with a moderation of inflation and eventually a restoration of price stability.

*Lyle E. Gramley is a member of the Board of Governors of the Federal Reserve System. Reprinted from the *Voice*, November 1980, a publication of the Federal Reserve Bank of Dallas.

If fiscal and monetary policies both aim at reducing inflation over the long run, the prospects for success in this effort will surely be greater.

How much help can we really expect from supply-side economics in curing inflation? As I think about that question, I cannot help but remember the enthusiasm with which economists of my generation embraced the old fiscal doctrines 30 years ago. We spent a large part of our energy elaborating the theory of aggregate demand management, as it was so often called, and testing its conclusions against the facts. We tried our best to make fiscal policy work in ways that would reduce unemployment and idle capacity, keep the economy operating close to its full-employment potential, and yet avoid periods of excess demand that create fresh inflationary forces.

In retrospect, our principal mistake was a failure to recognize the severe limitations of aggregate demand management in an economy as complex as ours. We tried to achieve results that simply could not be realized.

The same danger exists now, I believe, with supply-side economics. Steps to increase the potential output of our economy and to improve productivity can make a vital contribution to dealing with inflation. However, unless we recognize the limits of supply-side economics, and design our economic policies accordingly, we could end up making our inflation problem worse instead of better.

What do we mean by supply-side economics? Conceivably, a wide range of things could be included—energy policy, manpower training, Federal support for higher education, and other programs that might increase the growth of supply or enhance productivity. I propose to focus today on three principal areas in which public discussion of supply-side economics has centered in the past several years: first, tax reductions on earned income—that is, on wages and salaries—to increase incentives to work; second, tax incentives to businesses to increase the rate of capital formation and thereby to improve productivity; and third, tax reductions on investment income to encourage a larger volume of private savings.

In discussing these three ways to increase aggregate supply, I do not propose to break any new ground. My objective is merely to make some common-sense observations on the potential contribution of this fiscal policy approach to solving our inflation problem.

TAX REDUCTIONS ON EARNED INCOME

Tax reductions for wage and salary income, if they contributed to the fight against inflation, would certainly have the enthusiastic support of a large number of our citizens. The average American gives up about one-fifth of his income in the form of direct tax payments to government; upper-bracket rates are, of course, much higher—up to 70 percent for the Federal personal income tax. Reducing these tax rates significantly might increase the willingness of individuals to work, and it could do so in a variety of ways—by increasing hours worked per day or per week, inducing large numbers of women to enter the labor force, encouraging postponements of retirement age, or making people willing to work harder. Is it possible that the aggregate supply of labor, and hence the output of goods and services, would rise substantially as a consequence of such tax reductions?

A bit of thought and introspection should raise some doubts in our minds. Work hours tend to be set by institutional arrangements as much as by individual decisions. Objectives for working, moreover, are complex and varied; many of us work for reasons other than simply the income we earn. Moreover, it is difficult to predict whether a completely rational economic man would work more of less if taxes were lowered. Lower rates of taxation increase the take-home pay that can be earned from an additional hour of work or a second job, but they also make it possible to attain any given standard of living with less work.

Studies of the effects of taxation on the available supply of labor both in the United States and in other countries are numerous, but their conclusions are ambiguous. Even in countries where tax rates are considerably higher than in the United States, such as the United Kingdom, it is not clear that labor supply would increase if taxes were lower. In a summary of the available evidence two years ago, the Congressional Budget Office concluded that labor supply probably would increase if taxes on earned income in our country were reduced. The effect, however, would be small; total hours worked might increase by perhaps 1 to 3 percent for each 10-percent rise in after-tax wages.

Reductions in taxes on wages and salaries stimulate demand as well as supply. Estimates of the increase in demand that would result from such tax reductions are also controversial. Nonetheless, the available evidence indicates that the increase in aggregate demand would be substantially larger than the increase in aggregate supply, possibly 5 or 10 times as large, or maybe more.

Tax reductions on wage and salary incomes, therefore, are not the most promising way to cure inflation. Indeed, unless the effects on aggregate demand were neutralized by raising other taxes or cutting budgetary expenditures, such tax reductions—if undertaken on any substantial scale—could make our inflation problem worse.

This does not mean that our Government should be insensitive to the burden of taxation that Americans are bearing. Certainly, our chances for healthy economic growth will be greatly enhanced if the share of our national resources devoted to Federal uses is reduced and the rate of taxation is lowered. But it does suggest that the principal contribution that supply-side economics can make to fighting inflation lies elsewhere.

INVESTMENT INCENTIVES AND PRODUCTIVITY

Providing tax incentives for business investment is another form of supply-side economics, one that we know more about. On several previous occasions during the postwar period, incentives to business capital formation have been increased through accelerated depreciation or an investment tax credit or a reduction in corporate profits tax rates. We therefore have some basis on which to judge their efficacy in stimulating capital formation and productivity growth.

A number of proposals have been put forward recently to stimulate investment through tax incentives. For example, in the Administration's recently announced fiscal program, allowable depreciation rates for new plant and equipment would be increased by 40 percent, and the investment tax credit would be liberalized somewhat. The cost of these incentives, in terms of loss of Federal revenues, would initially be small but would reach $25 billion per year by fiscal 1985. Corporate tax payments in that fiscal year would be reduced by approximately 17 percent as a result of the new tax incentives.

It has been estimated that these investment incentives would increase the long-term growth rate of productivity in our economy by about 0.4 percent per year—not right away but after several years. Judging by studies of the effects of investment incentives introduced in the past, this is a fairly generous estimate, but a reasonable one. To put this amount of improvement in perspective, we might note that productivity in the past five years has been rising on average at about 1 to 1½ percent a year. With an improvement of 0.4 percent, the trend would be up to 1½ to 2 percent. If improvements in productivity growth occurred for other reasons as well, we might hope to regain the 2½-percent average annual rise that characterized the first two decades of the postwar period. To put it another way, an improvement of 0.4 percent in annual productivity growth would lead, over the course of a generation, to an increase of 10½ percent in the potential output of our economy. Such an increase would make possible a welcome improvement in standards of living, in addition to its potential contribution to moderating inflation.

TAX INCENTIVES TO INCREASE SAVINGS

Increased investment expenditures, however, must be financed by increased savings. Otherwise, they, too, may add to inflation rather than reduce it. Let me turn next, therefore, to the third area of supply-side economics that I mentioned earlier: Are reductions in taxes on investment income an effective way to increase savings?

Unfortunately, in this area, too, we do not know as much as we need to know to justify bold action. Like reductions in taxes on earned income, tax reductions on investment income cut two ways. By raising the after-tax earning power of every dollar saved, they increase the benefit to the consumer of postponing purchases today in order to increase buying power tomorrow. But because of that, they reduce the amount that a consumer has to save to assure his ability to achieve a given living standard later on.

No one knows for sure which edge of the blade cuts more deeply. Some studies have concluded that if our tax structure were changed in ways that reduced the taxation of investment income, and raised the level of taxes on other forms of income, there would be no effect at all on private saving. Others suggest beneficial effects on private savings. This state of affairs should not prevent us from experimenting cautiously with changes in the tax structure that might encourage more saving. In light of the uncertainties, however, it is hard to imagine that tax incentives to foster savings can play more than a minor role in our battle against inflation, at least in the relatively near future.

Fortunately, there is a surer way of increasing the amount of savings available to finance a higher rate of business investment. It is an old-fashioned method, and one that has not been used much in the past two decades. It is to reduce the deficit in the Federal budget through restraint on Federal spending as rapidly as economic conditions warrant, and eventually eliminate it altogether. Surpluses in the Federal budget, used to retire debt, would return funds to financial markets that could finance the additional business investment needed to improve productivity and growth. That is also the way to increase the prospects that improved productivity growth will actually result in lower inflation. Let me turn to that issue next.

PRODUCTIVITY AND INFLATION

Increasing productivity growth through tax incentives for business investment appears to me to be the most promising route for moderating inflation through supply-side economics. But will it work? And how well?

Unfortunately, there is no guarantee that improved productivity will automatically reduce inflation. Indeed, among the major industrial nations of the world, rates of inflation during recent years have not been closely correlated with rates of productivity increase. From 1974 to 1979, for example, manufacturing productivity rose faster in France than in any other major industrial country. Yet, the rate of inflation in France during that period was higher than that for the United States and Canada, and far above that for Japan and West Germany.

How much an improvement in productivity contributes to reducing inflation depends on the responses of businesses and workers. If businesses do not, or cannot, increase their profit margins, the slower rise in costs that higher productivity brings will show up in smaller increases in prices. If workers then accept smaller wage increases because inflation is moderating, costs would rise still more slowly and the inflation rate would come down further. The inflation rate might ultimately decline by two to three times as much as the initial increase in productivity.

The potential reduction in inflation made possible by a higher rate of advance in productivity will be realized, however, only if conditions in labor and product markets promote the necessary response in wages and prices. Product markets must be sufficiently competitive so that businesses are motivated to pass reductions in their costs through to lower prices. Markets for labor must be sufficiently slack so that workers are encouraged to accept smaller wage rate increases as the rise in prices moderates. That is why prudent monetary and budgetary policies—policies that aim for slower growth of money and credit and for movements of the Federal budget toward surplus—are a necessary adjunct to supply-side economics. Unless these two work hand in hand, the promise that supply-side economics holds for reducing inflation could easily be lost.

Let me try to pull the threads of my argument together. Tax incentives to stimulate business capital spending appear to be the surest way of increasing our aggregate capacity to produce. At a cost of about $25 billion annually by 1985, in terms of revenue loss to the Treasury, we might reasonably expect productivity growth to increase by about 0.4 percent per year. Under favorable economic conditions the inflation rate might be brought down by about 1 percentage point, or perhaps a little more, through this means. These are, I believe, realistic estimates of the costs and benefits of going the route of supply-side economics.

If the cost is that high, you may ask, is it worth it? I would respond: What better alternatives are there? Certainly, it is preferable to use tax policy to increase productivity and our capacity to produce than to try to squeeze out inflation by relying solely on highly restrictive fiscal and monetary policies, with the inevitable losses of jobs and real output that would be entailed.

Supply-side economics is obviously no cure-all for inflation. But the problem of inflation is so intractable that no single measure to deal with it will suffice. Our only hope for making substantial progress against inflation over the next several years lies in keeping the fight against inflation at the forefront of every economic policy decision. If we recognize its limitations as well as its strengths, supply-side economics can play an extremely useful role in that endeavor.

21

Can Supply-Side Economics Cure Inflation?*

RAYMOND J. SAULNIER

Construing supply-side economics literally as related to measures having an impact on the volume and efficiency of production, its proposed policy measures will almost certainly in time have a retarding effect on inflation, though necessarily a limited one. But construing it as standing for the Reagan program as a whole, which has come to be the widely-accepted meaning, I have no doubt that supply-side economics greatly enhances the prospects for lowering the inflation rate. And, given a chance, it could in time even cure inflation.

First, I think supply-siders, by which I mean the Reagan group as a whole, have a better understanding of what causes inflation than their predecessors had. I expect them to give more attention to basics in their efforts to solve it: to what happens to the money supply, to the rate of increase of federal spending, and to the difference between income and outgo in the federal budget. Having a better understanding of what causes inflation, there is less chance they will be drawn, as others have been drawn, into unproductive, even counterproductive, efforts to stem it, such as the now-abandoned wage and price stabilization programs. Understanding the problem is not a bad start toward solving it.

Second, whether this can be called supply-side economics or demand-side economics turned right side up, the intensity of the administration attack on federal budget outlays, and on the outlays of agencies operating outside the budget—which is totally unprecedented, is bound to have an anti-inflationary effect. When federal spending rises 17 to 18 percent a year—as it has been rising recently—there is not only a direct upward push on costs and prices, but the chances of mounting an adequate monetary attack on inflation and sustaining it long enough to produce results are virtually nil. Money policy must be tighter, and in-

*Reprinted from *Economic Outlook USA*, Spring 1981, published by the Survey Research Center, University of Michigan. Raymond J. Saulnier is Emeritus Professor of Economics at Barnard College and Columbia University.

terest rates higher, by wide margins over what would otherwise be necessary; and the impact on the private side of the economy, where the brunt must be borne, is so severe and so obviously unfair that political pressure to abandon the effort is inevitable. Bowing to this pressure means a return to the double-barreled expansionism—fiscal *cum* monetary—that produced inflation in the first place.

Third, it will take time, but tax changes that increase incentives to save and invest, and promote higher ratios of capital to labor, will help raise productivity (slow the increase of labor cost per unit of output) and help slow inflation. The contribution is necessarily limited, but achieved along with a slowing of compensation costs through monetary and fiscal restraint it could be spectacular. For example, the GNP implicit price deflator, a good measure of overall inflation, could be cut a third by a combination of (1) raising output per hour from the −0.4 percent estimated for 1980 to a more normal 2 percent and (2) slowing the increase of compensation costs from 1980's 10 percent to 8 percent. In short, when things work together, and in the right direction, the total effect can be great. What the supply-siders are striving to do in the already well-advanced area of reforming government regulatory practices works toward the same end.

Fourth, I wish I could say there is nothing in the supply-side package that could complicate carrying out the anti-inflation program, but I fear that is not so. Judgments differ on this point, and it is hard to know what is right, but it seems to me not yet time for large cuts in personal income taxes. Taxes are high, and counterproductive in many ways, even perilously so; and just about everyone wants them reduced. The question is when to do it, and by how much. Tax cuts, especially those affecting consumption, are bound to dilute the anti-inflation effect of budget spending reductions. In the circumstances of 1981, some dilution of this effect is probably not a bad idea, but it could easily go beyond what might be justified on economic stabilization grounds. I am less confident than supply-siders on the extent to which income not taken in taxes will be saved, and less confident than they appear to be on how much income that now evades taxation because of high rates will surface and accept it at lower rates. And the argument that lower personal income taxes will pay for themselves by generating a greatly increased stream of taxable income is worrisome when the top policy priority must be reducing inflation, since inflation could be aggravated if the increase in income is large enough.

It will all depend, of course, on the kind of tax bill that is enacted, and on how tax reductions prove in the end to be timed with spending economies. Opportunities for tax reduction on a large scale will be available soon if there is as much success in slowing the increase of federal spending as now seems possible. We will be able then, at long last, to enjoy the benefits of "fiscal dividends" which year after year have been preempted by more than offsetting increases in federal spending.

Finally, it will be enormously helpful in the fight against inflation to move budget toward balance, as the supply-siders are determined to do. Monetarism teaches that balancing the budget is not a total guaranty against inflation, and that a budget deficit does not make inflation inevitable, which is correct. But the monetarist argument misses certain critical points. Budget deficits absorb savings, require interest rates higher than necessary to balance capital and credit markets under noninflationary conditions, and thus discourage capital formation and productivity improvement. They can tip the balance in credit markets toward cruch conditions that make recession inevitable. They raise inflationary expectations, which supply-side economics understands. And, when large enough, deficits can stymie the monetary authorities and completely defeat the monetarist cause.

It is good that the monetarist element in the present administration is strong enough, as I judge it is, to assure support for an adequately disinflationary monetary policy. But it is also a comfort, and a good augury for success in bringing down the inflation rate, that the program put forward is sufficiently nonmonetarist to take a budget balance seriously.

All things considered, and having in mind especially what supply-side economics can be expected to do in supporting a disinflationary money policy and pushing a similarly disinflationary federal spending policy, I look for significant progress toward curing inflation—some in 1981 and considerably more in 1982. At the same time, and strictly from the efforts of the supply-siders, a momentum is being built up with strong public support to stimulate capital formation and saving and to redress the balance between public and private effort, which in my judgment has been shifted unduly to the public side. From these efforts I expect everyone to benefit.

22

Supply-Side Tax Cuts: Will They Reduce Inflation?*

THOMAS M. SUPEL

There is wide agreement that the fiscal policy that has resulted in successive and large budget deficits in the United States could be modified to play a more constructive role in shaping our overall economic performance, but there is much disagreement as to precisely how to modify it. One point of view on this issue is that of supply-side economics, which stresses that in order to enhance economic performance, fiscal policy needs to take account of incentives to save, invest, and work. By taking advantage of these incentives, according to supply-side advocates, properly constructed tax cuts could increase productivity and thereby help offset inflationary pressures in the economy.

This conclusion—while having considerable intuitive appeal—is, in fact, open to question on at least two grounds. First, it is based partly on economic models that are seriously flawed. Supply-side models are traditional macroeconomic models that have been reworked to reflect the supply-side thinking on incentives, productivity, and inflation. Supply-side models may be improvements over the earlier models for purposes of forecasting under a given historical policy. But they have not solved the major problem of the traditional models they were designed to replace: they are still incapable of assessing the effects of a change in policy by simulating alternative policy actions. The conclusion that tax cuts can increase productivity and thereby reduce inflation is questionable, secondly, because the relationship between productivity and inflation is much less certain than many supply-side advocates acknowledge. The empirical evidence suggests that this relationship is extremely tenuous. My point is not that fiscal or tax policy should stay the same—in fact, a tax cut that is balanced by an expenditure cut may be warranted—but that some of the key arguments that

*Reprinted from the Federal Reserve Bank of Minneapolis *Quarterly Review/Fall 1980*. Mr. Supel is a senior economist with the Research Department of the Federal Reserve Bank of Minneapolis.

the supply-side advocates use to justify cutting taxes alone or cutting taxes more than expenditures are not supported by the evidence.

DEFECTS OF TRADITIONAL MODELS

Supply-side models are attempts to correct the defects of traditional models and thus produce better assessments of the effects of alternative policies. They were developed after the traditional models repeatedly and spectacularly failed to produce accurate assessments of the policies that were begun in the 1970s.

The traditional models, based on Keynesian macroeconomics, seemed to be working well in the 1960s. They appeared to be able to explain the relationship between inflation and unemployment that had been observed in the United States and other countries during the 1960s, a relationship shown in Chart 1. In general, these models interpreted this relationship as a trade-off or a menu of choices, implying that policy-makers could reduce unemployment by accepting a little more inflation. In 1964, the models' implications were put to the test: taxes were cut in an attempt to reduce unemployment. In this case, the economy appeared to behave as the models said it would. Inflation did not increase very much, but unemployment dropped sharply from roughly 5.5 percent in 1963 to nearly 4 percent in 1965. The traditional models thus gained respect in academia and in Congress.

In the 1970s, however, the models' predictions were so far from the mark that they were difficult to take seriously anymore. The problem was not just that prices were rising faster than the models had predicted at any given unemployment rate. It was that, in addition, unemployment was going up along with prices, as seen in Chart 1, a state of affairs which the traditional models could not explain without incorporating factors that were originally outside the model. With inflation and unemployment rising together, it was clear that the traditional models were defective, and economists began to alter them to make them conform better to the facts.

SUPPLY-SIDE MODELS: CONSIDERING INCENTIVES

Some economists believed that the principal defect of the traditional models was that they ignored incentives to work, save, and invest, in-

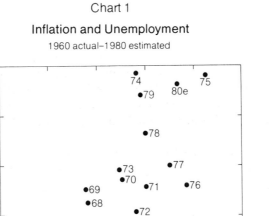

Chart 1

Inflation and Unemployment
1960 actual–1980 estimated

Source: U.S. Department of Commerce

centives that affect people's decisions to produce goods and services and thus affect the supply side of the economy. An adverse shift in supply could indeed explain the adverse shift in the relationship between unemployment and inflation. So economists devised ways to incorporate such incentives into the traditional models. They did this, specifically, by adding policy variables (such as variables that incorporate the rate of taxation) to versions of the equations that appeared in the older models, so that a change in taxes would lead directly to a change in consumption and labor supply.

For example, in the 1972 version of the Wharton model (McCarthy 1972), a well-known traditional model, one of the equations that represents how economic agents decide to consume (that is, the consumption decision rule) is basically constructed this way:

(1) Consumption of nondurable goods *depends on*
- past consumption
- disposable income

- the price of nondurable goods relative to other consumer goods.

This equation, of course, is greatly simplified here, but it is detailed enough to illustrate the evolution to supply-side models. In the 1980 version of the Evans model (Evans Economics 1980), which is representative of supply-side models, the equation for consumption is similar, except for the addition of one policy-specific term:

(2) Consumption of nondurable goods *depends on*
- past disposable income
- the price of nondurable goods relative to other consumer goods
- the real after-tax rate.

In both models, a tax cut encourages consumption by increasing disposable income. In the Evans model, though, a tax cut also has an opposing effect—it discourages consumption by increasing the real after-tax interest rate and thereby encouraging saving.[1] The real after-tax interest rate, presumably, was added to represent the direct incentive to save instead of to consume when taxes on income are reduced. Without actually simulating the model, it is impossible to tell if the effects of the real after-tax interest rate outweigh the effects of disposable income. Nevertheless, the Evans model does take into account some incentives to save instead of to consume that were not explicitly considered in the traditional Wharton model.

In the equation that determines the labor supply, the Evans model also attempts to improve on traditional models, such as the Wharton model, by adding terms that take account of incentives. In the Wharton model, as in most traditional models, the amount of labor supplied is determined by labor demand—that is, there is no decision rule for the supply of labor. In the only equation related to the supply of labor.

(3) The civilian labor force *depends on*
- civilian employment
- lagged unemployment.

The term *lagged unemployment* means that a previous unemployment rate or an average of several previous rates has been used.

---

[1] Most economic researchers have been unable to show a clear direction to the impact of a change in the interest rate on the consumption-saving decision of the consumer. Boskin (1978), however, found that an increase in the real after-tax rate of return leads to an increase in saving. The Evans model is consistent with this work.

In the Evans supply-side model, labor supply is expressed as a decision rule. It is disaggregated into age-sex groups, and a typical decision rule is that

(4) The labor force participation rate for females ages 25-54 *depends on*
   • lagged inflation
   • lagged unemployment
   • the real after-tax wage rate.

This is a decision rule because it contains variables that are relevant to the labor-supply decisions of optimizing consumers. For our purposes, the most significant variable is the real after-tax wage rate, which is supposed to capture how incentives to work affect labor supply. In the Wharton model a cut in the wage tax does not directly affect labor supply because it does not determine either employment or unemployment. In the Evans model, however, a cut in the wage tax increases labor supply by increasing the real after-tax wage rate—that is, by increasing take-home pay. In future periods it increases it further by decreasing unemployment and, perhaps, inflation.

The consumption and labor-supply equations contain the major differences between the Wharton and Evans models. Given the supply-side emphasis on the investment decision, one might also expect to find that the investment equation of the new models also differs in important ways from that of the old models. This, however, does not seem to be the case. The fiscal parameters included in the new supply-side models, such as the corporate tax rate and the investment tax credit, have been integral parts of traditional models, at least as far back as the 1972 Wharton model.

The differences between the consumption and labor-supply equations in the Wharton and Evans models imply that a tax cut in a supply-side model should increase consumption less and increase the labor supply more than in traditional models. A larger share of output, therefore, is potentially available for capital investment. Increasing investment leads, over time, to a larger capital stock and allows producers to have better tools and technology, so that productivity (output per worker) increases. Thanks to the increased productivity and the increased labor force, a tax cut in a supply-side model eventually leads to a greater increase in goods and services than a tax cut would in a traditional model. In fact, the output effect in the supply-side model may be so large that the rate of inflation falls. Traditional models, in contrast, always show a tax cut increasing inflation. In short, the supply-side argument is lower taxes, higher productivity, and possibly lower inflation.

It is important to note that the supply-side argument for a tax cut is more precisely an argument for a *net* tax cut. This distinction is critical. As the simulations presented in Evans 1980 clearly show, a tax cut alone increases inflation. Only a tax cut accompanied by an expenditure cut (which is smaller than the tax cut) can reduce both inflation and the unemployment rate in the Evans model. Recognizing this, Senator Lloyd Bentsen of the Joint Economic Committee (U.S. Congress 1980, p. 2) supports supply-side policies and "continues to believe that the Federal Government must put its own financial house in order."

THE SUPPLY-SIDE INTERPRETATION OF A TAX CUT

Based on supply-side models, some economists make very precise forecasts of what would happen if tax rates were changed. Michael Evans (1980, p. 9), the creator of the Evans model, recently told Congress that the "total increase in the labor force caused a 1 p.p. [percentage point] reduction in the tax rate would be 0.26%, or approximately 270,000 workers at the present size of the labor force." Similarly, Otto Eckstein (1980, p. 53), using another supply-side model, has estimated that

> ... a 1 percent rise in the real tax burden discourages 0.04 percent of our workers from the labor force. Since 1965, the real tax burden has increased by almost 50 percent, driving 1.9 million people from the labor force according to the equation.

Policymakers sometimes treat such estimates with too much respect. For example, Senator Bentsen (U.S. Congress 1980, pp. 1-2) comments that the Eckstein supply-side model

> ... shows that tax policies, such as depreciation schedule adjustment, can lower the inflation rate substantially over the decade.... This new model is an important tool which will help policymakers implement the supply side policies which are being advocated by the Joint Economic Committee.

Such confidence may be misplaced. Although the new models purport to take adequate account of incentives, their forecast that tax cuts will lead to lower inflation is questionable.

The validity of the supply-side analysis can be questioned on two grounds. First, the new supply-side models have not remedied the major defects of the old models. Consequently, there is no reason for believing that they can better predict the results of changes in economic policy. Second, the empirical evidence is not adequate to support the supply-side proposition that inflation can be reduced by stimulating productivity. There seems to be little, if any, direct empirical relationship between productivity and inflation.

DEFECTS IN SUPPLY-SIDE MODELS

Supply-side models have not corrected the fundamental problem of the traditional models, the problem that makes them incapable of quantifying the results of a previously untried tax cut or other policy change. The problem is that supply-side models, like traditional ones, are constructed so that they do not agree with the theory they are supposedly based on.

Their underlying economic theory, hardly controversial, is that economic agents *optimize* or, in other words, take action to obtain the goods and services they want the most, limited by only a few major constraints—their wages, prices, available technology, and time, for instance. Both supply-side and traditional models are based on this theory. According to this generally accepted theory, consumers face a single optimization problem. They must make a simultaneous decision about how to divide their time between work and leisure and how to divide their income between current consumption and saving (or future consumption). These cannot be separate decision, because a decision to work more will lead to a higher income, and this higher income, in turn, should change their decisions about consuming and saving. Consumers solve this optimization problem—that is, they make their decisions— according to their own individual tastes and preferences, using whatever information they feel is pertinent and worth the cost of acquiring.

To be consistent with the theory of optimizing agents, an economic model must have at least two properties:

- *Internal consistency*. Because consumers solve a single optimization problem, the equations representing labor supply and the demand for consumption goods must be systematically related. If people decide to work less, for instance, they must make a corresponding decision to consume less. (Of course, if there is some change in the available technology or another of the constraints so that their standard of living rises, then they can work less and consume more—but this is another issue altogether.) A model is internally consistent only if the consumption and labor-supply deci-

sions are systematically related.
- *Policy consistency*. Because they optimize, consumers make their decisions only after they have considered all the relevant information, such as the future values of wages and taxes. To form their expectations in a way that is consistent with the theory of optimizing agents, they cannot ignore readily available information that can determine their future well-being. Therefore, if there is a change in the government's taxing strategy, consumers must change their decisions in accordance with it. The underlying economic theory, in sum, tells us that when policy changes, the values of the coefficients in the equations representing decision rules (such as labor supply and consumption) must also change to reflect the new decisions that consumers make. (This point is discussed more fully in the appendix.)

SUPPLY-SIDE MODELS VS. ECONOMIC THEORY

Unfortunately, the supply-side models are not consistent with the theory of optimizing agents, for they do not have these two key properties. They have neither internal consistency nor policy consistency.

The Evans model, for instance, is internally inconsistent because consumers can change how much they consume without making any change in how much they work. In other words, the equations that represent consumption and labor supply in this model can change independently of each other, as if they were unrelated. This model, in effect, divides a person's life into two unrelated halves—one that works, one that consumes.[2]

Similarly, the new supply-side models are not consistent with the theory of optimizing agents because the coefficients of the decision rules do not change when policy changes. A radical change in policy that is well-announced and well-understood by the people in the relevant markets—such as a substantial tax cut, the nationalization of the oil industry, or a declaration of war—will have no immediate effect on

---

[2]Wallace 1980 describes the problem of unrelated decisions (or partial equilibrium) with an analogy to the standard textbook descriptions of macroeconomic models. In a typical text there is essentially one chapter for each macro relationship, and that relationship is purported to be explained by the assumptions (theory) of that particular chapter. One problem with this textbook approach is that there is no guarantee that the assumption of different chapters, such as the one on consumption and the one on labor supply, are consistent, and hence no guarantee that there is a coherent underlying theory of the decision rules of the model.

people's expectations in these models. In some circumstances in these models, people begin to notice after a while that things have changed, and in perhaps a year or two they adjust to the changes completely. In other circumstances, they never learn and are repeatedly fooled by a continuing long-term policy. But except when the present and future policy happens to be the same as the policy in force when the models were estimated, people do not optimize and consider information that can drastically affect their well-being, even though the underlying economic theory says they must. The problem is not that they are ignorant, but that they are foolish; even when they have the information they need, they refuse to use it in an efficient way. Thus, the models assume that agents do not optimize when they form their expectations of future events, contradicting what they assume elsewhere. (For a more detailed discussion, see the appendix.)

SUPPLY-SIDE MODELS VS. THE EVIDENCE

Although the supply-side models are not compatible with the theory that underlies them, it is still possible that they have, by chance, recommended policies that will do what they claim. That is to say, the tax cuts that supply-side advocates recommend could help fight inflation, even though this result is not supported by supply-side models. The empirical evidence, however, does not support the advocates of a tax cut without an expenditure cut.

According to supply-side advocates and their models, stimulating productivity reduces inflation. If this were the case, then lower inflation would generally tend to accompany higher productivity. The evidence I have examined, though, seems to say that lower inflation and higher productivity do not necessarily go together.

I have examined time series regressions of the logarithms of the consumer price level on the money stock and productivity (output per worker) for the United States and seven of our major trading partners: Canada, Denmark, France, Germany, Japan, Sweden, and the United Kingdom. Over the period from 1950 to 1973 (prior to the surge in oil prices which, many have argued, has adversely affected productivity growth), none of the eight countries shows a statistically significant negative elasticity of price change with respect to an increase in productivity. That is, in none of these countries has an increase in productivity been associated with a decrease in inflation. In fact, all the countries except the United States and Sweden show a statistically significant positive elasticity. This suggests that higher productivity and lower inflation do not necessarily go together.[3]

For the period from 1950 to 1979 (which includes the period of the large rise in oil prices), the evidence from the regression analysis adds only a bit of support to the supply-side approach to inflation. Over this period, both the United States and Sweden show statistically significant negative elasticities. Nevertheless, the other six countries show positive elasticities, some of which are significant. There is thus no strong evidence based on these regressions that higher productivity accompanies lower inflation.

The cross-section data raise still further doubts about the supply-side approach to inflation. The trends in inflation and productivity in the United States and the seven foreign countries are shown in Chart 2. The plotted observations are the trend rates of growth of consumer prices and productivity (real GNP per worker) over the post-World War II period. This simple correlation across countries suggests that if there is any relationship between productivity growth and inflation, it is positive, not negative.[4] In brief, I was again unable to find that an increase in productivity is generally associated with a decrease in inflation.[5]

So it is by no means clear that a government tax policy designed to induce more rapid productivity growth would really lower inflation.

[3]These simple regressions are meant to be suggestive and not definitive. The potential for simultaneous bias exists, since we have not tested for exogeneity of productivity with respect to inflation.

[4]Chart 2, however, does not represent as strong a case against supply-side models as the time series regressions, since it does not take account of differences across countries in such things as monetary policies.

[5]In fact, inflation is higher in some countries when their rate of increase in productivity is higher. Yet it is commonly held that for a given rate of wage increase, an increase in productivity will lead to a slowdown in inflation, since firms could maintain their presumably fixed profit-margin mark-ups over labor costs at lower prices. Should Chart 2 then be dismissed as simply recording a spurious correlation? Not necessarily.

Even under the theory that wages are the predominant cause of inflation, this correlation can be explained. The actual inflation rate is affected by the growth in nominal wage rates which is affected by expectations of both productivity growth and inflation. If workers expect their output to increase, they will attempt to bargain for at least part, if not all, of this output increase. It makes no sense to talk of a given wage increase when productivity is expected to change. Furthermore, as implied by the discussion in the appendix, the relationship between wages and inflation could change when there is a new expected productivity path. Inflation could thus increase even when productivity is increasing.

The positive correlation between productivity and inflation can also be explained under the alternative theory that inflation is determined by monetary and fiscal policy while output is determined largely by productivity. If monetary and fiscal policies are fixed, a spurt in the growth of productivity (caused, for example, by a major technological change) would likely produce price levels lower than what they would otherwise have been. Under these conditions, too, output would likely increase. However, if the higher productivity growth is induced by some change in monetary or fiscal policy, then the effects are much harder to determine. It is possible that the inflation-raising aspects of the policy stimulus would swamp the inflation-lowering aspects of the increase in productivity.

Chart 2

Inflation and Productivity Growth

1950–79 in the U.S. and Its Major Trading Partners

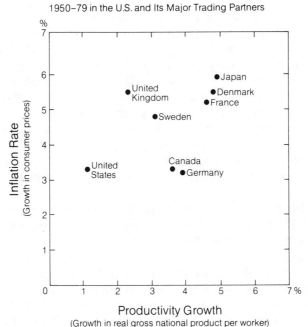

Productivity Growth
(Growth in real gross national product per worker)

Source: International Monetary Fund

The evidence against the supply-side view is certainly strong enough to make us question the validitiy of supply-side prescriptions.

BETTER MODELS AND METHODS

Both economic theory and empirical observations suggest that tax cuts which are rationalized by the new supply-side models are by no means a certain way to reduce inflation, although tax cuts may be warranted for other reasons. As this paper demonstrates, these models cannot be used to assess the effects of a tax cut or any other new policy, because they are not stable when policy changes. Although they can provide reasonably accurate forecasts when policy is constant, they simply cannot deal with a change in policy in a way that is consistent with the theory they are based on. Like the traditional models, therefore, they cannot be trusted to tell us how the economy will react to a tax cut, not even approximately. As this paper also demonstrates, these models cannot be used to assess the effects of a tax cut or any other new policy, because they are not stable when policy changes. Although they can provide reasonably accurate forecasts when policy is constant, they simply cannot deal with a change in policy in a way that is consistent with the theory they are based on. Like the traditional models, therefore, they cannot be trusted to tell us how the economy will react to a tax cut, not even approximately. As this paper also demonstrates, the relationship between productivity and inflation, which the supply-side advocates hope to exploit, is highly uncertain and is very likely influenced by factors—both cyclical and secular—other than tax policy. (See Denison 1979.) Because of this, one must be suspect of the notion that there is a direct negative relationship between productivity and inflation.

Even to begin to comprehend how the economy works, we need economic models which are capable of analyzing alternative economic policies, models that remain stable when policy changes. Although considering such models is beyond the scope of this paper, it is worth noting that such models will require an entirely new approach, not merely the simple alterations of traditional models that have resulted in supply-side models. One strategy for building economic models that is consistent with the underlying economic theory is provided by Lucas and Sargent (forthcoming).[6] Unfortunately, it is likely to be some time before this strategy produces models that can be used for meaningful policy simulations.

Until meaningful macroeconomic models are available for policy simulation, policymakers will have to use more modest tools. They can rely, for instance, on some microeconomic models which do not have the serious defects of the supply-side and traditional models. (Such models are discussed in detail in Kareken-Wallace 1980.) These micro models, however, may not encourage cutting taxes in order to reduce inflation. Some, in fact, suggest that the larger budget deficits created by cutting taxes are themselves inflationary. (See Miller 1980 and Miller-Struthers 1980.) In addition, policymakers can supplement these models by examining previous experience, not only from recent U.S. history, but from other times and places. One important study by Sargent (1980), for example, shows that four countries in this century stopped inflations that were much more severe than our own, not by

---

[6] See also Miller-Rolnick 1980. Meese (1980) has recently argued that although the data do not strongly support the theoretical restrictions implied by rational expectations, the methodology described in the Lucas-Sargent (forthcoming) volume "may prove to be the most useful approach to employ in future work" (p. 153).

boosting productivity, but by stopping the growth of unbacked government debt. Such tools are more difficult to use than macro models because they do not produce policy simulations, but at present they are the best tools we have.

Editor's Note: The Appendix referred to in this article is not included in this reprint. Please see the original article.

23

George Gilder on Why Supply-Side Economics Will Work*

JACK F. KEMP

Mr. Speaker, President-elect Reagan will bring with him to office an economic package which comprehensively addresses our economic problems of high inflation, high unemployment, and sluggish productivity. The package includes tax and regulatory reform to restore economic incentives, and budgetary and monetary reform to end inflation and restore order to financial markets.

George Gilder is one of the most articulate spokesmen of the economic and social thought behind this program. I therefore read his recent article on supply-side economics, which appeared in the New York Times, with great interest. I recommend the article to my colleagues as a brief and clear explanation of why tax-rate reduction is an integral, indispensable element in President-elect Reagan's plan for economic recovery and stabilization.

The article follows:

[From the New York Times, Nov. 23, 1980]

FORUM—INSIDE THE SUPPLY SIDE

IT ENCOURAGES WORKERS TO WORK AND INVESTORS TO INVEST

In recent months the subject to supply-side economics has widely engaged the public. But after a Presidential race in which Ronald Reagan's supply-side programs were a major issue, confusion still reigns on the meaning and significance of the term.

By diluting his supply-side arguments during the course of the cam-

*Reprinted from the *Congressional Record*, 96th Congress, 2nd Session, Tuesday, December 2, 1980.

paign, Mr. Reagan himself has contributed heavily to the confusion. And by consulting chiefly with conventional economists since his election, most leading economists and financial writers have concluded that he has little enduring commitment to supply-side theory and that he has no way of escaping the economic tribulations that have afflicted the Administrations of Jimmy Carter and Margaret Thatcher.

To understand why these experts may be wrong, it is necessary to comprehend that supply-side theory is not a mere fashion of concern for "the supply-side" of the system but an entirely different and coherent model of how government affects the economy. Developed by the economists Norman B. Ture, Arthur B. Laffer, Paul Craig Roberts, Robert A. Mundell, Jude Waniski, Alan Reynolds, Michael K. Evans and others, this view of economics has captured the imaginations of the most influential Republican senators and representatives.

Let us assume that the Reagan-endorsed tax proposal put forth by Representative Jack Kemp of Upstate New York and Senator William V. Roth Jr. of Delaware is enacted and its 30 percent reduction in tax rates is applied over three years. The demand-sider believes that this measure will immediately stimulate total, or aggregate, demand by increasing the disposable incomes of consumers.

The supply-sider, however, denies that a tax cut can have any immediate effect on total disposable income or real aggregate demand. For every dollar of increase in disposable income from the tax cut, there will initially be $1 less of disposable income either for recipients of Federal aid or for purchasers of government bonds that would otherwise have to be sold to cover the deficit. Some people will have more money, others will have less; the result is essentially a wash. Lacking a net immediate increment of aggregate demand, there can be no major short-run stimulus to the demand side of the economy.

The Kemp-Roth bill will work not by increasing total disposable income but by increasing the incentives of workers and investors to supply additional goods and services to the market. Supply-side theory focuses on marginal tax rates, the rates that apply on the margins of the economy to additional income that earners might choose to pursue, whether by working overtime, withdrawing from tax shelters, foregoing consumption, rejecting leisure, selling gold, purchasing stocks, starting a business, taking extra training or otherwise accepting additional risk to earn more money.

By definition a marginal tax rate is the rate applying to the next dollar of income for a worker or investor. So cuts in these rates will tend to induce workers to work harder for such additional dollars and investors to limit their consumption in order to earn more dollars in the future. The cuts will reduce the rewards of sheltering income from taxes through investments in untaxable activities or through work "off the books." By this process of changing incentives, tax cuts can lead to a long-run expansion of aggregate demand as a noninflationary result of expanding production of goods and services.

The only way a tax cut might contribute to inflation is by increasing the Federal deficit by a larger amount than personal and corporate savings, thus pressuring the Federal Reserve to expand the money supply. However, a cut in marginal tax rates, which Kemp-Roth would accomplish, would generate enough new revenue to eliminate the deficit or reduce it to manageable size. In addition, Kemp-Roth would yield enough new savings to remove pressure on the Fed to print money to cover any remaining deficit.

Marginal tax rates inflict a double penalty on saving. A particular marginal tax first deters the worker from earning the additional money that he is most likely to save. And, second, it deters him from saving it by taxing the income from savings at the highest rates. Because of this double inhibition, cuts in these rates impart a double stimulus to savings.

Not only have revenues increased in many countries, as well as the United States, after every previous cut in marginal rates, but there are also special conditions in this country today that make such results easily predictable now.

The economy is currently contorted by taxes. In recent years taxes have been growing 80 percent faster than inflation and 20 percent faster than personal income. In fact, one good reason for skepticism toward high taxes as an antedote to inflation is that for 15 years taxes—the price of government—have been the fastest-rising major cost in the economy.

Not only have these taxes been diffused into all the prices in the system, but the country has also developed a vast underground system of tax avoidance; a flourishing realm of cash and barter, financial finagling, investments in gold, baubles, flimflam films, subsidized real estate and an array of collectibles.

These shelters, hedges and other tax dodges exist almost exclusively as a result of the insidious interplay of rapid inflation and high marginal tax rates and would shrivel overnight under a rational tax system.

The marginal tax rate average Americans will face in 1981, though, as estimated from a study for the American enterprise Institute by Edgar K. Browning and William A. Johnson, will be more than 50 percent when all Federal, state, and local levies are combined with transfer payments that must be given up as earnings rise. This means that for the majority of Americans, rich and poor, it is more profitable to conceal a dollar of existing income than to earn an additional dollar.

For savers, however, the situation is worse. As Alan S. Blinder of the National Bureau of Economic Research recently testified before the Congressional Joint Economic Committee, most "unearned" income from savings such as interest and dividends, now faces tax rates substantially greater than 100 percent when adjusted for inflation. Most of these taxable "earnings" become losses when translated into uninflated dollars, but the I.R.S. continues to take a bite of up to 70 percent on these false gains, while state and local governments pile on further levies.

Moreover, by reducing expenditures on unemployment and compensation, welfare, early retirement and other recession-related government burdens, the Reagan program can facilitate cuts in government spending. Finally, by increasing the take-home pay of private-sector workers, tax cuts can diminish the pressures of the wage-price spiral. Supply-side economics thus provides an effective escape from the painful impasse of conventional economic theories and policies. That is why the theory will now be tested and prevail.

24

An Econometric Model Incorporating Supply-Side Effects of Economic Policy*

MICHAEL K. EVANS

To summarize the results of the previous section, we find that:

1. A 1 p.p. change in the tax rate will change labor force participation in the opposite direction for primary workers by a minuscule 0.05% but will change the participation rate for secondary workers by 0.37%.
2. A 1 p.p. change in the tax rate will change employment-hours in the opposite direction by 0.5%. Much of this change stems from the change in hours worked.
3. A 1 p.p. change in the tax rate will change the average wage rate in the same direction by 0.4% on impact, and 0.7% when the interaction between prices and wages is considered.

Thus a reduction in the personal income tax rate would increase the supply of labor, increase the number of hours worked, and reduce the gain in average wage rate. An increase in the demand and supply of labor would expand the maximum productive capacity of the economy. Thus inflation would be reduced both through a lower wage rate and a higher level of maximum capacity, thus widening the gap between actual and maximum capacity.

MAJOR LINKAGES IN THE SUPPLY-SIDE MODEL

One of the reasons that demand-oriented policies have been used almost exclusively in the past 15 years is that all of the current large scale

*Reprinted from *The Supply-Side Effects of Economic Policy,* Federal Reserve Bank of St. Louis, 1981. Michael Evans is President of Evans Economics, Inc., Washington, D.C.

econometric models have indicated that these policies will benefit the economy more than supply-side changes. Embedded in these models is the implicit assumption that an increase in demand will automatically trickle down to increase aggregate supply, thus insuring balanced, non-inflationary growth.

However, there is nothing magical about the balance between aggregate demand and supply. If incentives are lacking for investment, capital formation will stagnate. If incentives are lacking for labor, labor force participation will decline, the amount of labor offered by those already in the labor force will be reduced, and productivity will diminish. As a result, total productive capacity of the economy will grow more slowly than total demand, and bottlenecks, shortages and higher inflation will eventually result.

According to Keynesian demand economics, this higher inflation must then be fought by causing a recession and reducing aggregate demand. It is true that the gap between aggregate demand and supply must be widened in order to diminish inflationary pressures. However, surely there are two ways to accomplish this aim. One is indeed to diminish demand, thereby causing higher unemployment. The other is to increase aggregate supply, thereby raising the production possibility curve of the economy and increasing jobs and output at the same time that inflation is being lowered. This is the fundamental hypothesis underlying our supply-side modeling.

As already noted, most fiscal policy analysis of the past 15 years has been based on the belief that an increase in government spending will lead to a larger rise in demand and output than an equivalent reduction in taxes. The reasoning which leads to this conclusion is straightforward if inaccurate. If the government increases its spending, the entire dollar is used to raise aggregate demand. If taxes are cut, however, some of each dollar is used for saving. Since existing Keynesian models do not incorporate the links between saving and investment, demand does not rise as much.

Furthermore, these models also state that a personal income tax cut has a larger effect than a corporate income tax cut, and for much the same reason. Individuals spend a larger proportion of the extra money they receive from reduced taxes than do corporations, and that left-over saving does not contribute to economic growth or prosperity.

The supply-side model which we have built gives exactly the opposite result: an income tax cut has a larger effect on the economy than an increase in government spending. The supply-side mechanisms which support this conclusion can be qualitatively summarized as follows. In particular, a reduction in personal and corporate income taxes will set in motion the following chain of events.

1. An increase in the after-tax rate of return on personal saving occasioned by a reduction in personal income tax rates raises the incentives of individuals to save. This increase in saving leads to lower interest rates and higher investment.
2. A reduction in the effective corporate income tax rate, either through lower tax rates, a higher investment tax credit, or more liberal depreciation allowances, improves capital spending directly by increasing the average rate of return.
3. An increase in both personal and corporate saving leads to greater liquidity and less loan demand, thereby lowering interest rates. These effects help both capital spending and residential investment.
4. A rise in the ratio of investment to GNP leads to higher productivity, which means that more goods and services can be produced per unit of input. As a result, unit costs do not rise as fast and inflation grows more slowly.
5. A reduction in personal income tax rates leads to a rise in labor force participation and work effort, thereby increasing the supply of labor necessary to produce more goods and services.
6. Thus labor supply, capital stock, and productivity are all increased by lower tax rates, thereby expanding the maximum productive capacity of the U.S. economy.
7. As a result of higher maximum capacity the inflationary pressures of shortages and bottlenecks diminish, thereby reducing the rate of inflation.
8. An increase in maximum capacity also permits the production of more goods and services for export markets. This improves our net foreign balance and strengthens the dollar, thus leading to lower inflation because imported goods decline rather than advance in price.
9. Lower personal income tax rates lead to smaller wage gains, since wage bargaining is based at least in part on the level of after-tax income. This in turn reduces inflation further.
10. Thus lower tax rates cause a reduction in inflation through several channels. Inflationary pressures decline as the gap between actual and maximum potential GNP rises; productivity increases, thereby lowering unit labor costs; the dollar strengthens, causing less imported inflation; and wage rates rise more slowly.
11. Lower inflation leads to higher real disposable income, since bracket inflation is mitigated. The rise in income leads to an increase in consumption, output, and employment.
12. Lower inflation leads to lower interest rates, stimulating investment in both plant and equipment and in housing.
13. The increased demand for goods and services stemming from low-

er inflation is matched by the rise in the maximum potential capacity of the economy to produce these goods and services, thereby resulting in balanced, noninflationary growth.

One of the most important sets of linkages in the supply-side model is the relationship between saving and investment. For if saving rises and these funds are just used to increase idle cash balances, investment may not expand. However, these links are well documented in our model.

A $10 billion increase in personal saving raises time deposits by $3.0 billion and thrift institution deposits by $1.6 billion. In addition, it reduces loan demand by $3.6 billion.

As a result of these changes in the balance sheet of commercial banks, demand for U.S. government securities by the banks increases by $11.5 billion. This results in approximately a 1% decline in interest rates and a 3.2% increase in stock market prices.

These changes have two related effects on investment. First, lower interest rates and higher stock prices stimulate fixed business investment. Second, easier credit increases housing starts and mobile homes and, to a lesser extent, producers durable equipment.

As would be expected, nonresidential construction is more sensitive to changes in interest rates and stock prices than is equipment. Thus we find a $2.5 billion increase in structures, as compared to a $1.3 billion rise in producers durable equipment from a $10 billion increase in personal saving. Residential construction rises $1.5 billion because of credit easing and $1.2 billion because of lower interest rates. These are, of course, only first-round effects which do not take into account the increase in investment stemming from higher income and output. However, these results do document the strong linkages between saving and investment which exist in the supply-side model. For if these linkages are not strong, the second-round effects will not be observable either.

Another important breakthrough in our supply-side model is the endogenous explanation of productivity, which we have already discussed in the first section.

A 1% increase in productivity will not only expand maximum potential GNP by that amount; it will initially lower prices by 2/3%, since labor costs consist of 2/3 of total factor costs. This is only the first-round effect, since lower prices will lead to lower wages and further declines in unit labor costs and prices. The total effect of a 1% increase in productivity is to reduce prices by about 2%.

We are also able to introduce other innovations into the supply-side model because of the endogenous treatment of maximum capacity. In particular, the model introduces the concept of the cumulative gap, already discussed in the first section, which we define as the cumulative difference between 99% of maximum GNP and the actual level of GNP *when this gap is negative*. When it is positive—i.e., actual GNP is below maximum potential output—inflationary pressures do not build because of bottlenecks and shortages. However, when it is negative, prices start to rise faster than would be indicated by the cost of factor inputs alone.

So far this term does not sound greatly different than an index of capacity utilization, although it is much more inclusive in that it covers all sectors of the economy. However, we have *cumulated* this gap for all periods when the gap is negative. The term therefore indicates that inflationary pressures build up over many years and do not disappear every time a mild recession occurs. The inefficiencies and distortions which occur when the economy is operating near full capacity are not reversed overnight, and remain as a legacy until the cumulative gap once again returns to zero. This term may also represent the gradual buildup of inflationary expectations.

The final area of the model in which supply-side economics has been incorporated is the integration of the international sector with the U.S. economy. Again, this is an area where theoretical economists have long posited strong links, but they have never been empirically documented within the context of a macroeconomic model.

Supply-side effects are important in two specific areas. First, an increase in the gap between actual and maximum potential GNP raises exports, since the greater capacity of the U.S. economy permits the production of more goods and services for export markets as well. A 1% increase in this gap raises net exports by about $0.7 billion per year; since the gap is cumulative, this figure continues to increase linearly and is, for example, $2.1 billion after three years.

The second major effect is the link between the trade-weighted average of the dollar, which is itself closely tied to the size of the net foreign balance, and the overall rate of inflation. We find that a 10% decline in the value of the dollar relative to a trade-weighted average of the Deutschemark, French franc, Belgian franc, Dutch guilder, and Japanese yen raises the producer price index 1.3% and the consumer price index about half that much after a period of two years.

Thus we can document several supply-side relationships that have a significant effect on inflation as well as the rate of growth. All these figures refer to the change in the CPI and are impact estimates only. First, a 1 p.p. decline in the personal income tax rate will lower wage rates and thus prices by about 0.5%. Second, a 1% increase in productivity will lower prices by 2/3%. Third, a 10% improvement in the trade-weighted average of the dollar will reduce inflation by about 0.6%. Fourth, after a three-year period, a 1% increase in the gap between actual and maximum GNP will lower prices by 0.4%. It is worth repeating that all of these figures are impact estimates only and do not take into account the interaction between wages, prices, productivity, and other factors of production. Indeed, the final changes in prices are between two and three times the initial impacts, depending on cyclical conditions at the time.

Thus we find that the nemesis of demand-side economics, namely that output must be reduced and unemployment increased in order to dampen the rate of inflation, is only one of several alternatives. Inflation can also be reduced by increasing productivity, reducing personal and corporate tax rates, and strengthening the value of the dollar. We would not quarrel with the statement that the size of the gap between actual and maximum potential GNP is one of the factors determining the rate of inflation, but do believe that other factors must be considered as well.

The actual reduction in the implicit GNP deflator for the high-growth, high-deficit case is only 1.3% by 1990, although even this represents a marked change from the usual finding that inflation would be higher. The two principal reasons for this discrepancy are a) the lag structure and b) the large deficit. The changes in productivity do not immediately translate into lower prices, since both changes in wages and prices react to change in economic stimuli with a substantial lag. In addition, the benefits to higher productivity from higher investment are not felt immediately.

The second and more important reason is that the huge budget deficit pushes up interest rates, thereby contributing to higher costs of doing business and also raising the CPI through higher mortgage interest rates.

Because of the fact that the implicit GNP deflator declines in this high growth scenario, we find that the reflows are rather modest. Hence the *ex post* deficit in 1990 is approximately $500 billion in spite of the higher growth generated. While such a deficit is economically feasible because the dissaving by the government is funnelled into saving by the private sector, we do not think it would be politically feasible, nor do we consider it the optimal solution.

For this reason we have calculated another high-growth scenario, one with a balanced budget, which is generated by reducing transfer payments. This alternative high-growth scenario, which we then adopt as our preferred run, also provides additional information about the timing and magnitude of government spending multipliers.

GENERATING A HIGH-GROWTH SCENARIO:
THE BALANCED BUDGET CASE

To generate this simulation, we made only one change from the previous high-growth run: we reduced transfer payments enough to generate a balanced budget. This resulted in transfer payments increasing only 2.2% per year (current dollars) instead of the 11.4% per year increase which is included in both the baseline and high growth-large deficit scenario. The total reduction in transfer payments by 1990 is approximately $500 billion per year.

Before examining the economic ramifications of such a reduction, it certainly is worth asking whether it would be possible to cut transfer payments by this amount while still retaining the present social fabric of the United States. Figures on the projected growth of transfer payments over the next decade under alternative assumptions are given in Table 5.

For purpose of this analysis, we can divide transfer payments into three categories: retirement benefits, medical care payments, and other transfers, which are largely veterans benefits and welfare payments. Under the baseline case, retirement benefits are expected to grow at a rate equal to the annual average increase in the CPI plus the average increase in the population over 65. A similar formula would apply for medical care benefits, although there we use the increase in the CPI for medical care. Other transfer payments are expected to grow at a rate of increase equal to the average rise in the implicit GNP deflator plus the average gain in total population. These figures are all given in Table 5A.

The figures in Table 5B are adjusted for lower inflation, and also incorporate the assumption that retirement benefits would be indexed to the implicit deflator for consumption rather than the CPI, since the tendency of the latter to overstate price increases because of its overdependence on the cost of buying and financing a home is now well known. Thus switching to the higher-growth lower-inflation scenario, plus this one sensible adjustment in the indexation scheme for social security benefits, reduces transfer payments by almost $200 billion per year by 1990.

While this $200 billion is indeed an impressive saving, it is far less than the $500 billion which is needed to balance the budget. Table 5C provides the arithmetic to indicate how these remaining savings are achieved. From an economic point of view, the following changes are instituted:

1. The retirement age is raised from 65 to 70. There is nothing sacrosanct about the number 65 for a retirement age; indeed, if we use the most recent actuarial tables, we find that a retirement age of 65 in the mid-1930s (when social security was originally implemented) now corresponds to an age of almost 70, and that figure will probably rise to 72 by the end of this decade.

As might be expected, the savings in postponing the retirement age are substantial. Each additional year of postponement—e.g., from 65 to

Table 5   Projected Growth of Transfer Payments

	1980 (billions)	Annual Increase Due To:			Total Annual Change	1990 (billions)
		Inflation	Pop.	Change in Coverage		
A. Baseline						
Retirement Benefits	$157	9.9%	2.0%	0.0%	12.1%	$490
Medical Care	38	10.1	2.0	1.0	13.4	134
Other	98	8.3	1.0	0.0	9.4	241
TOTAL	293				11.4	865
B. Adjustment for Lower Inflation Only						
Retirement Benefits	$157	6.1%	2.0%	0.0%	8.2%	$344
Medical Care	38	7.8	2.0	1.0	11.0	108
Other	98	7.5	1.0	0.0	8.4	222
TOTAL	293				8.7	674
C. Lower Inflation and Cutbacks in Program						
Retirement Benefits	$157	6.3%	2.0%	−9.0%	−0.7%	$147
Medical Care	38	7.8	2.0	−5.0	5.0	62
Other	98	7.5	1.0	−3.7	4.6	154
TOTAL	293				2.2	363

[a] Implicit Constant Deflator instead of CPI.

66—saves the government $18 billion at current levels of benefits and population. If we adjust this figure upward for the increase in the implicit consumption deflator and the growth in population over 65, by 1990 this figure amounts to $40 billion for each year the retirement age is postponed. Thus raising the retirement age to 70 would save a whopping $200 billion, in which case retirement benefits would actually be somewhat below present levels.

The other cuts are less drastic. The reduction in medical care benefits could be accomplished, we believe, by simply adding a deductible and coinsurance whereby the patient would pay the first $100 per year of medical expenses and 90% of the remainder up to some fixed limit which might be equal to, say, 10% of his annual income. For example, if an individual had an income of $20,000, he would be required to pay no more than $2,000 in medical premiums that year regardless of the extent of his actual bills. This would provide 100% coverage for catastrophic illness while alerting patients to the substantial cost of medical services which is borne by society at large. We estimate that the deductible and coinsurance as outlined above would cut the growth of medical care payments in half.

The remaining cuts would occur in the phasing back of existing programs, such as food stamps for college students, a cap on black lung payments, reduction in the Aid to Families with Dependent Children as these parents returned to work, and other similar welfare programs.

Of the three major areas, these cuts are proportionately the smallest and the most politically feasible.

It should be made quite clear that workers who no longer receive retirement benefits at ages 65 through 69 will remain in the labor force, but the higher growth rates will certainly provide the additional jobs necessary to support these older workers. As we have already mentioned above, the U.S. economy will shift from a labor surplus to a labor shortage economy by 1990, and the jobs which these older workers retain will mitigate the labor shortage problem. Hence the gradual raising of the retirement age—increasing it, for example, six months every year over the next decade—would fit hand in glove with the need for more workers and the redirection of resources from the public to the private sector.

COMPARISON OF THE TWO HIGH-GROWTH SCENARIOS

Based on traditional multiplier analysis, one might expect that the $500 billion decrease in transfer payments would result in a far slower rate of growth because of the resulting decline in consumption. However, this is not at all what happens. The reduction in the federal government budget deficit lowers interest rates, thereby stimulating capital formation. Furthermore, the lower rate of inflation which stems from higher productivity growth also reduces interest rates. Finally, since income is redistributed to those who are working away from those who are not, labor force participation rises, which provides the additional labor inputs needed to complement increased capital spending.

The comparison for several key variables is given in Table 6. In particular we note that while real growth is about ½% per year higher for the largest deficit case in the early 1980s, the pattern is completely reversed in the second half of the decade, and by 1990 real GNP is increasing almost ½% per year faster for the balanced budget case. As can be seen, the rate of inflation is approximately 1% per year lower for the balanced budget case after 1985.

LOW-GROWTH SCENARIO

We have generated a high-growth scenario with a balanced budget by cutting corporate and personal income tax rates dramatically and then

Table 6 Comparison of Two High-Growth Scenarios

	1981	1982	1983	1984	1985	1986	1987	1988	1989	1990
Real GNP, % Growth										
Large deficit	2.6	6.2	4.4	1.0	2.1	3.4	3.9	4.4	4.8	5.0
No deficit	2.5	5.9	3.8	0.2	1.6	3.2	4.1	4.7	5.2	5.4
Implicit GNP Deflator, % Growth										
Large deficit	9.2	8.7	8.8	8.6	7.6	6.6	6.1	5.6	5.3	4.9
No deficit	9.2	8.7	8.6	8.2	6.9	5.7	5.0	4.5	4.2	3.8
Federal Budget Surplus or Deficit, billions of $										
Large deficit	-78	-70	-92	-148	-199	-239	-284	-348	-416	-508
No deficit	-65	-19	-2	-15	-16	-2	13	15	16	-4
Government Spending/GNP, ratio										
Large deficit	37.1	35.5	34.5	34.8	35.1	35.2	35.2	35.2	35.2	35.2
No deficit	36.6	34.0	32.2	31.9	31.6	31.1	30.4	29.9	29.4	29.0
AA Utility Bond Rate, %										
Large deficit	11.5	11.3	11.7	13.0	13.6	14.1	14.6	15.5	16.6	18.0
No deficit	11.5	11.0	10.9	11.8	11.5	11.3	11.0	11.2	11.5	12.2

balancing the budget through lower transfer payments. The low-growth alternative, however, cannot realistically be generated by raising tax rates the same amount they were cut in the high-growth alternative, for no one expects the statutory tax rates to be raised during the 1980s, although rates may drift up because of bracket creep. Thus we must lower growth directly by reducing growth in the labor force and by lowering the rate of growth in productivity. This can be done by a combination of a) higher tax rates through bracket creep, b) higher costs of government regulation, and c) higher relative energy prices.

Thus we have approached the low-growth scenario in a much different manner, and have changed those variables which impact directly on labor force growth and productivity *other than* income tax rates. The changes which we have introduced to generate this scenario are the following;

1. Energy prices, both imported and domestic, grow at a faster rate.
2. The cost of government regulation doubles over the decade.
3. Labor force participation rates grow more slowly.
4. Transfer payments grow 15.6% per year instead of 11.4%. The average tax rate increases from 24.9% to 38.3% by 1990—but that is entirely due to bracket creep and does not reflect any rise in the statutory rate.

In addition to these four changes, we have also cancelled any personal or corporate income tax cuts over the decade which are included in the baseline, held depreciable lives at 1980 levels, and terminated the investment tax credit. However, it should be stressed that these do not account for the bulk of the decline in growth which occurs in this scenario—that is due to the four factors listed above.

V
REAGANOMICS

Part V explains how supply-side economics evolved into a major political philosophy supported and fostered by President Reagan. In treating this topic, both pros and cons of so-called Reaganomics are presented.

25

Supply-Side Economics and How It Became a Presidential Program*

ROBERT W. MERRY
KENNETH H. BACON

WASHINGTON—Economist Norman Ture has been following public-policy debates since the Truman administration and has never seen anything like the rapid emergence of the idea called supply-side economics.

"It's one of the most dramatic, revolutionary developments I've ever seen," he says. "I don't know the like of it."

Mr. Ture should know; he is a supply-sider himself. Five years ago, most other economists dismissed him as something of a dreamer. Some still consider him that, but they can't disregard him today. Mr. Ture is the Reagan administration's under secretary of the treasury for tax policy.

In that post he is working to apply the supply-side doctrine that sharp cuts in tax rates will simultaneously spur higher economic growth and lower inflation. Several years ago Mr. Ture was part of a small, largely ridiculed band of supply-side guerilla fighters battling an army of Keynesian economists who for a generation have guided government policy more toward controlling economic consumption than promoting production.

RESPECTABLE NOW

President Reagan and his Cabinet now lead the supply-side movement. Today Mr. Reagan will announce to Congress and the nation a program of individual income-tax cuts, combined with extensive budget

---

*Reprinted by permission of *The Wall Street Journal,* © Dow Jones & Company, Inc. 1981. All rights reserved. Robert W. Merry and Kenneth H. Bacon are staff reporters of *The Wall Street Journal.*

reductions and a call for tighter monetary policy by the Federal Reserve Board.

The program will be controversial in Congress, and many conventional economists still doubt that supply-side nostrums can produce the fast economic growth and low inflation that Mr. Reagan will forecast. The President's program thus will provoke an epic economic debate.

"We're at one of those great moments where the opportunity to reverse the steady slide of our economic system exists and where new ideas are being offered to accomplish the turnaround," says Otto Eckstein, a Harvard economics professor and president of Data Resources Inc., a forecasting firm. But he warns that much of the supply-side theory hasn't been tested, and he worries that its rapid adoption "would be a gamble with our economic system."

At the heart of the debate is a fundamental question: What drives an economy? To the followers of the famous British economist John Maynard Keynes, the answer is aggregate demand—the willingness of people to trade their dollars for goods and services. In this view, if the government puts dollars in people's pocket through spending programs or tax cuts, they will spend much of the money, creating incentives for production. In other words, demand creates supply.

Not so, say the supply-siders. People produce not *only* because other people are ready to buy. They produce, in the words of New York's Rep. Jack Kemp, a leading supply-sider, "for after-tax income, after-tax profit, after-tax rewards." Individual tax cuts help, but they help more in brackets where people are more apt to invest and produce than they are to spend. If the rewards of production are stifled through high taxes and burdensome government regulations, potential producers won't engage in productive enterprises. Instead of working, saving and investing, they will spend their money—or dump it into nonproductive tax shelters and inflation hedges, such as gold.

That is happening in the U.S. now, the supply-siders argue, and it is stifling economic growth. They call for sharp cuts in tax rates designed to make both work and investment more rewarding, and thus to stimulate production, increase the supply of goods and services, and cool inflationary pressure.

Supply-siders reject the Keynesian idea that government can manage the economy by adjusting taxes and spending to achieve a balance between inflation and growth. They argue that increasing government spending to fight unemployment when taxes are high spurs inflation by increasing the demand for goods without increasing the supply. They also contend that tax increases to suppress demand and cool inflation— a policy sometimes advocated by Republicans—only produce recessions.

"Over the past several years, economic policy has been used to fight short-term swings in economic activity rather than to promote long-term growth of productive capacity," says Treasury Secretary Donald Regan. The Reagan team thinks it can produce simultaneous economic growth and milder inflation, rather than trade one for the other as the Ford and Carter administrations tried to do.

STOCKMAN'S CONCLUSION

"None of the standard Keynesian policy models, with government as the central instrument for economic improvement, seems to work," concludes David Stockman, President Reagan's budget director and an ardent supply-sider.

He and other supply-siders also criticize the argument—long posed by Republicans but more recently by Democrats as well—that taxes shouldn't be cut until the budget is balanced. Although balanced budgets are desirable, in the supply-side view, it is impossible to eliminate government deficits as long as high taxes stifle economic growth.

President Reagan agrees. In his recent economic address, he complained of "those who always told us taxes couldn't be cut until spending was reduced." He added that "excessive taxation of individuals has robbed us of incentive and made overtime unprofitable." And Secretary Regan, who says "I was a supply-sider before I ever heard the term," argues that holding tax cuts "hostage" to budget-balancing efforts would only continue "business-as-usual" no-growth policies.

Capturing the Executive Branch of government was an amazing victory for the supply-side movement, which hardly existed a mere eight years ago. It emerged in the thinking of two economists—Arthur Laffer, now at the University of Southern California, and Robert Mundell of Columbia—whose ideas captured the imagination of an editorial writer for this newspaper, Jude Wanniski.

Mr. Wanniski, who now runs his own economic-consulting firm, combed Washington for receptive politicians and finally found his man—Rep. Kemp, who in 1977 was co-author of the Kemp-Roth bill to slash individual income-tax rates 30% over three years. Soon, Republican staffers on Capitol Hill were picking up supply-side ideas and guiding converted legislators in pushing alternatives to the ruling Democrats' economic programs.

CONVERTING A CANDIDATE

Meanwhile, Mr. Kemp set out to convert Mr. Reagan, whom he considered the most receptive of the potential Presidents. It wasn't difficult. "Reagan has understood this stuff all the way along," says Mr. Wanniski.

But the supply-side outlook has some passionate critics. President Reagan's own vice president, George Bush, called it "voodoo economics" when he was running against Mr. Reagan in last spring's primaries. Walter Heller, former chairman of the Council of Economic Advisers, says the theory is supported by only "a few thimblefuls of questionable evidence." Sen. Paul Tsongas, a Massachusetts Democrat, derides it as "bumper-sticker economics."

Many economists reject the supply-siders' view that the best way to spur productivity is through deep cuts in individual income-tax rates. Even many Republicans in Congress argue that cutting individual taxes so sharply would merely generate new demand without immediately expanding supply and thus would worsen inflation. They prefer tax breaks for business and investors.

But supply-siders contend that people react quickly to reductions in their "marginal" tax rates, the amount of tax they pay on increased income. The theory is based on an abundant faith in Americans' work ethic, entrepreneurial spirit and investment savvy. When people realize they can keep more of each additional dollar earned, they will "shift into work out of leisure and into investment out of current consumption," says Paul Craig Roberts, a former Wall Street Journal editorial writer soon to become assistant treasury secretary for economic policy.

DOUBT EXPRESSED

Many economists doubt, however, that cuts in marginal rates would produce an explosion of new work and investment. Mr. Heller says, "The eager beavers will work harder, and the laid-back people will work less."

Mr. Heller was chairman of the Council of Economic Advisers when the last major cuts in marginal rates took place. Although he concedes that the 1964 Kennedy-Johnson tax cuts spurred economic growth and thereby increased tax revenues even at the lower rates, he worries that sharp rate cuts now would encourage demand more than supply—and hence worsen inflation. The inflation rate was only 1.2% when the 1964 tax reductions occurred, compared with about 13% today, he notes, adding:

"The enormous preponderance of evidence is that there's a relatively slow and modest supply response."

Supply-siders retort that Keynesian economists are prisoners of their conventional demand-side computer models, which can't predict the future because they ignore supply-side incentive effects. The Reagan team predicts that its tax cuts, combined with sharp federal spending curtailments and a tight monetary policy, will lead to a rapid reduction in inflation even as the economy booms. Its projections for 1984 are bright: inflation, between 5% and 6%; economic growth after inflation, over 4%. In 1980, consumer prices rose 13.5% and the gross national product, adjusted for inflation, slipped by 0.1%.

"The world is dominated nine to one" by people who believe that the momentum of inflation can't be slowed as quickly as the administration predicts, says John Rutledge, president of Claremont Economics Inc. and a Reagan adviser. He contends that the President's program will quickly convince people that inflation will slow, causing rapid declines in interest rates and an easing in wage and price pressures as lenders, workers and everyone else becomes less frantic about keeping ahead of inflation.

THE MONEY SUPPLY

Besides, the Reagan team assumes that the Federal Reserve Board will curb money-supply growth so as to moderate inflation, which Treasury Secretary Regan defines as "primarily a monetary phenomenon." He adds, "Stable prices are impossible if money-growth rates outstrip the growth of goods and services."

And so the Reagan team predicts that its program will quickly lower inflationary expectations, affecting prices "much faster than any of those white-coated econometricians would guess," in the words of Mr. Rutledge. The standard economic models, he adds, don't properly account for the boom in financial markets that will result from lowered inflation expectations and the willingness of people to forgo consumption in favor of investment.

Although many economists are skeptical, they're beginning to pay attention. For example, Richard Berner of Wharton Econometric Forecasting Associates Inc. is designing a new economic model that incorporates some of the supply-side thinking. Others may soon follow. "A new element has been injected into the ongoing economics debate," says Lawrence Klein, who won the Nobel prize for developing the Wharton econometric models.

26

The Reagan Program for Economic Recovery: Economic Rationale (A Primer on Supply-Side Economics)*

JAMES R. BARTH

The Reagan administration has proposed a four-part economic program to spur economic growth while simultaneously reducing inflation. The specific parts of this program are reductions in marginal tax rates, cuts in the growth in government spending, a slow and steady growth in the money supply, and regulatory reform. Critics of President Reagan's Economic Recovery Program contend that it is very unlikely that this program will achieve its twin goals of lower inflation and greater economic growth. They argue instead that the proposed program will more likely result in continued inflation and sluggish growth.

To judge whether or not the economic program proposed by President Reagan will be successful requires an understanding of the program's economic rationale. Although most people now know that the rationale is "supply-side" economics, that is about all they know about it. What exactly encompasses this particular approach to economic policy still remains largely a mystery. This article attempts to eliminate the mystery by explaining the administration's program in terms of supply-side economics.[1]

TAX CUTS

The centerpiece of the administration's economic program is the recently enacted cuts in personal tax rates and business taxes. The per-

*Reprinted from the *Economic Review*, September 1981, published by the Federal Reserve Bank of Atlanta.

†The author wishes to acknowledge the helpful comments of: Joseph Cordes, William Cox Manuel Johnson, Michael Marlow, Frederick Ribe, Stephen Sheffrin and especially George Iden.

[1] For additional information about supply-side economics, the reader is urged to consult the references cited at the end of this article. (See *Economic Review*, September 1981.)

sonal part of the tax package calls for a 25 percent across-the-board three-year reduction in marginal tax rates.[2] These cuts are intended to provide incentives to work harder and save more. The cuts are in marginal rather than average tax rates because it is believed that it is at the "margin" where people make decisions. "Marginal tax rates" are the rates paid on a dollar of additional income.

According to supply-side economics, such tax reductions first and foremost affect relative prices. Specifically, tax cuts alter the relative price of work versus leisure as well as the relative price of saving versus consumption. Supply-side proponents argue that an individual chooses between working an additional hour or devoting the hour to leisure based upon the after-tax real wage for that hour. If marginal tax rates are reduced, the after-tax real wage for working an additional hour rises. In other words, the price of work relative to leisure falls. Individuals are therefore induced to trade-off leisure for work at the margin.

This relative price effect is supposed to provide an incentive for those persons currently working to increase hours worked and/or reduce absenteeism. Persons not currently working presumably will have a greater incentive to seek employment, while persons currently working in the "underground economy" (to reduce their tax burden) will be induced to reenter the regular economy.[3] Of course, if the tax cuts do result in an expansion in total employment, then the economy should grow faster.

The predicted impact of marginal tax reductions on work effort, however, is theoretically questionable. As a result of an increase in after-tax real wages, people may work less, not more. The reason is that with higher after-tax real wages an individual may be able to work fewer hours, while still maintaining or even improving upon his real income or standard of living. This means that although the tax rate cut will change the relative price of work vis-a-vis leisure and thus induce a "substitution effect" of work for leisure, this may be more than offset by the "income effect" that induces people to work less and devote more time to leisure.

Whether or not a cut in marginal tax rates will therefore increase employment is an empirical issue. The empirical evidence, unfortunately, is mixed. Some studies find that tax cuts significantly increase the supply of labor, while others do not. The more recent studies, however,

---

[2] The tax package has been referred to as the Kemp-Roth tax cut because the "Tax Reduction Act of 1978" (the Kemp-Roth bill) also represented a commitment to a very large tax cut over a period of three years.

[3] It is also assumed that the incentive to avoid taxes through "tax-shelters" will diminish with cuts in marginal tax rates. This is considered important because it is believed that tax shelters siphon off funds from investment in productive plant and equipment. More generally, the tax cuts are across-the-board so as to avoid the distortions generally associated with targeted or selective cuts.

seem to find almost unanimously a positive employment effect resulting from tax cuts, at least for secondary workers.[4] There thus seems to
be an emerging empirical consensus that tax cuts do stimulate employment. But even though one may find a significant positive impact on
employment resulting from tax rate reductions, it is not clear that the
resulting employment is sufficient to contribute substantially to the
growth in output.

Regarding the impact of reductions in marginal tax rates on the decision to save or consume, the story is somewhat similar. An individual
uses his after-tax income to consume and/or save. The decision to save
today, however, is simply the decision to consume tomorrow. The more
one consumes today therefore, the less one consumes tomorrow. By
increasing saving, an individual is able to increase future consumption.
The exact link between saving and future consumption is determined
by the after-tax rate of interest. Future consumption is equal to current
saving plus the after-tax interest earnings on that saving.

A tax cut thus raises the price of current consumption relative to
the price of future consumption. Specifically, a reduction in marginal
tax rates decreases the relative price of future consumption to current
consumption. People therefore will have an incentive to consume more
in the future, which means to save more today. In short, the tax cut increases the after-tax rate of return to saving and thus provides an incentive to save more and to consume less.

Once again, there are theoretical reasons to question this predicted
result. As the after-tax rate of return rises due to a tax cut, an individual
may save less and yet still maintain or even increase future consumption.
The reason should be clear. Higher after-tax rates of interest applied to
a lower level of saving may still lead to an increase in total interest earnings, meaning that future consumption need not fall. Although tax cuts
provide people with an incentive to save more and to consume less, this
substitution effect may be more than offset by the income effect resulting from increased after-tax interest earnings. Whether or not people
save more or less as a result of a tax cut, therefore, cannot be determined on theoretical grounds alone.

The issue is instead an empirical one and empirical results, again, are
mixed. Some studies find that reductions in after-tax rates of return
significantly increase saving, while others do not. Furthermore, even in
those cases in which there are statistically significant positive saving
effects, it is unclear whether the enacted reductions in marginal tax
rates provide enough of an incentive to increase saving substantially.

The increase in private saving, which as a share of income is at an
historically low level, is a crucial component of supply-side economics

---

[4] Secondary workers are to be distinguished from primary or head-of-household wage earners.

because presumably most, if not all, of the increase would be channeled directly and indirectly through financial institutions into corporate securities, both bonds and stocks.[5] Business firms thus would be provided with the funds necessary to finance the acquisition of new plant and equipment. To stimulate capital formation further, the Reagan program also provides investment incentives in the form of greater depreciation allowances. More specifically, the business part of the tax package calls for more rapid write-offs of investments in newly acquired plant and equipment.[6]

Although it is generally agreed that this action will stimulate investment, there is some concern that there may be distortions in the type of investment stimulated. Critics contend, for example, that industries (such as the automobile and steel industries) already employing rapid depreciation write-offs and/or experiencing losses will gain little from these tax actions. Administration officials expect increased saving and investment resulting from the tax cuts to generate the additions to the capital stock necessary for improved productivity and greater economic growth. Presumably, of course, the federal tax cuts would not be offset by tax increases at the state and local level, over which the administration has little control.[7]

Thus, according to supply-side economics, the tax cuts will change two important relative prices and thereby provide the necessary incentives for people to work and to save more and for business firms to invest more. This additional work, saving and investment will improve productivity and increase the supply of goods and services in the U.S. economy, though the exact timing of these effects is not known with any degree of certainty. Hence the term supply-side economics. The increase in supply, moreover, gives rise to the income to create the necessary increase in the demand for goods and services.

This approach to economic policy is in contrast to demand-side or Keynesian economics. According to traditional Keynesians, the first and foremost effect of tax cuts is to increase consumption and thus the demand for goods and services, due to the increase in after tax or dis-

---

[5] It should also be pointed out that the tax cuts should reduce consumer borrowing, which represents negative saving, because the benefits of deducting the interest expense from taxable income are reduced. Such a reduction in consumer borrowing should channel more funds into the business sector of the economy.

[6] Specifically, business tax relief includes faster write-off of capital expenditure over 3, 5, and 10 years for various kinds of equipment, rather than over the so-called useful life of an asset. Most buildings could be written off over 15 years.

[7] Since the U.S. tax system is not indexed, inflation has tended to push people into higher tax brackets over time. The cuts in marginal tax rates will contribute to offsetting "bracket creep." Furthermore, starting in 1985, annual adjustments will eliminate "bracket creep." Nevertheless, questions will remain about the duration and magnitude of any incentive effects resulting from the tax cuts.

posable income. The resulting increase in demand, in turn, creates the necessary increase in supply. For supply-siders, therefore, supply creates its own demand and for demand-siders or Keynesians demand creates its own supply. This, at least, appears to be the view of administration advocates of supply-side economics.

In sum, supply-side economics emphasizes the longer-run aspects of fiscal policy (the increased supply due to tax rate cuts), whereas Keynesian economics emphasizes the shorter-run stabilization aspects of fiscal policy (the use of tax-rate cuts to increase demand when supply is below its potential). A more important distinction, perhaps, is that Keynesians contend the tax cuts stimulate demand and thereby create additional output but only at the cost of higher inflation, whereas supply-siders contend that the increased supply resulting from tax cuts will lower inflation so long as the Federal Reserve behaves properly. More will be said about this below.

SPENDING CUTS

Another important element in the administration's economic program is a reduction in the rate of growth in government spending. To understand the importance of spending reductions, it is important to realize that government spending must be financed by taxes, by borrowing from the public and/or by printing money. Given that cuts in tax rates have been enacted, unless government spending is correspondingly reduced, a deficit may arise.[8] A deficit arises when government spending exceeds tax revenues. If tax revenues fall as a result of tax cuts, then a deficit will be created so long as government spending remains unchanged.

It is, however, theoretically possible for tax revenues to rise as a result of tax rate cuts. According to the "Laffer Curve," there is some range over which tax rate reductions will increase tax revenues, not decrease them. This is perhaps more fully grasped by realizing that when the tax rate is zero, so too are revenues. Similarly, when the tax rate is 100 percent, the incentive to earn income disappears and tax revenues are again zero. As the tax rate rises, in other words, revenues will rise until at some tax rate they finally begin to fall toward zero as the disin-

---

[8] The size and persistence of any deficit depends upon the exact timing and magnitude of any positive supply-side effects. Unfortunately, however, there is no direct evidence pertaining to the length of the lags associated with stimulating the economy as the supply-siders propose going about it.

centive effect of the higher tax rate causes income to fall faster than the rate rises.

Having said this, however, there is no clear evidence that the U.S. economy currently is operating in the perverse tax rate range. If not, then tax cuts will reduce tax revenues and thus create a deficit (or increase an existing deficit). Since the administration predicts a deficit, the full Laffer effect (tax cuts that finance themselves) does not appear to be an integral part of the administration's economic program. In other words, supply-side economics as being interpreted and implemented by the administration does not depend upon the specific positioning of the economy on the Laffer curve. However, although the administration does anticipate a deficit in the shorter-term, it expects that the predicted growth in the economy will produce a balanced budget within three years.

Given the government budget restraint, any deficit created by tax cuts must be financed by printing money and/or borrowing from the public. Under the administration's program, the deficit is intended to be bond-financed, not money-financed. Administration planners believe that financing the deficit in this manner will not be inflationary. Due to the tax cuts, disposable income will rise, providing people with the additional funds with which to purchase the U.S. government securities being sold. According to that premise, people will use their increase in disposable income to save rather than to consume so that demand does not increase. As a result, the predicted deficit will not be inflationary.

Keynesians, however, contend that even a bond-financed deficit will be inflationary because U.S. government securities are considered to be part of private wealth. An increase in the amount of these securities outstanding resulting from the financing of the deficit therefore leads to an increase in private wealth. According to traditional Keynesian economics, as people become wealthier they will increase their spending or consumption. But if consumption increases, so too does aggregate demand. And the increased demand for goods and services will put upward pressure on prices.[9] [10]

---

[9] Keynesians do contend, however, that in periods of substantial unemployment increases in demand are only moderately inflationary, if at all.

[10] There is a more subtle argument, based upon "ultra-rational" behavior by taxpayers, that bond-financed deficits do not add to demand and thus are not inflationary. According to that argument, the government bonds that are issued to finance the deficit impose a liability on the federal government. To pay the future interest on these bonds, future taxes must also be higher. This implies that the present discounted value of the bonds is offset by the present discounted value of the tax liability. As a result, there is no "wealth effect" to stimulate demand; people will not view government bonds as a component of their wealth because of the offsetting tax liability. The asserted equivalence of debt and taxes is usually referred to as the "Ricardian equivalence theorem." It should be noted that there are both theoretical and empirical objections to this "theorem." Many simply find the degree of foresight and rationality required by

If the supply-siders believe that deficits resulting from tax cuts are not inflationary when bond-financed, then why were spending cuts proposed? Actually, the administration proposed changes in the mix of government spending. The question therefore should be, more specifically, why are social expenditures being cut while defense expenditures are being increased substantially?

The answer seems to be that this change in the mix of government spending toward defense and away from social programs is broadly consistent with the administration's goal to provide work incentives. Some claim, for example, that the current level of government expenditure on welfare benefits, unemployment benefits and public-service jobs deters individuals from obtaining productive work. Reductions in government spending, furthermore, reduce the size of the deficit and thus the amount of borrowing from the public, thus providing more funds for private investment (i.e., the amount of "crowding out" is lessened). More generally, the spending cuts probably reflect a belief that federal expenditures are simply too high: that goods and services are being provided that could be provided more efficiently by the private sector if such goods and services are actually desired.[11]

SLOW AND STEADY MONEY GROWTH

Another key part of the Reagan Economic Program is a slow and steady rate of growth in the money supply. The administration looks to the Federal Reserve to implement this part of the program. Although many contend the Federal Reserve has been unable and/or unwilling to pursue such a strategy, the administration assumes in its planning that this will no longer be the case. If the Federal Reserve is unsuccessful, some would argue that the time has finally arrived for a return to the gold or some other commodity standard to provide discipline over the money supply.

Under the proposed economic program, the Federal Reserve is assigned the responsibility of reducing money growth to a slow and steady rate. Such a policy is expected to bring the inflation rate quickly down,

this argument "hard to swallow." More seriously, it is contended that either people do not fully discount the future tax liability or do not expect the government ever to redeem its securities. In the latter case, government bond-financed and money-financed deficits are essentially the same, and both are inflationary. Less than full tax discounting implies a wealth effect and thus an inflationary increase in demand.

[11] Interestingly enough, the government spending cuts may also moderate the inflationary fears of those concerned about the size of the tax cuts.

but not by producing sluggish growth in the economy. The administration believes that a publicly announced commitment by the Federal Reserve to this policy will generate the credibility necessary to alter the "inflationary psychology" that currently exists. This should lead to lowered "inflationary expectations." Lowered inflationary expectations, in turn, should reduce the rate of wage increases and thus price increases. A reduction in the expected inflation rate should also lead to a decline in the nominal interest rate.

All of this occurs, contrary to the belief of Keynesians, without slowing output growth. The reason is that as long as the Federal Reserve fulfills its commitment, people's expectations about inflation coming down will be realized. Without any surprises, the slower money growth should affect only prices and wages. Keynesians, however, believe that wage rigidities will upset this process. Slower money growth will drive up real wages and thus reduce employment, producing slower growth.

The administration's confidence in its expected result is based upon the belief that the Federal Reserve will be better able to pursue a policy independent of fiscal actions. Until now, it is argued, the Federal Reserve has responded to ever larger budget deficits by monetizing ever larger parts of them to moderate upward pressure on interest rates or government borrowing costs. As budget deficits grew under the old regime, ever larger amounts of government securities had to be sold to the public to finance the deficits. To borrow such increasingly larger amounts, it was assumed that interest rates had to rise to induce the public to part with its funds.

It was believed that, historically, the Federal Reserve moderated the rise in interest rates by monetizing a portion of the deficit. But this required ever larger expansions in the money supply and thus put continual upward pressure on prices. The resulting inflation, it is argued, generated inflationary expectations which only led eventually to higher, not lower, interest rates. The administration proposes to put a halt to this process, relying on the Federal Reserve to bring the money supply under control, so that it grows at a slow and steady rate.[12] It is not expected to monetize budgetary deficits or to attempt to hold interest rates down. If it accomplishes its assigned task, the result should be a decline in both the inflation rate and interest rate.

The historic record of the Federal Reserve's ability and/or willingness to control the money supply is considered by many to be mixed. Some contend that the Federal Reserve has exacerbated fluctuations in interest rates and contributed to inflation, while others, though prob-

[12] Steady growth is considered to be important so as not to convey false signals about the intentions of the Federal Reserve. Steady growth, in other words, contributes to credibility of the monetary authorities. The time frame during which these events are expected to take place is a matter of considerable conjecture.

ably far fewer in number, contend just the opposite. Whether the Federal Reserve will accomplish its task to the administration's satisfaction is debatable. Whether or not the administration's inflation forecast will be achieved in any event, depends largely upon what happens to future money growth.

REGULATORY REFORM

The last important part of the administration's economic program is regulatory reform. On February 17, 1981, President Reagan issued Executive Order No. 12291 on regulatory reform calling for a cost-benefit analysis before issuing any new federal rule or regulation. By comparing the economic and social benefits and costs of individual rules, the administration aims to make the regulatory process more cost-effective, thereby reducing the "hidden tax" (including paperwork requirements) of complying with federal rules which do not contribute to the public welfare.

More generally, regulatory reform is intended to curtail government intervention into the economy, thereby placing more reliance on the workings of the market for the pricing and allocation of resources. This view assumes that in many cases the profit motive is more likely to generate the desired outcome than existing regulations. Some Reagan advisors believe that an insufficient use of cost-benefit analysis in the past has led to excessive regulation that has contributed unnecessarily to a misallocation of resources and to inflation.

AN HISTORICAL COMPARISON

As we have seen, there are both theoretical and empirical reasons for questioning to some degree the predicted outcome of President Reagan's Economic Program. Tax cuts (even if sufficient to initially offset and to eventually eliminate bracket-creep and social security tax hikes) may actually reduce employment and saving, or at least not increase them very much. If this were to happen, it might not be possible for the administration to simultaneously reduce inflation and increase economic growth. Furthermore, interest rates may not come down significantly and productivity may not show much improvement. But, of course, the opposite scenario cannot be dismissed out of hand.

Given the substantial skepticism toward its economic program, the administration has been under constant pressure to provide evidence that its program will work. Thus far, the main evidence supporting supply-side economics has taken the form of a retrospective look at what happened after the Kennedy tax cuts of February 1964. It is claimed that the recent tax cuts are quite similar to the earlier cuts and therefore should have essentially the same effect. According to the administration, the economic events which followed the Kennedy tax cuts provide evidence bearing on the likelihood of the supply-side effects. As a result, it is worthwhile examining this historical period.[13]

When examining the effect of the Kennedy tax cuts, it is useful to concentrate on what happened to saving. The reason is that the claim that the tax cuts will raise saving enough to more than offset any resulting deficits has received the most skepticism. This is because Keynesian theory maintains that a tax cut will increase after-tax income and thereby increase both consumption and saving. But the tax cut will also produce a deficit which will more than offset the increase in saving, unless government spending is sufficiently reduced and/or enough new tax revenues are produced. According to Keynesian theory, it is very unlikely that the economy will grow fast enough as a result of the tax cuts for this to happen.

The administration view, however, is quite different. The tax cuts will increase the after-tax rate of return to saving, thus causing saving to increase. This increase is in addition to the increase in saving resulting from the rise in after-tax income. In other words, the tax cuts will produce an increase in saving even if income were held constant. Correspondingly, of course, these across-the-board cuts will produce a decrease in consumption at each and every level of income. If the after-tax rate of return effect is strong enough, tax cuts can even cause a net reduction in consumption. In this case, a $1 cut in taxes will cause more than a $1 increase in saving since after-tax income goes up $1 and consumption actually declines. This increase in saving is expected to more than offset the deficit resulting from the tax cuts, especially given the reductions in government spending.

What actually happened to saving following the Kennedy tax cuts, the purpose of which, interestingly enough, was "not to create a deficit but to increase investment, employment, and the prospects for a balanced budget?"[14] As Chart 1 shows, if one considers the entire 1963-

[13] This raises the issue regarding not just this administration's forecast, but any forecast, which is by how much and for how long does reality have to fall short of expectations before one declares a program unsuccessful.

[14] President Kennedy, Special Message to Congress on Tax Reduction and Reform, January 24, 1963.

Chart 1
Personal Saving Before and After Kennedy Tax Cuts

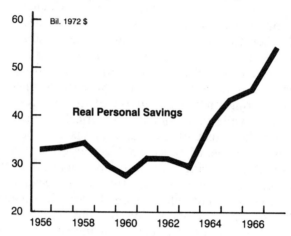

Source: U.S. Treasury Department.

64 period to be the relevant point of departure rather than simply late February 1964 when the tax reduction bill was passed, personal saving did indeed rise markedly following the tax cuts. Furthermore, as has been pointed out by the Reagan administration, real consumer spending actually declined as a percentage of income while the real saving rate rose markedly.[15] From 1963 to 1969, business capital spending in real terms also grew at a 7.6 percent rate, up from 4.2 percent between 1959 and 1963. Chart 2 provides information as to why the budget position was close to balance in 1965 despite the tax cut. As may be seen, in real terms, federal revenues increased markedly and were substantially above the trend of the years prior to the tax cut.

Certainly, all of these figures are consistent with supply-side economics. But they are also consistent with other views about how the economy operates, including Keynesianism. The reasons is that relative to the four-year period preceding enactment of the Kennedy tax cuts, real output growth increased more than 37 percent in the subsequent period. Such rapid cyclical output growth, according to Keynesian theory, should lead to substantial increases in the level of real saving, a rise in the real saving rate and a fall in the real consumption rate.[16] Increases

[15] The figures and charts which follow are based upon Paul Craig Roberts, "Reagan's Tax-Cut Program: The Evidence," *The Wall Street Journal*, Thursday, May 12, 1981, p. 6.

[16] If the real consumption function is written as $c = a + by$, it is easy to show that consumer spending (c) as a percentage of income (y) will fall as income rises (which also implies that the saving rate increases).

Chart 2
Real Federal Receipts in the Kennedy Tax-Cut Years

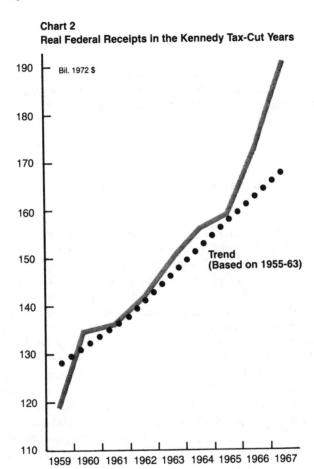

Source: U.S. Treasury Department.

in investment spending are also not unexpected under Keynesian theory, given the magnitude of the output growth. The same applies to the increases in real federal receipts.

The problem with simply examining growth rates in various key variables visually (as has been frequently done) is that the variables incorporate many different effects. As a result, it is not possible to identify the separate effects. But until this is done, one can only conclude that the Kennedy tax cut episode is evidence that is not inconsistent with Keynesian theory. Such evidence for supply-side economics must therefore be viewed as circumstantial.

Apart from these difficulties, one must be extremely careful in extrapolating events from the past to the present. After all, the economic environment in 1963-64 was vastly different from that in 1981. Furthermore, whereas President Reagan considers a reduced rate of growth in the money supply an important part of his economic program, the money supply accelerated both before and after the Kennedy tax cuts. The Kennedy program also placed no emphasis on the need to reduce the growth in government spending. In short, the administration's money and government spending growth program is quite different from those prevailing during the Kennedy period.

THE MAJOR CONTROVERSY

At the outset of this article it was noted that the administration's economic program is designed to reduce inflation while simultaneously spurring economic growth. Although there are many supporters of this program, there are also critics. As the foregoing discussion has by now no doubt made clear, there are theoretical justifications and empirical evidence supporting both sides. This means that the economic rationale for the Reagan program for economic recovery cannot be simply dismissed as "voodoo economics." However, one can legitimately question the likelihood that the program will achieve its stated objectives. In other words, even if one supports the economic program as proposed, will it simultaneously lower inflation and improve economic growth?

The main controversy that remains after all has been said and done is whether the administration's predicted deficit is inflationary or not. The related issue is whether output growth will be sluggish or not if the deficit is not inflationary. The best way to summarize all that has been discussed thus far is as follows. It is well known that

$$(1) \quad MV = PY,$$

where M is the money supply, V is the velocity or turnover rate of money, P is the price level, and Y is real income or output. It therefore follows that

$$(2) \quad \%\Delta M + \%\Delta V = \%\Delta P + \%\Delta Y.$$

This equation states that the growth rate in the money supply plus the growth rate in velocity equals the rate of inflation plus the growth rate of output.

Now the tax and spending cuts as well as the regulatory reform parts of the administration's program are designed to stimulate supply or to increase output growth, %ΔY, without increasing demand, %ΔM + %ΔV. This growth in output should contribute to a reduction in inflation, %ΔP. The remaining part of the program calls for a reduction in money growth, %ΔM. This reduction in %ΔM should further contribute to a reduction in inflation, %ΔP. The actual administration scenario is shown in Table 1. As may be seen, according to the administration, between 1980 and 1986 the inflation rate will decline to 4.9 percent from 9.0 percent, while simultaneously real output growth rises to 4.2 percent from -0.1 percent.

What concerns the skeptics of this forecast is the implied increase in velocity that must take place. As may be seen, velocity must increase to a growth rate of 5.7 percent from a rate of 2.5 percent. Not only is such an increase considered unlikely based upon the historical record, but even more unlikely given the forecast that interest rates will be falling during this period (see Table 1).[17] This concern is perhaps best reflected in the following quote: "More troublesome (than the administration's predicted rise in velocity), the rapid rise in money velocity is assumed to occur simultaneously with a substantial drop in interest rates."[18] However, this concern is based upon the unadjusted nominal interest rate.

But the more appropriate interest rate is the after-tax rate. As Table 1 shows, when one examines the after-tax interest rates (those reported should only be considered suggestive), depending upon whether one is referring to individuals or businesses, interest rates fall by only 0.7 percentage points or 3.7 percentage points. These declines are in sharp contrast to a decline in the before-tax interest rate of 5.9 percentage points. Since the quoted statement is based upon the before-tax rather than the after-tax interest rate, what is "substantial" may be only modest and therefore what is "more" troublesome may be only slightly troublesome. But if velocity does not grow or grows more slowly than expected, something has to give. In other words, if the increase in %ΔV falls short of the administration's expectations, one would expect inflation to be reduced less and/or output growth to be smaller. Most skeptics contend that the most likely result will be less of a reduction in inflation and more sluggish growth than advertised.

The administration's response appears to be that the historical record for velocity is not a good guide for the current period and that there have been periods in which velocity has risen while interest rates fell. Perhaps more importantly, they argue that there is no theoretical reason that velocity cannot grow more rapidly while interest rates decline

---

[17] Lower interest rates are thought to increase the demand for money, thereby reducing, not increasing, velocity.

[18] See Congressional Budget Office, *Economic Policy and the Outlook for the Economy*, March 1981, p. 71.

Table 1. Actual and Forecast Growth Rates in Selected Economic Variables 1980-1986

(Percent change, except for the interest rate)

| | Administration's Forecast | | | | | After-tax Interest Rate | |
	%ΔM (money supply M1B)	%ΔV (velocity)	%ΔP (GNP deflator)	%ΔY (real growth national product)	Interest Rate (3 month U.S. Treasury Bill)	Individuals in 70% marginal tax bracket	Corporations
1980	6.4	2.5	9.0	-0.1	11.5	3.5	8.4
1981	5.9	5.1	9.9	1.1	11.1	3.7	8.1
1982	5.4	7.1	8.3	4.2	8.9	3.6	6.9
1983	4.9	7.1	7.0	5.0	7.8	3.7	6.2
1984	4.4	6.1	6.0	4.5	7.0	3.5	5.6
1985	3.9	5.7	5.4	4.2	6.0	3.0	5.0
1986	3.4	5.7	4.9	4.2	5.6	2.8	4.7

NOTE: The money growth rate figures are based upon the administration's economic scenario which "assumes that the growth rates of money and credit are steadily reduced from the 1980 levels to one-half of those levels by 1986." (See **A Program for Economic Recovery**, February 18, 1981, p. II-23.) The choice of M1B is based upon the following statements by David Stockman: "During the past 4 years, the growth of M1B, the basic money supply measure, has averaged nearly 8%. Over the next 5 years, however, the administration expects the rate of money growth to decline by approximately one-half." (See Statement of David Stockman before the House Committee on the Budget, March 26, 1981, p. 9.) Also, it is reported that the reduction in the rate of growth is expected to take place in one-half percentage point steps.

simultaneously.[19] Finally, the administration seems to contend that if the forecast for velocity growth is too optimistic, then the inflation forecast is too pessimistic.[20]

CONCLUSIONS

The Reagan Program for Economic Recovery consists of four inter-related parts: (1) tax cuts, (2) spending cuts, (3) slow and steady money growth, and (4) regulatory reform. The economic rationale for this four-part package is supply-side economics. If fully implemented, the President contends that this program will reduce inflation while simultaneously providing the incentives necessary for improves productivity and faster economic growth. Given the fact that the theoretical and empirical support for supply-side economics is not beyond dispute, it is not surprising that people have been and are still opposed to implementing the entire package and/or skeptical about the predicted outcome. Although Congress has recently enacted, with modifications, the spending and tax cuts requested by the President, many members of Congress, like the Wall Street bond traders, are still concerned that the tax and spending cuts will create inflationary deficits, despite the administration's claims to the contrary.

This concern already seems to have put the administration on the defensive, as many, including administration officials, now talk openly about larger deficits than originally predicted and thus the necessity for additional budget cuts. If a much larger deficit actually materializes, will it be a crippling blow to supply-side economics and thus the economic forecast? Furthermore, would such a deficit lead to a movement away from supply-side economics and toward Keynesian economics (which supply-siders blame for our progressively worsening economic

[19] If the demand for money function is written as $M = a_0 r^{-a_1} Y^{a_2}$, where M is money demand, Y is income and r is the rate of interest, it follows that velocity, V, is given by $V = 1/a_0 r^{a_1} Y^{(1-a_2)}$. Appropriate manipulation can show that even though the interest declines, velocity need not fall.

[20] Some claim that large-scale macroeconometric models that the administration's economic program will not lower inflation and spur economic growth as much as predicted. However, it should be pointed out that these models, apart from not being truly supply-side models, are subject to the "Lucas critique." This means that the users of these models use historically estimated relationships to predict what will happen if the administration's program is implemented. But the use of historical or fixed relationships to predict the impact of a new policy can produce inaccurate predictions (as the evidence amply demonstrates), since economic behavior will change as a result of the new policy. The administration is therefore skeptical about criticisms of its policies based upon forecasts obtained from the large-scale macroeconometric models. Whether or not the administration bases its forecast on a model not subject to this criticism and/or instead "informed judgment" is not publicly known.

performance during the past fifteen years or so), or perhaps closer to Monetarism, thereby implying a new and different economic forecast? Alternatively, are the spending cuts being mentioned meant to mollify those concerned about the possibility that the deficits resulting from the tax cuts will be inflationary?

The answers to these questions are, of course, not known at this time. Recent economic news further clouds the picture. On the one hand, a recent report that the economy grew by an annual rate of 8.4 percent in the first quarter of 1981 doesn't help the administration's contention that broad tax cuts are essential to speed up economic growth. On the other hand, reports that the rate of growth in consumer prices has dropped below 10 percent in recent months could mute the fears that the tax cuts will have a substantial inflationary impact.

27

The Reagan Economic Plan Supply-Side, Budget and Inflation*

JAMES TOBIN

It's nice that you have a visitor from the East every four years, at the beginning of a new Administration. I'd like to assure everybody that the first article I published, to which President Balles just referred, was, like many of my subsequent ones, an anti-Keynesian paper.

A speaker who casts doubts on President Reagan's Economic Recovery Program is likely to be as unwelcome as a ghost at a wedding feast. After viewing the euphoria of the joint session of Congress when the President displayed his resilience and his oratorical magic, I hate to be a wet blanket. I wish that his was a cause to which I too could rally. I would like to be enthusiastic about the dawn of the New Beginning.

There are several ways in which we might view the Program. We could examine its *micro*-economics, how it reorders the nation's priorities, reallocates income, wealth and power among individuals, groups, and regions. These may be the most important issues, the most fundamental new directions. The Reagan counter-revolution proposes to shift resources from public sector to private sector, from civilian government to national defense, from the Federal government to state and local governments, from beneficiaries of social programs to the taxpayers, from the poor and the near-poor to the affluent and the very rich. These proposals deserve to be considered in detail, item by item, and evaluated in terms of their economic efficiency and equity.

However, the Administration bills and sells its program primarily as a *macro*-economic policy. The President and his spokesmen appeal for support of their counter-revolutionary reallocations and redistributions not on their intrinsic merits, but on the grounds that they are necessary and sufficient to solve the problem of stagflation. Here, we are told, is the remedy, the only remedy, for high unemployment, high inflation,

*Reprinted from the *Economic Review* of the San Francisco Federal Reserve Bank, May 1981. James Tobin is Sterling Professor of Economics at Yale University and Robert Hall is a Professor of Economics at Stanford and also a Hoover Fellow.

low growth, and lagging productivity. We are asked to swallow the micro-economic medicine not because it tastes good but because it is good for what ails us. So far, it appears, Congress, press, and public readily accept the program as the necessary remedy of our macro-economic ills.

It is the macro aspect of the program that I propose to discuss, as is only appropriate at a central bank. I'll begin by remining you that there is precious little evidence in international experience that successful macro-economic management is inversely correlated with size of government, tax burdens, public debt, and social transfers. Some countries whose macro-economic performance we envy have much larger public sectors, more generous social welfare programs, greater tax burdens, and higher budget deficits.

The Reagan recovery program, viewed as macro policy, has a fiscal side and a monetary side. Together they are projected to accomplish the disinflation and the real economic growth shown in columns four and five of my Table 1 and columns one and three of my Table 2.

A NEUTRAL FISCAL PACKAGE

The fiscal policy, viewed from the standpoint of conventional aggregate demand analysis, does not seem to be a significant factor of either stimulus or contraction over the five years for which it is projected. It is important to judge the impact of fiscal policy against what is and has been going on, last year and this year, and not to use as a hypothetical reference path President Carter's January budget. The Carter budget, since it eschewed tax cuts to offset fiscal drag, would have tightened fiscal policy dramatically over the next few years. The Congressional Budget Office (CBO) compares the Reagan budget program with a more realistic baseline, the Carter budget modified for 1982 and 1983 by some business tax reductions and by a 10 percent personal income tax reduction and by unspecified tax cuts to maintain effective tax rates constant after 1983. The CBO projections show little difference between the Reagan budget and this baseline in macro impacts. If anything, the Reagan program is a little tighter than the assumed baseline. Reagan spends less and taxes less, and the net effect is close to neutral.

Actually the high employment budget deficit (calculated for, say, 6-percent unemployment) declines slightly over the next few years under the Reagan proposals, even when the Administration's optimistic inflation scenario is replaced by the more pessimistic price forecasts of the CBO and private model-builders (see Table 3). These are conventional Keynesian calculations, without supply side optimism. (Neither

Table 1
Monetary Growth Targets vs. Reagan Projections of Inflation and Real Growth Implications for Monetary Velocity
(percent per year, yearly averages)

Year	(1) Monetary (M–1B) Growth $\left(\frac{\Delta M}{M}\right)$	+	(2) Velocity Growth $\left(\frac{\Delta V}{V}\right)$	=	(3) Nominal GNP Growth $\left(\frac{\Delta \$GNP}{\$GNP}\right)$	=	(4) Price Inflation $\left(\frac{\Delta P}{P}\right)$	+	(5) Real GNP Growth $\left(\frac{\Delta Q}{Q}\right)$
1980 actual	6.7		2.2		8.9		9.0		-0.1
	Announced Policy Implied by Other Columns				**Reagan Administration Projections***				
1981	3.5 - 6		7.6 - 5.1		11.1		9.9		1.1
1982	3 - 5.5		9.8 - 7.3		12.8		8.3		4.2
1983	2.5 - 5		9.9 - 7.4		12.4		7.0		5.0
1984	2 - 4.5		8.8 - 6.3		10.8		6.0		4.5
1985	1.5 - 4		8.3 - 5.8		9.8		5.4		4.2
1986	1 - 3.5		8.3 - 5.8		9.3		4.9		4.2

*Office of Management and Budget, *Fiscal Year 1982 Budget Revisions*, March 1981, Table 6, p. 13.

Discrepancies between (3) and (4) + (5) are in original sources, and are due to second-order effects $\left(\frac{\Delta P}{P} \cdot \frac{\Delta Q}{Q}\right)$, quarterly compounding, and rounding.

Table 2
Real Gross National Product and Unemployment, 1980-86
Reagan Scenario compared to Conventional Estimates

	(1)	(2)	(3)	(4)	(5)	(6)
	GNP (1980 $billion)		Unemployment (%)		GNP (1980 $billion)	Reagan Scenario GNP Relative to
	Reagan Scenario	Estimated Potential at 6% Unempl.	Reagan Scenario	CBO Alternative	Conventional Estimate for Reagan Unempl.	Conventional Estimate
1980	2629	2746	7.2	7.2	—	—
1981	2658	2815	7.8	7.8	2663	.998
1982	2769	2886	7.2	7.9	2802	.988
1983	2908	2958	6.6	7.8	2914	.998
1984	3039	3032	6.4	7.7	3001	1.013
1985	3167	3108	6.0	7.5	3108	1.019
1986	3300	3185	5.6	7.2	3217	1.026

(1) and (3) Office of Management and Budget, *Fiscal Year 1982 Budget Revisions*, March 1981, Table 6, p. 13. GNP converted to 1980 dollars by deflator projections given in same scenario.

(2) and (5) Author's estimates, assuming (a) Potential GNP grows at 2.5% per year, (b) $Y^* - Y = Y[.025(U-6.0)]$ where Y^* is potential GNP (2), U is unemployment percentage (3), .025 is the assumed Okun's Law coefficient, and the equation is solved to give Y, "actual" GNP (5).

(6) = (1)/(5). For 1986, the Reagan scenario gives real GNP 2.6% higher than its unemployment projection would indicate in a conventional Okun's Law calculation.

(4) Congressional Budget Office estimate of unemployment conditional on Reagan budget with less optimistic economic forecast. CBO, *An Analysis of President Reagan's Budget Revisions for Fiscal Year 1982*, Staff Working Paper, March 1981, Summary Table 3, p. xviii.

Table 3
The Federal Budget, 1980-84
Outlays, Revenues, Deficit, High Employment Deficit

| | Budget Outlays ($billion) | | | Budget Revenues ($billion) | | CBO Alternative Inflation Scenario |
| | (1) | (2) | (3) | (4) | (5) | (6) |
	Reagan Estimates	CBO Estimates for Reagan Scenario	Estimates for 6% Unempl. and CBO Inflation	Reagan Estimates	Estimates for 6% Unempl. and CBO Inflation	% increase in GNP Deflator
1980	580	580	577	520	554	10.3
1981	655	660	657	600	662	9.2
1982	695	708	716	650	710	8.6
1983	732	740	761	709	765	8.1
1984	770	782	812	771	827	

| | Deficit ($billion) | | High Employment Deficit ($billion) |
| | (7) | (8) | (9) |
	Reagan Estimates	CBO Estimates for Reagan Scenario	Estimates for 6% Unempl. and CBO Inflation
1980	60	60	23
1981	55	60	-5
1982	45	58	6
1983	23	31	-4
1984	-1	11	-15

(1), (4), (7) Congressional Budget Office, *An Analysis of President Reagan's Budget Revisions for Fiscal Year 1982*. Staff Working Paper, March 1981, Summary Table 1, p. xiii.

(2), (8) Reagan estimates plus subtotal for Alternative Programmatic Assumptions, Spending Rates, and Other Factors, CBO, *op. cit.*, Summary Table 4, p. xxi.

(6) CBO alternative inflation forecast conditional on Reagan program. *op. cit.* Summary Table 3, p. xviii. Compare Reagan scenario column (4) of Table 1.

(3) Column (1) plus Total Reestimates from CBO Summary Table 4, *loc. cit.*, less author's estimate of reduction in outlays due to difference between CBO unemployment projections in Summary Table 2 and 6%. In principle, column (3) differs from (1) by adding outlays due to higher CBO estimates of inflation and interest rates and by subtracting outlays, mainly unemployment compensation, due to projected unemployment rates above 6%.

(5) Column (4) multiplied by $(1 + 1.5(x-1))$ where x is the ratio of column (2) Table 2 to column (1) Table 2, i.e., potential GNP to projected actual GNP. The elasticity of revenues with respect to GNP is assumed to be 1.5.

(9) = (3) - (5) Negative figures are surpluses.

do they apply to the federal government the inflation accounting we recommend to private businesses, which would of course tell us that even the actual budget is already balanced.)

The composition of the budget, as well as its totals and its balance, affects its macro-economic impact. Under the Reagan program, federal purchases of goods and services rise because of the defense build-up. Transfers and taxes fall. The changes in composition are large, but I think they don't change the macro story just told. For the same budget totals, the shift to defense purchases is expansionary. On the other hand, the shift of purchasing power from liquidity-constrained transferees with high marginal propensities to consume to higher income taxpayers is moderately contractionary. Some economists believe that defense is intrinsically highly inflationary and cite with foreboding the fact that Reagan's projected build-up is comparable percentage-wise to Johnson's Viet Nam spending binge. The analogy is far from perfect. This defense build-up starts in an economy with a much larger amount of slack than there was in January 1966. And it lacks the compulsion to disregard costs and budget constraints that an actual war provides.

No observer of the current political scene can forebear comment on the ironies of the political parties' reversals of roles. Now the Republicans defend planned deficits against Democratic attack, advocate tax cuts not just to arrest recession but to sustain incipient recovery, and resist Democratic proposals to tilt tax reduction further toward businesses at the expense of individuals. It was a Democratic President who deliberately declined, ever since 1977, to recommend tax cuts to compensate for fiscal drag and bracket drift, and who sanctimoniously foreswore counter-cyclical fiscal measures to overcome the recent recession. It is the Democrats in Congress who now issue dire warnings of the inflationary effects of stimulating the economy by three years of tax reduction even when the unemployment rate is 7½ percent and capacity utilization is barely 80 percent. It is the Republicans—some of them, it is true, without full conviction in their new religion—who say that it is idle and self-defeating to try to balance the budget by higher and higher effective tax rates. The final irony is that it is a Republican budget, proposed by a President who is a free enterprise hero, to which the securities markets are currently registering a vote of no confidence.

The budget is taking a bad rap from those, whether liberal Democrats or conservative investment bankers, who say it is a reckless gamble to reduce taxes so much. To say this is not to agree with extravagant Administration claims that their package increases the national propensity to save, but only to say that it doesn't decrease it; clearly the tax cuts by themselves, without the expenditure cuts, would diminish saving relative to GNP. Nor is it to agree with Lafferite views that the tax cuts will actually maintain or increase revenues. That is most improbable, as I shall explain below.

In judging the fiscal package to be more or less innocuous in its macro-economic impact, I am not endorsing it. I have serious micro-economic and distributional objections, but I will confine myself here to two macro-economic reservations. First, I regret that once again opportunities are being lost to use tax reduction to gain ground on inflation. We could cut taxes that directly boost labor costs and prices, e.g. by reducing payroll levies. We could go further and offer tax inducements for disinflationary wage and price behavior. Second, we could aim for a different fiscal-monetary mix, one better designed to foster capital formation and growth. In my opinion, that would involve a tighter budget policy compensated by a monetary policy that would give us lower real interest rates.

MONETARY POLICY: DISINFLATION THE FED'S JOB

I turn now to monetary policy, where the greatest inconsistencies in the Reagan recovery program occur. The President and his Administration have assigned the Federal Reserve responsibility for inflation. You take care of prices, they say in effect, and we'll get the economy moving again. Criticizing imperfect markmanship of the past, the President and his economic policy-makers order the Fed to cut the rate of monetary growth in half over the next five years. This was already the Fed's policy, as anyone who listens to Paul Volcker knows. Now he has Beryl Sprinkel and other monetarists looking over his shoulder, if not waiting in the wings.

The monetary targets of the Fed and the Administration are shown in the first column of Table 1. The idea that money and prices can be detached and delegated to central bankers while Congress and the Executive independently take care of budget, taxes, employment, and output is the kind of fallacy that makes exam questions for freshman economics, a fallacy now elevated to Presidential doctrine. If Amtrak hitches engines at both ends of a train of cars in New Haven station—we still do have a railroad there—one engine heading west to New York, the other east to Boston, and advertises that the train is going simultaneously to both destinations, most people would be skeptical. Reagan is hitching a Volcker engine at one end and a Stockman-Kemp locomotive to the other and telling us the economic train will carry us to Full Employment and Disinflation at the same time.

This inconsistency is shown in Table 1. The third column is the official Administration projection of nominal GNP, equal to the totals of columns four and five, the Reagan scenarios for inflation and real output growth. Subtracting the monetary targets of column 1 from the dollar-GNP projections of column 3 gives the implied growth rates of velocity of M1B, column 2. The two numbers correspond to the M1B target brackets.

There has never been a two-year period over which the average growth of M1B velocity has exceeded 5 percent. It would have to beat that in each of the next five years, hitting 7, 8, almost 9 percent to make the Reagan scenario come true. These increases in velocity are beyond historical experience, even in the recent decade of unprecedented financial innovation. Finance is one sector where American technology remains the best in the world, and the possibility of even faster progress in economizing cash can't be completely ruled out. But if policy-makers were to accept rescue from velocity miracles, or *a fortiori* from further regulatory changes, they would be substituting shadow for substance, appearance for reality. Although the Fed might be tempted by any escape route from the credibility impasse they have painted themselves into, I assume the Fed really means to do literally no more than what their targets say, and to do less if the spirit of the policy so dictates.

This translates, whether the Administration realizes it or not, into significantly lower rates of growth of dollar spending on GNP than the official projections (column three). Of course, another way to achieve high velocity growth is to engineer even higher nominal and real interest rates than those we're now suffering. But they would surely be inconsistent with the substantial recovery of real and nominal GNP promised by the President (columns three and five). On the other hand, if the inflation and interest rate projections of the Administration were realized, velocity would slow down.

MISSING: A STRATEGY FOR DISINFLATION

As devastating as this inconsistency is to the credibility of the President's program, the scenario contains a more fatal flaw. This is the division of nominal GNP, column 3, between inflation, column 4, and real output growth, column 5. It defies historical experience to expect price inflation to subside as rapidly as shown in column 4 while output recovers as vigorously as projected in column 5. Experience tells us the combination is a most unlikely one, given the stubborn inertia of existing patterns of inflation. Experience tells us that disinflation requires recessions, prolonged slack, and high unemployment. What entitles this Administration to expect to cut inflation in half while output is growing faster than its sustainable potential for five years?

The only answer that has trickled out of Washington is an appeal to self-fulfilling expectations. The public will read column 5. Observing the decisive budgetary moves of the new Administration, believing them to be the proper medicine for inflation as advertised, the public will act to make the predictions come true. That means they will negotiate lower wage bargains and slow down price increases. Previous optimistic inflation forecasts from the White House have not been self-fulfilling or otherwise fulfilled, but maybe this time will be different.

This is an expectations argument, but certainly not a rational expectations theory. Rational expectations require a model that makes sense, one that truly connects policy action to results. Rational expectations not only generate but are generated from such a model. In this case no such model exists, and Robert Lucas and Robert Hall are as unlikely as Lane Kirkland and Sam Church to believe and act upon the advertised disinflation.

The two major English-speaking democracies are in conservative economic hands, but the policies and public stance of Margaret Thatcher in Great Britain are very different from those of Ronald Reagan in the United States. Their Prime Minister threatens workers, managers, and plain citizens like an authoritarian schoolmaster disciplining an unruly class. You won't have jobs, profits or prosperity until you stop inflating your wages and prices. Our President promises disinflation without tears, indeed with prosperity. He encourages unions and managements to carry on business as usual. After all, inflation is only the government's fault, and all we citizens are asked to do is to accept tax goodies and stop indulging the poor. The Federal Reserve, it is true, has been following a Thatcher-like policy but in whispers. I am one of the thousand or so Americans who hear and read Paul Volcker and know that M1B is not an army rifle. I pay attention to Henry Wallich too. I believe they will do what they say they will do, and I am duly scared. If *I* were Lane Kirkland, I would take the monetary threats seriously and tell my constituent unions to take it easy.

The Fed's muted threat is quite different from Her Majesty's First Minister's standing up in Parliament and throughout her country to say that she doesn't care how much unemployment there is for how long, or what is the real rate of growth or decline; she will stick it through whatever the pain, however long it takes to eliminate inflation. Reagan has said nothing like that, and Volcker isn't well known in Peoria or Spokane, in the shops and offices where wages and prices are made. Federal Reserve threats are hears in financial circles all right, but the bond market does not seem to be impressed. In summary, if the Reagan anti-inflation strategy depends on expectations, the Administration has done and said nothing to make expectations work in its favor.

Let there be no illusion. There is no way to reduce inflation in this country so long as wage increases proceed at 10 percent a year. There is no possible miracle of productivity that can validate such a trend in money wages. Our lost 2 percent per year productivity trend may reappear as mysteriously as it vanished. If we are very, very lucky, policy to speed investment and research and development might add another half point or full point, not this year or next but some years down the road. But with the best of good fortune we would be left with domestic core inflation of 7-8 percent unless the money wage pattern is broken—and it may be more difficult to break it when workers can claim to have earned more via improved productivity. We must also expect an adverse trend in the terms of trade between American labor and resource-based commodities imported from abroad or produced within the country. This may be equivalent on average to a half point or full point of decline in worker productivity.

I emphasize the persistent inertial trend of money wages in the central non-agricultural "fixprice" sector of our economy, because no lasting solution of our inflation is possible unless it is brought much closer to the sustainable trend of productivity. In short runs, especially month to month and quarter to quarter, popular price indexes can vary widely around this core inflation rate, from the weight of flexible prices loosely tied to U.S. wages. In the next eighteen months, for example, the volatile elements in the Consumer Price Index might be favorable, and the Administration might be able to point to some apparent sucesses in its battle against inflation. If mortgage interest rates stay put or fall, the housing component will contribute less to CPI inflation news than in 1979-80. Perhaps we have purchased a respite on the oil front by selling Awacs to Saudi Arabia, as well as by slowing down our economy and swallowing the decontrol of domestic oil prices in one gulp early this year. Our tight monetary policy, if it does nothing else, is appreciating the dollar against other currencies; this may be bad for the U.S. export-import position but it lowers dollar prices of some imports and world-traded commodities. Food price prospects, always uncertain, are not so favorable, given the end of the grain embargo and the low level of world stocks. My purpose is not to predict prices but to warn that transient luck in the volatile elements of price indexes does not signify final victory, any more than transient misfortune justified panic about runaway inflation acceleration in 1979-80.

At the beginning of my talk, I pointed out that countries with enviable inflation records in recent years are not invariably those with Reagan-like fiscal policies. If the successful countries have a common characteristic, it is that they have some kind of handle on money wage decisions.

Here in the United States whoever was the victor in the November 1980 election had, I thought, the rare opportunity to use the window of good feeling that Americans open at the start of a new Presidential term to gain control over our wage-price spiral. To engineer disinflation without a protracted dose of recession and economic stagnation, I believe it is necessary to give everybody assurance that everybody else is going to disinflate. Otherwise the fear and suspicion of each group that it will lose real and relative income lead it to stick to the existing inflationary pattern. This makes tough going for a Thatcher policy, and even tougher going for a contractionary policy without a clear and credible threat.

For this reason, I have favored a preannounced schedule of gradually declining standards for wage increases over a five-year transitional period. Inducements to obey the guideposts would be provided by payroll tax rebates for employees in complying firms, and for employers too if their percentage markups do not rise. The guidepost schedule would be consistent with a macro-economic disinflationary policy to which the Administration, Congress, and Federal Reserve would be solemnly and visibly committed. Since nominal GNP growth and wage-cost inflation would decline in concert, there would be neither suppressed demand-pull inflation nor the damage to real economic performance caused by cutting monetary demand growth while money cost inflation proceeds unabated.

Such a policy clearly requires a consensus among labor, business, and government, and such a consensus clearly requires strong and persuasive leadership by a popular President. We lost that opportunity this year, just as we lost the chance to follow a "cold turkey" policy with some chance that inflation would melt faster than previous statistical evidence leads us to believe it will.

SUPPLY-SIDE ECONOMICS: NO FREE LUNCH

But can't we take hope from the recent discovery that the economy has a supply side? This remarkable revelation plays a big role in the rhetoric that rationalizes the Reagan program, although, as I argued above, the fiscal program as macro strategy does not really depend on Laffer-Kemp calculus. The official macro-economic scenario does contain a small bit of supply-side magic. Real GNP five years out is somewhat larger, relative to the projected unemployment rates, than received "Okun's law" wisdom would allow. (Table 3, column 6) There appears to be on average an extra half percent per year of real growth, beyond what would normally accompany the unemployment reductions shown. It is not clear from what source these gains are supposed to come.

From labor supply? Supply-side wisdom is that the upward drift of marginal personal tax rates is drying up the supply of productive labor. That there has been such a drift, particularly since 1977, is undeniable, though it is not as great as often alleged. The Brookings Institution tax file permits calculation of the federal marginal rate of personal income tax, averaged over all brackets, faced by a breadwinner with spouse and two children: 1960, 18.8 percent; 1965, 15.9 percent; 1970, 18.2 percent; 1975, 18.0 percent; 1980, 21.6 percent. Yet it is hard to find evidence of a weakened propensity to supply labor in recent experience. Labor force participation, overtime hours of work, multiple job holding, weekly hours of work corrected for changes in industry mix—none of these indicators seem out of line with trends and cyclical effects dating from the 1950s and 1960s. Believe it or not, most of our seven million unemployed fellow citizens really do want work, and there are many "not in labor force" who do also. Finally, I observe that although the Administration's tax bill reduces marginal rates for taxpayers, especially those in high brackets, its budget cuts will seriously impair work incentives for low-income families and individuals dependent on welfare, food stamps, and other transfers.

In the belief that a Curve deserves a Theory, I have derived rigorously a Laffer Curve based on labor supply response to after-tax real wages. Indeed, I have derived two Laffer Curves, one for Tax Revenues and one for National Saving (more precisely for Tax Revenues plus Private Saving, which exceeds National Saving by the amount of Government Purchases, assumed constant.) These are pictured in Figure 1, which

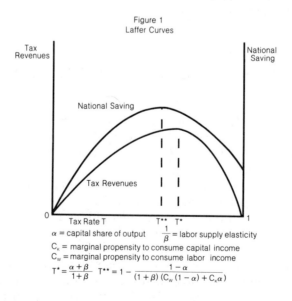

Figure 1
Laffer Curves

α = capital share of output $\dfrac{1}{\beta}$ = labor supply elasticity

C_κ = marginal propensity to consume capital income

C_w = marginal propensity to consume labor income

$$T^* = \frac{\alpha + \beta}{1 + \beta} \qquad T^{**} = 1 - \frac{1 - \alpha}{(1 + \beta)(C_w(1 - \alpha) + C_\kappa \alpha)}$$

also contains a rather cryptic, but I hope sufficient, explanation of their derivation. The important parameters are the Cobb-Douglas elasticity of output with respect to capital α, and with respect to labor, $1\text{-}\alpha$, and the elasticity of labor supply $1/\beta$. In the numerical example, I took both α and $1/\beta$ to be $1/3$. That is a generous estimate of labor supply response; the consensus guess is no higher than $1/6$. With these values my Laffer Curve peaks at a wage tax rate of $5/6$. The National Saving Curve involves also the marginal propensity to consume, which I took in the exercise to be .4 for capital income and .8 for after-tax labor income. The peak of this second, and more economically significant, Laffer Curve is at a tax rate of $3/4$. I doubt that we are on the wrong slope of either Laffer Curve now, and I hope we don't go there.

A more credible supply-oriented policy is to stimulate non-residential fixed investment, in the hope that accelerating the growth of capital relative to output and labor supply will raise productivity. As one of the Kennedy team that originated the Investment Tax Credit in 1962, I have some sympathy with this goal. Clearly I do not have time to discuss adequately the Reagan Administration's investment stimuli, so I will confine myself to four short remarks.

Figure 2

Derivation of Laffer Curves

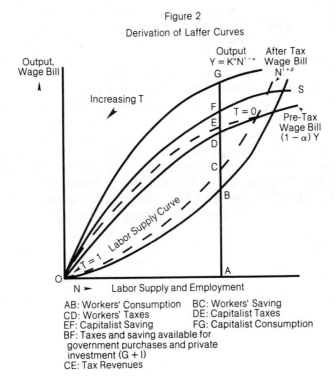

AB: Workers' Consumption   BC: Workers' Saving
CD: Workers' Taxes   DE: Capitalist Taxes
EF: Capitalist Saving   FG: Capitalist Consumption
BF: Taxes and saving available for
  government purchases and private
  investment (G + I)
CE: Tax Revenues

First, as I stated earlier, I regret that we cannot adopt a mix of macro-economic policies, fiscal and monetary, that would shift the composition of output toward capital formation. Why can't we? The main reason is simply the monetarist dogma embraced by the Administration, to which the Federal Reserve is hostage. This locks us into a particular path of a particular monetary aggregate, invariant to fiscal policy and other macro-economic circumstances.

Second, there are ways to provide investment incentives in the taxation of business that do not make a shambles of economic efficiency and tax equity, as the present proposals for accelerated depreciation do. If the intention is to make amends for the overstatement of taxable profits due to historical cost depreciation, there are straightforward ways of doing so without freezing into the tax code a depreciation system that will still be there if and when inflation abates. Anyway, this investment disincentive is offset, partially or fully, by another inflation distortion in the tax code, the deductibility of nominal interest.

Third, whatever investment incentive is enacted now should be effective immediately. Its impact is diluted by a gradual phase-in such as the Administration proposes, because this gives an inducement to delay investment projects.

Fourth, plant and equipment is not the only social capital. If we wish as a society to make better provision for the future, we should also be concerned with the preservation and improvement of human capital, natural resources, and public sector facilities and infrastructure, all of which are sacrificed in the Reagan budget, pervaded as it is by the ideology that only private business capital is productive.

The outlook, I am afraid, is for continued stagflation, with disappointing results on all fronts—inflation, unemployment, real output, interest rates, and capital formation. We will unwind the Great Society, redistribute income regressively, withdraw the Federal commitment to the environment, and we will have little or no macro-economic progress to show. The Program will not fulfill the promises that have led the country to support it. I wish I knew what will happen when the Administration, Congress, and the public confront this reality.

28

The Reagan Economic Plan*

ROBERT HALL

Balles. The discussant for Professor Tobin's presentation, presumably giving the other side of the story, is Professor Robert Hall, Professor of Economics at Stanford and also a Hoover Fellow. He holds a joint appointment at both institutions; he is, as well, a member of the Brookings' Panel on Economic Activity and head of the National Bureau's business cycle dating project. His research projects are many and varied, but he has been particularly interested in the microeconomics of labor markets and in the influence of those markets on the employment and inflation process. I'm informed that he's currently editing a book on inflation for the National Bureau. At various times, he's investigated the impacts of government tax policies, both on the level of business investment and on the supply of labor. Hence, he is very well-qualified to comment on the likely supply-side impact of the President's policy package as well as other matters brought up, or perhaps not brought up, by Professor Tobin. So let's welcome Professor Hall.

Let me start by saying that in no sense am I a spokesman for the President's program. The closest I came to participating in the formulation of the policy was serving as a member of the Task Force on Inflation, which made its report last November. Since them, I have been an academic on the sidelines.

What do economists and the public think is wrong with the American economy today? In the first place, the economy suffers from disap-

---

*Reprinted with permission from *The Reagan Economic Program*, presented at Economic Seminar Federal Reserve Bank of San Francisco, May, 1981.

pointing real growth. The disappointment dates back to 1973 in its worst form, but actually real growth as we knew it in the 1960s came to an end in 1969. Since then, periods of growth have alternated with severe recessions, and, over the whole period, net growth has been weak. The past few years have been especially bad. And the prospect for the economy today is for continuing disappointments in real incomes and real growth. As I understand it, the administration is very, very concerned with the growth issue.

The second problem, first on the public's list but second on mine, is inflation. People are very tired of struggling with a dollar that loses some 10 percent of its value every year. The public has been clear about its desire to end inflation. There is a very strong political commitment to end inflation. We as economists have an obligation to say, how can we do it?

The third item on my list is excess government control over the use of resources in the economy. There is simply too much intervention in various forms—regulation, taxing, and spending. A particular form of excess government intervention is the heavy taxation of the return to savings. There is virtually a crisis in the taxation of one of the most critical channels of savings and investment, equity-financed purchases of plant and equipment by corporations. Those transactions are taxed in the U.S. economy today at rates of something like 60 or 70 percent, which is simply excessive. On the other hand, as Professor Tobin points out, we have another problem today, that the tax system subsidizes tax shelters, because of the deductibility of interest. The tax system is completely out of kilter as a result of inflation, and we need to do something about it.

That's my short list of things that are wrong with the economy. Let me turn now to what we shouldn't do about it, and here you will find me in agreement with what Professor Tobin just said. The leading example of what not to do with the economy today is what the British are doing. Let me review the elements of the British macro policy as I see them. In the first place, the British have brought about a sharp reduction in money growth. And that has brought with it the usual symptoms of a financial crisis, including high interest rates, overvalued currency, and the like. Second, government expenditures are continuing to rise. That, I think, is the central problem they are facing. They simply do not have a handle on the budget in Britain. Part of the budget problem takes the form of direct government purchases of goods and services, including the continuing sad story of deepening government involvement in operating government enterprises, in spite of Margaret Thatcher's commitment to free enterprise. Another important source of budget strain comes from transfers, which have risen because of the reduction in real activity and employment. Finally, under the influence of, I think, a very basically incorrect interpretation of supply side arguments, the British have sharply raised commodity taxes and sharply cut income taxes at the same time. The net effect on the budget from these two moves was not large but it brought about a sharp increase in inflation. There is a large amount of feedback from the cost of living index to wages and transfers in the British economy. And the worsening of inflation has not been offset by any supply side response, either in theory or in fact. A fundamental supply side analysis says that the incentive to work depends on the ratio of take-home wages to prices. That's not affected by a move which increases take-home wages but also increases prices.

Let's not do what the British are doing. I'm happy to see that, by and large, the Reagan Administration is not moving in the British direction. None of the three elements that I've listed in the British example exist in the proposed policy of the Administration. So what should we do? Again, I have a list, and it differs from the Administration's policy only in one of its elements.

In the first place, we need to limit government expenditures. Here, I think, is probably the largest disagreement with what Professor Tobin has said. There are a great many federal spending programs, transfer programs, and regulations which the people don't want, which have an unfavorable effect on the public's spendable real incomes. We should make a list of all the rat holes that the government is pouring money into today, and we should eliminate them. If you go through the budget proposals of the Reagan Administration, you will find that the character of the expenditure reductions is largely, though not exclusively, elimination of rat holes. One can give countless examples. One which has been quite prominent is the Export-Import Bank—a good example of a program which simply does not have a proper role in a well-run economy. It certainly does not benefit the poor, and is something which should be dispensed with. Well, there are many, many things in the budget that should be dispensed with. My personal list would be considerably longer than the one the Administration has come up with. Furthermore, my cuts would be larger in those cases where the Administration has successfully identified a rat hold and then said, our way of dealing with the problem is to cut the budget by twenty percent. Having found a rat hole, I think we should simply stop pouring anything down it. Whole segments of the budget—like the Energy Department—are just collections of rat holes. Together, they consume a non-trivial fraction of real GNP.

Let me be very clear that I do not include in this category the types of expenditure which have virtually eliminated poverty in the United States over the past twenty years. I am very happy to see that anti-poverty programs like AFDC, supplemental security income, and food stamps have not been gutted. Though these programs are not completely satisfactory, they represent a very important step forward in improving the distribution of income in the most important way, by helping those at the very bottom. The President has been very clear on the need to retain anti-poverty expenditures. I think it's very unfortunate that a large number of opponents of the package have described it incorrectly as aimed primarily at eliminating expenditures on behalf of the poor. That's simply not correct. There are, of course, some attempts to improve the performance of transfer programs, but it seems to me that one can correctly characterize most of the expenditure cuts as eliminating rat holes.

President Reagan has also proposed large increases in military spending. I don't feel qualified to judge the desirability of this move, but I think that economists do have one very important thing to say with respect to military expenditures—macro policy is capable of delivering full employment and price stability for virtually any level of expenditures. Here I agree completely with what Professor Tobin said. There are good examples of economies which have much larger public sectors than ours, and have full employment and price stability. If necessary, we could support a much larger military establishment than we have now without automatically creating any significant macro-economic problems. Of course, resources available to the private sector for investment and consumption would necessarily be less in an economy that was devoting a large amount of its output to military or other government purposes. Within that limitation, the total level of output and the behavior of prices are things that policy can control. An increase in government spending is not by itself a threat to the performance of the overall economy. Nor is a decrease in spending. We ought to be able to design macro policies that handle any of these contingencies.

One of the most controversial features of the President's program is substantial reduction in tax rates. I emphasize that what's being proposed are rate reductions, and not necessarily revenue reductions. One does not have to accept the labor supply rationale of the Laffer curve to entertain the proposition that a tax rate reduction would increase revenue. A very good example of this is the reduction in capital gains tax rates that went into effect in 1978. In a recent study, the Treasury concluded that revenue remained about the same as a result of a large reduction in tax rates. Rate reductions can stimulate revenue because people have a good deal of discretion about how they arrange their affairs and how they fill out their tax returns. When tax rates go down, the incentives to shelter income are dramatically reduced; certainly that was the case with the capital gains reduction. And a fairly small fraction of total income actually flows through people's income tax returns. In spite of high apparent marginal rates, it's a curious fact of the U.S.

economy that only 11 percent of personal income is paid to the federal government as personal income tax. I agree completely that the evidence that people work harder when they are taxed less is not nearly strong enough to support the notion that revenue would respond favorably to a tax cut. What the reduction in capital gains rates suggests is that people's incentive to avoid taxes would be dramatically reduced by cutting top marginal rates, and that would mean that revenue at least would not fall nearly as much as a simple calculation might suggest.

Although I am skeptical about the strength of the supply response to reduced tax rates, I endorse tax cuts as a way to restore real growth. Perfectly standard macro analysis, in which labor supply is exactly inelastic with respect to real wages, will tell you that tax cuts are expansionary. The idea that was pushed very hard and successfully in 1961 through 1964 is correct today. And it seems to me that it should be pushed today. One doesn't have to believe in an exotic labor supply function to take the view that the time has come for tax cuts.

I also favor tax cuts as far the best way to keep expenditures under control. It seems to me that the reason that government expenditures haven't swollen worse than they have is Congressional fear of deficits. If we don't have a tax cut, there will be that much more room for pouring money down rat holes, which is not something I'd like to see happen.

The last topic on the fiscal side is investment incentives. As I said at the outset, heavy taxation of some kinds of investment income is one of our worst current problems. The President's proposal for accelerated depreciation—the 10-5-3 plan—is very much a stimulus to investment through reduced taxation of its return. I don't think it is the best way to cut taxes on investment, however. I would far rather see the following combination of changes: On the one hand, allow an immediate write-off of all corporate investment—this would be the ultimate extension of accelerated depreciation. On the other hand, we should deny all interest deductions under the corporate income tax. That combination of proposals would provide even more stimulus than 10-5-3, and it would eliminate the inefficient subsidy we now pay to leveraged investment as well. In the long run, such a tax has a zero effective rate on a corporation that has no monopoly earnings. In a sense, it amounts to a proposal to abolish the corporate income tax, which I don't think would be a bad idea. Even with 10-5-3, the corporate income tax would become a very small part of the federal revenue picture. The big engine of revenue in the U.S. economy in the future will be the payroll tax— not the corporate income tax and not the personal income tax.

With respect to monetary discipline, what is needed is the establishment of a long-run framework for monetary policy. We need to be able to promise a move toward monetary stability, and therefore to price stability, over the next half-decade or decade. We need a convincing way to express that policy. It's not a matter of adopting a harsh reduction in money growth over the next 12 months. Rather, we need a way to promise the American public that we will not push the economy too hard at any one time, but we will push it to long-run price stability. So far, the Administration's proposals have not been in the form I would like to seem—there has not been a strong announcement of a long-run monetary framework. Partly this is a recognition of the independence of the Federal Reserve System, and a reluctance for the President to appear to be trying to dictate to an independent branch of government what it should be doing.

What should the Fed be doing? The type of announcement I would like to see would state the target of monetary policy in terms of a path of nominal GNP. Take column 3 in Table 1 of Professor Tobin's handout and say, this is what monetary policy will achieve. We would love to accomplish what is shown in columns 4 and 5. We'd love to get inflation down that rapidly, we'd love to raise real growth to these exceptional rates year after year. We can't promise either. What we can promise through the use of a sensible long-run monetary policy is column 3. We can promise to use monetary instruments to keep nominal GNP growth at a reasonably high level, that is, not undergo sharp recession, and yet, reduce this growth gradually to a non-inflationary level. What I don't want to see, and what I am afraid I am hearing more and more from the Administration, is that money growth will stick, come hell or high water, to the predetermined target of column 1. We can see from the table that column 1 does not mesh with column 3. I couldn't agree more strongly with Professor Tobin's comments on this contradiction. There's simply nothing in the economy that's going to give velocity growth as high as is suggested by column 2. Furthermore, to the extent that a policy is successful in bringing inflation to an end, it will also gradually reduce interest rates. Lower interest rates should cause velocity to fall, so the problem is even compounded relative to Professor Tobin's discussion.

One of the things I like most about the new Administration is its commitment to strong real growth. To the extent that policy is successful in bringing growth, the economy will need more money. We shouldn't be afraid of money growth, if the reason we need it is growth in real GNP. The strict target of low money growth of column one just doesn't make sense in a rapidly growing economy. We can get out of the box by announcing a nominal GNP target instead of a money growth target. So far, the Administration's position has been incomplete in this area.

Taken together, the policy of reduced federal command over resources, lower tax rates, and investment stimulus adopted by the Administration promises progress in solving economic problems.If coupled with a good long-run framework for monetary and price stability, it would be a very large step forward in economic policy making.

COMMENTS BY SPEAKERS

Professor Tobin:

I knew that Bob Hall was a good macro economist, so I'm not sur-
prised that he tried to shift the debate—or shall we say, the discussion—
to the micro side of the budget program. Just a couple of comments:
First, I don't think it's fair to say that the Administration has not committed itself to column one of Table 1. The president's message in the
budget-revision document states that the growth of money stock must
be cut in half over a period of time. Although Hall interprets the inconsistency as delicate respect for the independence of the Federal Reserve,
another interpretation is that the Administration is setting up the Federal Reserve to receive the blame for the inconsistencies of the program.
In case the inflation rate doesn't go down as advertised, the failing would
be the Fed's because it had been assigned the responsibility. In case the
recovery falls short, failure to finance it could be the Fed's failing too.

Second, I want to stress the need for a *concerted* policy directed to
an agreed path of nominal income, or money spending on GNP (column
3). I was glad that Bob Hall endorsed nominal income targeting. But it
should be the policy of the Federal Government as a whole, fiscal and
monetary together, consistent as between the two. Similarly, in Congress, we need a concerted approach to macroeconomic strategy as between the various committees—those on the one hand that oversee
monetary policy, and those on the other that oversee budget policy.
We've had too much compartmentalization both in Congress and in the
Administration, as if the two areas of macro policy weren't connected
with each other. Desirable as an MV target policy may be compared to
concentrating on M1B (column 1), I am skeptical that it will succeed
without considerable pain and damage to the economy, and without
the help of an incomes policy to bring about a reduction in wage and
cost inflation consistent with the scheduled monetary disinflation. It is
interesting, by the way, to see the distance conservatives take pains to
put between themselves and British conservative policy, now that it
appears that Thatcherism isn't succeeding too well.

Third, the claim that taxes take as much as 60 or 70 percent of net
income generated by non-financial corporations seems a considerable
exaggeration. Summers and Feldstein have cited figures of that magnitude as estimates of *marginal* rates. But they seem to be well above any
estimates of average tax rates, and I suspect dubious as marginal rates as
well. And they're really not consistent with what Bob Hall said himself,
when he observed how little income appears on income-tax returns.
That's certainly true of interest income, dividend income, and pension
and annuity income—those kinds that reflect corporate-income
payments.

Fourth, I think it's a great mistake, both in the Reagan tax program and in previous tax legislation, to correct inflation-generated distortions in the tax system by introducing other kinds of distortions. Why not meet head-on the non-neutrality of the tax system with respect to inflation? The problem may be historical cost depreciation, but we're going to be stuck with 10-5-3 for the rest of time no matter what the inflation rate after Bob Hall gets inflation down. The 10-5-3 plan, at that time, will no longer be justified as compensating roughly for inflation's exaggeration of taxable income. It would be better to have something like the Auerbach-Jorgenson plan, which would give the full present value of depreciation on a new investment right now, computed at a real interest rate of 4 percent or some arbitrary reasonable number. This plan is automatically neutral with respect to inflation. I also agree with Hall on eliminating the tax deductibility of interest costs.

Fifth, we cannot be sure as economic theorists that shifting taxation from capital income to wage income is a useful method of increasing saving and investment. The life-cycle model tells us that the aggregate supply of saving is scaled to after-tax wage income. Whether a shift in taxation from capital income to wage income will actually increase the amount of saving depends on the interest elasticity.

Finally, about ratholes: It's not really true that all the items in the Stockman hit list are ratholes, that none touch the truly needy or those that should be protected by "safety nets." A lot of them have to do with welfare, with food stamps, with Medicaid. One consequence of the cuts is to turn these people over to the tender mercies of the states, not all of which are as benign as California, Connecticut, and Massachusetts. Also, inconsistent with the spirit of the program as a whole, the marginal tax rates of the poor and near-poor and working-poor are going to be increased by the emphasis on keeping all but the truly needy off the rolls. The sacrifice of benefits involved in earning additional income is going to be much larger than under present programs. Things like aid to "federally impacted" school districts and export-import loans are examples of ratholes, where we would all agree—both on efficiency and equity grounds—that cuts are justifiable. But by no means all Stockman's cuts are of this nature. Moreover, we could compile a list of items that deserve to be cut but have been spared. Consider tax expenditures, which are basically open-ended appropriations by the Federal Government to use resources at the discretion of tax-payers, often for doubtful purposes that would get the axe if they were on the other side of the budget ledger. We can't debate budgets this afternoon, but I don't think an inspection of the program would justify what Bob said about it.

Professor Hall:

Let me just discuss one topic, the taxation of savings and investment. As Jim said, the average rate of taxation of investment income is not as high as the example I gave of tax rates of 60 or 70 percent. It may help if I elaborate upon the example where rates are at that confiscatory level. A corporation issues new stock bought by individuals who are in the 40-percent marginal tax bracket, which is typical for the owners of common stock. All of the proceeds are then invested in a plant. There's no investment credit involved. There is no leverage, no borrowing in the debt market, so there is no deduction for interest. The combination of the 46-percent statutory corporate income-tax rate, 40-percent marginal personal income-tax rate, and historical cost depreciation at 10-percent inflation gives a total effective rate of 60 to 70 percent, which is excessive.

The big problem with the tax system is the coexistence of these high rates with negative rates on other types of investment, notably those with high leverage and large interest deductions. That's why, when you add everything together, the average tax rates on all types of investment turn out not to look very high. So the evidence Jim referred to does not contradict my point that some critical types of investment are highly taxed. The problem with the tax system—entirely attributable to inflation—is that it deals very harshly with equity-financed investment and very, very generously with leveraged investment. You find individuals going out and leveraging themselves like crazy, borrowing everything they can to create tax shelters—and corporations, who are reluctant to leverage, incurring very heavy tax rates and therefore finding that the current environment is not very favorable for investment. The problem needs to be solved by eliminating the subsidy to leveraged investments and reducing the taxation of equity-financed investments. The two together don't have large revenue implications, because we could get the revenue by eliminating subsidies of leveraged investments and applying the revenue to reduced tax rates on equity-financed investments.

Unfortunately, 10-5-3 is not the best way to make this kind of a change. I understand the Administration is at least considering some more fundamental tax reforms to be proposed after Kemp-Roth and 10-5-3 go through. There are some very badly needed structural reforms that would improve the incentive for plant and equipment investment by corporations.

29

Reagan's Tax Plan Makes Sense[*]

PAUL W. McCRACKEN[†]

Would a tax reduction along the lines of the President's proposal be a fiscally responsible action in this session of the Congress? It is this part of the President's program that has produced the most skepticism.

In the static sense, those skeptical of the President's tax program would have a case for at least two reasons. The fact is that economists simply do not know for sure to what extent movements in the economy are caused by fiscal policy, by monetary policy, by "external shocks" or by destabilizing forces internal to the private economy itself.

On these matters the profession has been all over the map during the last several decades. At one time it was assumed that the task of those managing monetary and budget policies was to counter the tendency for the private sector "on its own" to ricochet from boom to bust. Then we decided that the private economy was reasonably stable except when drawn off course by erratic economic policies of government.

At one time we were sure that monetary policy did not matter much, and fiscal policy would deliver sustained prosperity. By a decade ago monetary policy occupied center stage, and the old conventional Keynesian fiscal policy wisdom (as usually happens to old conventional wisdoms) was on the defensive. In recent years, however, the relationship between the money stock (however defined) and the pace of business activity began to blur—encouraging the agnostic view that what we know for sure about these matters remains limited.

*Reprinted with permission from *The Wall Street Journal*, June 1981.

†Mr. McCracken is Edmund Ezra Day University Professor of Business Administration at the University of Michigan, former chairman of the Council of Economic Advisers under President Nixon and a member of the Journal's Board of Contributors.

With uncertainty about the relative influence on the economy of the Federal Reserve's monetary and credit policies and the government's fiscal policies, prudence would seem to dictate caution about sharp changes in any policy.

DANGEROUSLY LOW SAVINGS

Moreover, in our low savings economy large budget deficits do crowd markets. The U.S. is now a dangerously low-savings economy, not only relative to such countries as Japan and the Federal Republic of Germany but relative to our own historical performance.

The problems with which economic policy must come to grips, however, are far more fundamental and dynamic than leaning against the zigs and zags of the normal business cycle.

The American economy seems to have lost its vigor. The causes of this deteriorating economic performance are numerous and deep, but two are clearly related to the fiscal operations of government. One is that because of inflation and our archaic accounting conventions, the federal government is collecting corporate taxes on fictitious profits, thereby contributing to the low-investment tendencies of the economy. National income data suggest that we are understating the cost of capital currently expiring by about $17 billion per year. If the profits taxes paid on these nonexistent profits were instead going into more capital formation, the economy would be less afflicted with a productive plant that is now too small and too old.

Another basic source of our troubles is that we have gone too far in making income available without regard to whether the recipient earned it through productive activity that enlarges the output of goods and services. This process shows up in the federal government's budget. If projections in President Carter's January Budget Message (adjusted for the usual initial underestimates) were to be realized for fiscal 1982, the rise in total public spending at all levels of government would have been equal to half or more of the projected increase in the total national income.

The tandem strategy that says we must first hold down spending until a budget surplus is achieved before considering tax reduction is in a sense unexceptionable. We would thereby have won the fight to a lower tax burden.

It also has a major flaw. It does not work.

Experience shows that this strategy leads not to a budget in the black, but to a budget with outlays and revenues both higher than would otherwise occur. It is a strategy that, particularly in recent years, has produced a public sector absorbing a large proportion of increases in the national income. It is the ineluctable end result because it is a strategy which in essence says that government has first claim on earnings, and those earning these incomes must make do with the remainder.

It makes sense, therefore, to try the opposite strategy. The thrust of public policy should be shifted toward giving higher priority to those doing the earning and producing and saving, with the public sector being required to accommodate to that part of their earnings that people are willing to have spend collectively. If that is to be the strategy, the trail should be blazed far enough ahead so that the private sector can have enough confidence to alter its long-range plans.

This is the real significance of a three-year tax proposal. The effort to limit the tax program to one year, if it were to be successful, would be a major victory in the effort to avoid that fundamental change in the direction of national policy so essential to start the process of economic revitalization.

This the "big spenders" understand well enough. If they can hold the tax structure essentially intact, they win. In the years ahead more money would then be spent on more public programs than if government commits itself to a tax reduction program with a multi-year time horizon—long enough so that people and businesses can start to make the basic plans that this arthritic economy needs. This is why conservatives genuinely concerned about budget deficits find that they are joined by the spenders in trying to limit the scope of tax reduction—the spenders also, of course, voicing concerns about deficits, which have caused them little loss of sleep for decades before this year.

In fact, the President's program might be criticized for its modesty. As for taxes on corporate income, the Administration priced out its recommendations at a $2.5 billion tax reduction for this fiscal year and $9.7 billion for fiscal 1982. For an economy whose capital formation ought to be running $50 billion per year above current levels, if it is to get back on the track, these are not extravagant figures.

Moreover, if the National Income Accounts estimates are reasonably correct—that we are underestimating the cost of capital currently expiring by $17 billion per year—it is not until fiscal 1983 that the administration's tax program would get beyond eliminating this tax on phantom profits. It's a tax which we should never have been collecting in the first place. (It has been the most clear-cut case of a penalty tax on economic progress.)

INCORRECT IMAGE

Clearly the most controversial part of the President's tax program is the proposal pertaining to individual income taxes. The administration has been talking to conservative House Democrats about the possibility of fashioning a three-year cut with figures different than its original proposal of a 10% reduction in three successive years. Whatever three-year package results from this process, it is here that the image emerges of revenues going *down*.

For the sake of argument, we will work with the administration's original 10-10-10 proposal and address the opposition's assumption that revenues will go down a like amount, or 30%. This is not correct. The administration projected revenues from individual income taxes at $311 billion in fiscal 1983, 27% above the $244 billion realized in fiscal 1980.

What the President's proposal here does is little more than to neutralize the tendency for a progressive tax rate structure over time to increase the proportion of the national income going for taxes as the national income rises (either because of inflation or rising real incomes).

We see this clearly by comparing the projections for future years by President Carter in his January Budget Message and President Reagan's projections. In fact, with the President's tax package the proportion of aggregate personal incomes going for individual income taxes in the next fiscal year would be about a half of one percent only below that in 1980, and with full implementation of the program by fiscal 1983 the proportion would be only one percentage point lower.

Individual Income Tax Receipts As Percent
Projected Personal Incomes

FY	Carter	Reagan
1980	11.7%	11.7%
1981	12.1	11.9
1982	12.6	11.1
1983	13.1	10.7
1984	13.8	10.6

Sources: Basic data from: "Budget Message of the President, January 1981" and "Fiscal Year 1982 Budget Revisions."

What 10-10-10 essentially does, in short, is to avoid an unlegislated increase in the proportion of people's earnings which would accrue to government from inaction. This is clearly evident in the Carter budget, which projected a persistent rise in the share of incomes going to the tax collector.

The President's tax program, in short, is an essential element in the strategy to regain control of spending as well as to revitalize the economy. The spenders understand this. Hopefully the conservatives will also.

30

Will Reaganomics Unravel?*

PAUL CRAIG ROBERTS

The Reagan Administration's economic program consists of a fine balance between three different points of view, each with a dominant goal. There are the supply-siders in the Treasury, who are primarily concerned with increasing the rate of real economic growth. There are the monetarists in the Treasury and on the Council of Economic Advisers, who are primarily concerned with lowering the inflation rate as fast as possible. And there are the traditionalists at the Office of Management and Budget, who are primarily concerned with making good on their promise of a balanced budget by 1984.

WAITING FOR A BREAKDOWN

A great deal has been made in the press of alleged inconsistencies between these points of view. The Administration's opponents are convinced that sooner or later a program based on mutually incompatible strategies will break down in internal warfare. They are so convinced that a breakdown is imminent that they are doing little to help it along, to the frustration of liberal columnists like Hobart Rowen, who keeps exhorting the Democrats, without effect, to "fight Reagan on the economy." Veterans like Thomas P. "Tip" O'Neill, the Speaker of the House, have been quite clear on the matter—why fight a popular President if his program is going to self-destruct?

*Paul Craig Roberts, Assistant Secretary of the Treasury for Economic Policy, is one of the architects of Reaganomics. Reprinted from *Fortune*, November 16, 1981.

In fact the three viewpoints are compatible. Supply-siders realize that inflation could cancel the tax-rate reductions and thereby the supply-side effects that they are counting on to raise the real growth rate. They fully support a policy of moderate and predictable growth in the monetary aggregates. Supply-siders also realize that budget deficits draw down the pool of private-sector savings, offsetting their efforts to raise the savings rate, and so they strongly support OMB's efforts to reduce the growth of spending.

The Administration's monetarists are pleased to have their war against inflation aided by a higher saving rate and a larger supply of incentives—such as tax breaks and less government interference—that spur production and raise productivity. Without such help, monetarism can veer into its most extreme form, in which the economy starts to close down, causing output to fall along with demand, thereby keeping price levels higher than they otherwise would be. It is easier to bring down prices if better incentives and higher after-tax rates of return are expanding production. Although the evidence seems clear that money growth, and not budget deficits, explains inflation and interest rates, monetarists support smaller deficits in order to reduce the temptation for the Federal Reserve Board to finance the debt by inflating the money supply.

The Republican traditionalists, who believe that a balanced budget is the prerequisite for a sound economy, appreciate the contribution that supply-side and monetarist policies make to lowering expenditure growth. They understand that higher real economic growth reduces budget expenditures and helps bring the budget into balance. If better incentives mean more jobs, then expenditures for income-support programs will be lower. Also, less inflation means lower expenditures for the indexed and over-indexed pension and transfer programs.

ACHILLES' HEEL

It is on the revenue side that the traditionalists have their doubts. In their view revenues depend on *nominal* GNP and tax rates. Since our tax system taxes nominal income at progressive rates, the higher the inflation and the tax rates, the higher the government's revenues.

If the Administration's program has an Achilles' heel, it is here. Much has been said—erroneously—of a split between supply-siders and monetarists. But when the traditionalists focus on the revenue side of the budget, it pits them against both supply-siders and monetarists.

This is not generally understood, because supply-siders have been mistakenly portrayed as "Lafferites," promising higher revenues from from lowered tax rates. In fact, what they have promised is that *some* of the revenues will be recaptured because of a larger tax base, and that the deficit remaining after budget cuts will be easier to finance because of an increase in the savings rate. Nevertheless, if your success indicator is a balanced budget, it doesn't get you off the hook to point out that the deficit you do have is financed out of higher savings. The more the Administration focuses on the deficit per se, the greater the likelihood that monetarism or supply-side economics, or both, will be abandoned.

The tensions have been present since before the inauguration when work began on the February scenario, which the press mistakenly calls a forecast. Since the Administration was proposing major changes in policy, it could not forecast how the economy would behave until it knew to what extent Congress would implement its policy. It was called a scenario rather than a forecast to stress that it was an estimate of the effects that the proposed policy changes would have on the economy.

SWALLOWING "CORE INFLATION"

The tensions in this exercise were not between monetarists and supply-siders, but between the traditionalists and the other two points of view. Due to revenue considerations, the beginning date for the tax cuts assumed in the scenario was moved from January 1 to July 1, 1981. The monetarists had to swallow "core inflation" (the notion that some part of inflation is so embedded in the economy that it won't respond to monetary policy) and accept a higher nominal GNP growth path than was consistent with tight money. Later, in the negotiations on the tax bill, the traditionalists supported scaling down and further delaying the tax cut so that no significant revenues were at stake until the last half of 1982—a slippage of 18 months in the supply-side timetable.

This created a new problem. According to supply-side analysis, enacting a tax cut in the present to be effective in the future creates incentives for people to shift income-earning activities to the future when tax rates will be lower. The result could be a downturn in economic activity in the near term. In addition, incentives are created for people to shift tax deductions and exemptions to the present while the rates are higher, thus lowering the government's tax revenues near term.

By January 1982 the Administration will have to convert its estimate of the economic effects of its proposals into a forecast based on actual Fed policy and the actual tax and spending cuts that have been enacted. Since the effective date of the final tax bill was pushed back from the original proposal, the beneficial effects will also be delayed. This may adversely affect the deficit projections. If so, there is bound to be more pressure from the traditionalists to delay further the effective dates of the tax cuts or even to reduce their size.

This dynamic may already be in play as a result of OMB's "September offensive" on the budget. OMB saw an opportunity to turn congressional concern over high interest rates into a drive for further budget cuts. If the high interest rates could be blamed on the budget deficit, the pressures Congress was feeling from constituents about high rates could build support for a second round of budget cutting. All that was required was that the Administration abandon its monetarist explanation of interest rates and adopt the deficit-centered view of its Wall Street critic, Salomon Brothers economist Henry Kaufman. The transition began on August 10 and was completed by September 8.

The tactic wasn't without merit, and everything would have been fine except that Congress balked at the extra spending cuts. Stymied on the spending front, and having blamed high interest rates on the deficit, OMB had no place to turn but to the revenue front. The Administration proposed revenue-raising measures. There are some user's fees that are sensible enough, such as those that would apply to airplane and boat owners who use federal facilities and services, but the idea has crept in of balancing the budget by reducing "tax expenditures," or "loopholes. Some abuses need to be addressed, but the general problem with "tax expenditures" is that most are as well defended by organized lobbies as are the spending programs. So naturally many eyes have turned to the tax cuts scheduled to take effect in mid-1982 and mid-1983.

EASIER POLITICS

Key elements of the coalition that gave the Administration its tax-cut victory—Senate Republicans and "boll weevils" in the House—are already handing around tables showing how to balance the budget by further delaying and reducing the tax cut. People always forget that delaying the incentives adversely affects the projected GNP growth path, They "balance" the budget on paper by applying the higher tax rates to the higher growth path that is projected on the basis of the lower tax rates. They overlook the fact that higher taxes mean less real economic growth, thus offsetting some of their projected revenue gains and, in addition, raising budget expenditures. After the adverse feedback effects, the budget isn't balanced, and there is less saving out of which to finance the deficit.

Nevertheless, politicians may think that it is easier to take away tax cuts that aren't yet in anyone's hands than to pull bigger chunks of the budget out of hands that are already tightly grasping them. That is easier politics, perhaps, but bad economic policy without doubt. Regardless, Congress now thinks that revenue-raising measures are an alternative to budget cutting. It is an indifferent trade-off once you are "Kaufmanized." And once you abandon the monetarist explanation of interest rates, there's not much to keep you from using a little inflation to balance the budget.

To keep the September offensive from snatching defeat from the jaws of victory, something has to give. The Administration's program can succeed only if it adheres to its original balance of viewpoints. Neither monetarists, supply-siders, nor traditionalists can be allowed to impose their overriding goal as a single constraint on policy. If the inflation rate becomes the single constraint, then we risk lower growth and larger budget deficits. If balancing the budget by an arbitrary date becomes the single constraint, we risk higher inflation and higher taxes. After years of rising inflation, mounting budget deficits, and declining real economic growth, victory should be defined as declining inflation, declining deficits, and rising real growth. If the policymakers forget the multiple constraints, they will unravel the President's program and fulfill Tip O'Neill's expectations.

INCENTIVES ARE BEING RESTORED

Most recent Administrations have been dominated by economic events. What plans they had were soon abandoned or revised beyond recognition. The Reagan Administration came to town with a coherent view of what had gone wrong in the economic-policy arena and what needed to be done about it. Much has been accomplished in a short period of time. Federal spending is coming under control and incentives to work, save, and invest are being restored. Inflation is falling, the dollar has been riding high in the foreign-exchange markets, and the price of gold is down from panic levels. The risk in the economic arena is not a veto from Wall Street, but that the Administration might forget what it came here to do in the first place. I am confident that the Administration will see its program succeed.

VI

CONCLUSIONS
WILL IT WORK?

Part VI contains articles showing the possible integration of demand-side and supply-side ecomics. This is a more practical approach as opposed to the alternates: (1) that supply-side economics is going to become the new economics replacing Keynesian economics, or (2) that supply-side economics is going to fade away after making its initial impact on economic theory.

In addition, this part treats the possibility that most economists have accepted some of supply-side economics just as most of them eventually accepted Keynesian economics as a tool of economic analysis. Finally, it looks at the possibility of success for supply-side economics.

31

The Integration of Demand-Side and Supply-Side Policies*

Tax reductions which induce additional saving and investment will contribute to faster productivity growth, and this in turn will help reduce inflation. A number of critical questions arise, however, in determining the appropriate type, magnitude, and timing of any tax reductions. First, what kind of an increase in productivity might reasonably be expected from investment-oriented tax cuts of various sizes, and what would be the associated reduction in inflation? Second, to what extent would the improvements in productivity and other supply-creating aspects of a tax reduction offset the increase in aggregate demand they would cause? More generally, how would tax cuts aimed at increasing supply fit into the framework of fiscal restraint that is required to reduce inflation?

Although the effect on investment from a given loss of tax revenues would vary with the form of the reduction (accelerated depreciation, larger investment tax credit, or lower corporate income tax rates), the evidence suggests that each dollar of reduction in annual business taxes might, at the outside and after several years, generate slightly more than a dollar in business fixed investment. To increase investment by 10 percent, a business tax reduction of at least $30 billion—or about 1 percent of GNP—would be necessary. This larger volume of investment, maintained from 1981 through 1985, would increase the capital stock by about 5 percent after allowing for depreciation. On the basis of the historical relationships between output and capital, such an addition to the capital stock might generate a total increase in the level of productivity of at most 1.5 percent by 1985, or about 0.3 percent per year. In

*Reprinted from *The Economic Report of the President, 1981.*

view of the declining rate of productivity growth which the Nation has experienced in recent years, however, this small improvement would be significant.

Such a rise in the productivity growth rate would not be likely to induce a faster rise in money wage demands. Therefore, since the growth of unit labor costs is equal to the increase in compensation per hour minus the rate of growth in productivity, the faster productivity growth rate should lead to a slower rise in costs and prices. In turn, a slower rise in prices would help to reduce the growth of wages, leading to a still further slowdown of inflation. All told, an investment-oriented tax cut amounting to about 1 percent of GNP might produce a 0.3 percentage point rise in productivity growth that would translate, after several years, to just over one-half percentage point reduction in the inflation rate.

DEMAND VERSUS SUPPLY RESPONSES TO TAX CUTS

Tax reductions have two principal effects. On the one hand, individuals and firms will buy more goods and services. As a tax cut is spent and respent throughout the economy, the resulting increase in nominal GNP will exceed the original tax cut. As a result of this multiplier process, aggregate demand will rise by more than the tax cut. But tax cuts also increase the supply of goods and services. Since lower tax rates allow individuals and firms to keep a larger fraction of their income after taxes, the lower rates affect incentives to work, to save, and to invest the savings, increasing potential GNP.

Although the magnitude of the multiplier varies according to the nature of the tax cut, aggregate demand typically rises by about twice the size of a reduction in taxes. Thus, a tax cut equal to 1 percent of GNP will increase aggregate demand by about 2 percent. To match the increase in demand, a 2 percent increase in supply would also be required. To the extent that its supply response is less than the additional demand it creates, any reduction adds to the pressures of demand on the rate of inflation.

But there are two ways in which such tax cuts can be made while still restraining demand. First, tax reductions may offset increases in other taxes. As discussed earlier, inflation pushes taxpayers into higher tax brackets, so that the average effective tax rate—the ratio of tax revenues to GNP—rises. Consumption is depressed and economic growth reduced. In the years ahead, periodic tax reductions will therefore be both possible and necessary to keep aggregate demand from falling. Second, a tax reduction accompanied by Federal spending reductions of roughly the same magnitude will not change aggregate demand; hence, even if the supply response to a tax cut is smaller than the demand response, inflationary pressures will not be generated.

Thus, it is clear that the design and timing of supply-oriented tax cuts depend importantly on the specific relationship between the demand-side and supply-side responses. If such tax reductions fail to generate enough supply to offset the additional demand they create—and the evidence discussed below suggests this to be the case, particularly for personal tax reductions—they must then be integrated like any tax cut into policies of demand management.

THE SUPPLY-SIDE RESPONSE TO PERSONAL TAX CUTS

A 10 percent reduction in marginal tax rates on individuals (approximately a $30-billion personal tax cut in 1981) would increase the total demand for goods and services by $60 billion, or 2 percent of GNP. It could also lead to increases in individual work and saving in response to the lower tax rates and thereby increase potential GNP. How much of the increase in demand would be matched by such increases in supply?

The Supply of Labor

The additional production that results from lowering taxes on labor income depends both on changes in the quantity of labor supplied (i.e., the total number of hours worked) and on changes in the average productivity of labor.

Higher after-tax wages make work more attractive. This encourages new entrants to join the labor force and those already employed to work longer hours. Since after-tax incomes have risen, however, people can also afford to work less—to take longer vacations or to shorten their workweeks. Whether the former effect would or would not exceed the latter effect is hard to predict. A preponderance of the evidence suggests that for adult men the two effects approximately offset each other; that is, a cut in income taxes increases the supply of adult men in the work force only slightly, if at all. Women, on the other hand, and particularly married women, respond much more strongly to higher wages. In the past, the number of adult women in the work force may have increased by as much as 1 percent for every 1 percent increase in take-home pay. Although women are more responsive to changes in their wages than are men, men still outnumber women in the labor force and on average earn substantially more. Therefore, a reduction in personal income tax rates would increase the *total* supply of labor only slightly.

Whether an increase in the labor supply would be accompanied by an increase in productivity is uncertain. While most business investment enhances productivity, an increase in the labor supply would not improve productivity unless it increased the average quality of work performed or the intensity of effort. Productivity might actually fall as the supply of labor increased if the additional labor supply consisted, on balance, of less skilled or less experienced workers.

Alternatively, some have argued that the increased supply of labor from high-income, high-productivity workers would outweigh the increased supply from other workers, so that the average productivity of the labor force would rise. This could happen if high-productivity workers were more sensitive to a given percentage change in after-tax earnings, or if the tax reduction represented a larger percentage change in their take-home pay. Since high-income workers are a small fraction of the labor force, these influences would have to be large to alter total productivity significantly. Studies of high-income workers generally do not find them much more responsive to equal percentage increases in after-tax income. However, a 10 percent across-the-board reduction in tax rates would also mean a larger percentage increase in the after-tax earnings for these workers because their households are in high marginal tax brackets. A 10 percent tax cut is, therefore, likely to produce a somewhat larger change in the supply of high-income workers. Still, even in high-income households it is in fact second-income earners—generally those who have lower productivity—who are apt to be the most responsive to lower tax rates.

Balancing the two opposing forces—the lack of experience of new workers and the possibility of a greater-than-average influx of higher-income workers—it seems unwise to assume that the average productivity of the labor force will be improved by a personal tax cut.

Taking all the relevant factors into account, the limited response of the supply of labor and of productivity to a 10 percent reduction in personal income tax rates is likely to produce an increase in potential GNP of perhaps 0.2 percent to at most 0.6 percent. This result follows in part from evidence suggesting that such a tax cut would induce an increase in labor supply between 0.3 and 1.0 percent. According to past relationships between labor and production, such an increase in labor supply would lead to the modest increase in potential GNP mentioned above.

The Supply of Saving

A reduction in personal income tax rates increases both the income out of which an individual worker can save and the after-tax return to saving. It would also tend to discourage borrowing by reducing the value of the income tax reduction for interest payments. If the increases in personal saving find their way into additional business investment, productivity will rise.

Most empirical studies have concluded that changes in personal income tax rates would have only a small effect on personal saving. At best, a 10 percent reduction in tax rates would increase personal saving less than 3 percent. This means that the saving rate—the average share of personal saving in disposable income, which over the last 5 years has averaged 5.7 percent—would rise by no more than 0.2 percentage point. The additional saving would at most be equivalent to only about 0.2 percent of GNP.

Even if every dollar of personal saving that resulted from a 10 percent tax cut were invested in business plant and equipment—and some, in fact, would flow into housing—the effects on output and on productivity would be small. If the tax cut and the higher saving continued for 5 years, the additional saving and investment would increase potential GNP by less than 0.3 percent and lead to a negligible increase in the annual rate of productivity growth.

This examination of likely responses thus suggests that even under the most optimistic circumstances, a 10 percent reduction in tax rates would not induce enough additional work, saving, or investment to offset more than a fraction of the 2 percent increase in aggregate demand that would accompany the tax cut.

BUSINESS TAX CUTS

It was pointed out earlier that a tax cut that liberalized the business depreciation allowance or increased the investment tax credit could, after a time, have a fairly substantial effect on the Nation's productive potential. Such a tax cut, amounting to 1 percent of GNP, could raise potential output by perhaps 1½ percent over a 5-year period.

This would still be less than the 2 percent rise in aggregate demand that would also be generated, however. More important, the increase in demand would come relatively quickly, most of it within 1½ to 2 years. The increase in supply, on the other hand, would occur very gradually. As a consequence, the tax cut would tend to increase demand pressures, especially in the years immediately following it. While tax reductions that are effective in raising investment are essential in a long-term strategy to promote economic growth, business tax cuts, like personal tax cuts, must be designed to fit into an overall framework of fiscal restraint.

CONCLUSIONS

This analysis of the macroeconomic effects of Federal tax reductions suggests several conclusions for the development of fiscal policy:

First, specific investment-oriented tax reductions for business are likely to increase saving, investment, and productivity by a much more significant degree than cuts in personal income taxes.

Second, productivity-oriented tax reductions will yield improvements in the inflation rate that are helpful and significant, but still relatively modest in the context of a 10 percent underlying inflation rate.

Third, the supply response, while a critically important feature of any tax reduction, will be substantially less than the demand response, particularly in the short run.

Fourth, since reductions in both business and personal taxes will increase demand faster than supply, they must be designed and carried out in ways that are consistent with the demand restraint needed to reduce inflation.

It is sometimes alleged that the potentially inflationary effects of a large tax cut can be avoided if the Federal Reserve steadfastly pursues its goal of keeping the growth of the monetary aggregates within tight targets. But if taxes are reduced while the Federal Reserve pursues an unchanged monetary policy, aggregate demand will nevertheless increase, especially in the short run. The increase in demand would lead to a rise in interest rates that would dampen the increase in aggregate demand but not eliminate it. Additional inflationary pressure would then result.

A very large tax cut unaccompanied by the necessary spending cuts would lead to both an increase in inflation and a sharp rise in interest rates. Some, and perhaps all, of the stimulus to investment from tax reductions would be undone by the higher interest rates and the greater uncertainty engendered by a new round of inflation.

Monetary restraint is an absolutely essential element of inflation control and reduction. Tax measures focused on increasing supply can make a significant contribution. But there will be a continuing need for careful and prudent fiscal policies to restrain demand. In recent years the Nation has come to appreciate the potential value of supply-oriented tax policies. In the process of learning some needed lessons about supply-side economics, however, the Nation cannot afford to forget its hard-learned lessons about the need for demand-side restraint.

The three central elements of a macroeconomic policy to reduce inflation and advance the Nation's prospects for healthy economic growth have been set forth in this chapter: maintaining a persistent and prudent course of demand restraint; putting in place an improved incomes policy using tax incentives to induce wage moderation; and increasing the share of the Nation's output going to investment. The next chapter deals with the challenge of inflation and growth at the level of individual markets and sectors. It concentrates on measures to increase the economy's flexibility and capacity for adjusting to change.

Carrying out these policies will require patience and, in the interim, some sacrifice. But if they are followed with persistence they promise a substantial payoff in improved economic performance.

32

We are All Supply-Siders Now*

JOHN A. TATOM

The latest sensation in the popular press and among policymakers is the discovery of "supply-side economics" and the exciting promise of supply-side policies.[1] To provide a perspective on the current debate, this article reviews the conceptual basis for supply-side economics and examines the fundamentals of supply performance in the United States.

WHAT IS SUPPLY-SIDE ECONOMICS ALL ABOUT?

Supply-side economics is growth- and efficiency-oriented. It covers the entire range of economic decisions: what gets produced, how, for whom, and how fast production and consumption possibilities expand. The supply-side approach is not novel in economic analysis. Indeed, it has been the core of economic analysis since the first systematic analysis of scarcity and aggregate supply, Adam Smith's pioneering *Inquiry into the Nature and Causes of the Wealth of Nation's*, was published over 200 years ago.[2]

The recent emphasis on supply is novel, however, in at least one re-

*Reprinted from the *Review*, May 1981, Federal Reserve Bank of St. Louis.

[1] One of the first major policymaking endorsements of supply-side economics is contained in *Outlook for the 1980's,* Midyear Report and Staff Study of the Joint Economic Committee of the Congress (August 1979).

[2] For an historical perspective on supply-side economics, see Robert E. Keleher and William P. Orzechowski, "Supply-Side Effects of Fiscal Policy: Some Historical Perspectives," reviewed in the Federal Reserve Bank of Atlanta *Economic Review* (February 1981), pp. 26-28.

spect–the assertion that supply effects are of central importance in evaluating government efforts to improve the functioning of the economy. The conventional view of the functioning of the economy emphasizes a role for the management of aggregate demand as an appropriate macroeconomic policy for stabilizing the economy. The normal tools for influencing aggregate demand are monetary and fiscal policy, including spending for goods and services, transfer programs and taxation policies. By influencing demand for output, such policies are presumed to affect the levels of the nation's output, employment and prices, as well as their rates of change. Expanding the growth of the money stock or government expenditures for goods, services or transfer programs is viewed as "expansionary" in its effects on output and employment. Supply-siders reject such arguments as woefully incomplete. They emphasize that standard expansionary macroeconomic policies can significantly *reduce* the economy's ability to produce. In particular, they stress that individual choices affect the current and future availability of resources, as well as the efficiency of resource employment, effects that often are ignored in both macroeconomic analysis and policy decisions.

The supply-side view can be explained using a simple introductory economics framework. Suppose an economy has a given quantity of resources such as labor and capital (plant, equipment, knowledge, etc.) and an existing array of technologies for producing two goods called product X and product Y. At any time, resources can be completely devoted to the production of one or the other good, or both. If resources are used so that the largest production of X is obtained, for any given output of product Y, the production and consumption possibilities of the economy can be depicted as the curve AB in figure 1. Combinations of product X and Y output beyond AB (such as point C) are unattainable, given the technology and resources available, while those inside the curve (such as point D) are possible, but involve either unemployed resources, the use of inferior technologies, or both.

Given individual preferences and the distribution of resource ownership among individuals, an economy with free markets will tend to attain some equilibrium point (E), where the value of goods reflects the cost of production and where full employment of existing resources occurs. Competition among resource owners, the producers of the two goods and consumers will determine the prices of the products and resources, how much of each of the goods are produced, which of the available resources and technologies are used to produce each good, the income of individuals, and the distribution of goods produced among individuals.

An economy can improve its possibilities for consumption by shifting out its *production possibility frontier* (AB in figure 1). This occurs

Figure 1   A Simple Production Possibility Frontier

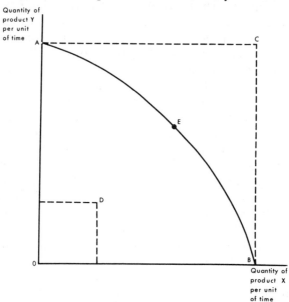

when the supply of labor or capital resources is increased or when technology is improved. Thus, individuals make choices that determine the rate of growth of income or the supply of goods producible under high-employment conditions. These choices involve foregoing present consumption so that resources can be used for research and development, innovation or the production of new capital goods. Figure 2 shows such a shift in production (and consumption) possibilities. When the production possibility frontier shifts from AB to A'B', individuals choose the opportunity to consume an output mix such as E'.

Supply-side economics focuses on two aspects of the simple framework above: first, that economic policy directly affects the rate of growth of resource supplies and the pattern of innovation, impinging on the rate at which the economy's production possibilities improve; second, that economic policy can alter the position of the current production possibility frontier.[3]

---

[3] A detailed discussion of the supply-side approach to macroeconomic policy may be found in Laurence H. Meyer, ed., *The Supply-Side Effects of Economic Policy* (Center for the Study of American Business and the Federal Reserve Bank of St. Louis, 1981).

Figure 2   A Shift in the Production Possibility Frontier

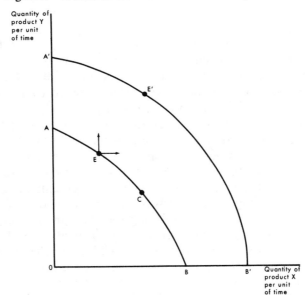

Supply-Side Effects of Regulation

Economic policies to regulate business can affect supply. In a market economy, the government can promote efficiency by regulating efforts to achieve monopoly control in resource or product markets. Such regulatory policies can also promote faster output growth by policing business practices that limit competition, technological development and innovation.

Regulatory policies can adversely affect consumption possibilities, however. Regulatory programs that mandate the use of inefficient technologies or that restrict the use of resources in some or all production processes cause the production possibility frontier to shift inward (for example, from A'B' to AB in figure 2). Such regulations can slow the rate of growth by retarding technological innovation or by reducing incentives to accumulate resources or improve their quality.

Supply-Side Effects of Government Spending

The decision to provide more of one good through government provision involves attracting resources away from the production of other goods (a movement *along* the production possibility frontier). Supply-siders emphasize, however, that the increased taxes levied to pay for the new goods can reduce the total resources available, *shifting* the frontier inward. Suppose the economy is initially producing and consuming at point E' in figure 2. An attempt by the government to increase the output of good X, moving along the frontier A'B', can lead to fewer available resources so that (1) the frontier shifts inward to a new frontier such as AB, and (2) production occurs at a point like C. The shift occurs because owners of human resources can forego supplying these resources in the marketplace, choosing instead to use labor resources at home or in leisure when confronted with larger taxes on labor income. Similarly, owners of capital resources can avoid taxes by reducing the use of existing plant and equipment, lengthening the useful life of assets, and spending the proceeds from current use of capital services on consumer goods instead of replacing the plant and equipment or investing in new assets. In the case of taxation of income of capital resources, the effects on the production possibility further tend to show up more heavily in the future through reduced growth of resources, rather than in immediate inward shifts of the frontier.

Taxation can also give rise to other forms of tax avoidance that shift the frontier inward. When taxes on resource incomes are different depending on the use of the resources, resource owners may continue supplying resources in the marketplace, but divert these resources to lower-taxed, less-efficient uses. While this lowers the total productivity of the resources, the after-tax incomes are larger than they would have been if resources were used in the high-tax sectors. Such tax avoidance leads to an inward shift of the frontier, even if the total supplies of resources remain the same.

Supply-Side Effects of Redistribution

Similarly, an economic policy aimed at changing the distribution of consumption goods among individuals can affect supply. A program that taxes income recipients in order to transfer existing output to particular groups can reduce the *total* consumption possibilities of the community. For example, increased unemployment benefits, food stamps and social security benefits involve increased transfers and taxes. Higher taxes can reduce the supply of resources available both now and in the future; in addition, higher transfer payments reduce some individuals' incentives to accumulate and supply resources in the marketplace. Both the programs and the higher taxes to support them can reduce resource supplies.[4] Reductions in resource employment reduce output. Government policies to transfer more of the goods produced at point E in figure 1 to a particular group can shift the overall production and consumption possibilities of the economy inward, as the higher taxes to pay for the redistributed goods and the increased availability of transfer payments reduce the total resources available for use in production.

Supply-siders emphasize that the critical factor in government transfer and spending decisions is that such expenditures are financed either by taxation, borrowing from the public or increasing the money supply. These methods of finance lead to reductions in the total supply of resources available for production. Higher tax rates discourage individuals from work, saving and productive investment. Financing through government deficits (borrowing), simply postpones taxes and "crowds out" private-sector investment in plant, equipment and consumer durables such as housing and autos, as financing costs are raised.

Supply-Side Effects of Monetary Policy

Attempts to finance expenditures by printing money similarly reduce the nation's production possibilities. A faster rate of money growth increases the rate of inflation (the rate at which the value of money declines). Inflation interferes with economic efficiency. For example, it creates uncertainties about the meaning of price changes. When a product's price is raised or when wages in an industry rise, it is less clear whether the increase reflects the scarcity of the product or resource, or the inflation process. Inflation also distorts the allocation of resources, as people employ scarce resources to economize on the higher cost of holding money. The disproportionate growth of resource employment in banking, financial intermediaries and financial management services is an example of such an inefficiency.

The supply-side effects of inflation also arise through the U.S. tax system. The principal characteristic of the tax system that creates supply-side disincentives when inflation occurs is its basis on historical *nominal* accounting of income. For the individual income tax, this has two important implications. First, when inflation is higher, investors require higher rates of return to compensate for the erosion of purchasing

---

[4]These considerations do not imply an aversion to redistribution schemes on the part of supply-siders. From a strictly positive view, however, supply-siders would tend to emphasize that the nation's distributional objectives can be accomplished more or less efficiently depending on the supply-side incentives involved.

power of both future interest payments and the original sum loaned. These higher interest rates simply allow the maintenance of the purchasing power of investors' portfolios. The added interest is compensation for a maintenance expense, not income. Nonetheless, these higher interest payments are taxed as income. The higher taxes on these non-income payments reduce the incentives to save and invest.

Second, the individual income tax is applied against nominal income in a progressive fashion. As a result, when wages and other income simply keep pace with inflation, individuals find themselves in higher and higher tax brackets, so that the purchasing power of their income declines. This process, sometimes called "bracket creep," subjects individuals to increasingly higher taxes on existing and any prospective additions to purchasing power. Consequently, workers have less incentive to work or save, despite the tendency of wages to keep pace with inflation.

For business, tax accounting again is based on historical nominal magnitudes. Thus, inventory expenses and depreciation are computed on the basis of the past dollar expenditures on goods, equipment or plant, instead of the current dollar costs of replacing the inventory or plant and equipment currently being used up in production. As a result, inflation leads to an understatement of the true costs and therefore an overstatement of business income and artificially inflated taxes. Since historical cost accounting subjects a given real cash flow of a business to higher taxes, businesses are discouraged from adding new productive assets during inflationary periods. Of course, the result of reduced savings and investment is to slow the pace at which the production possibility frontier shifts outward. For a given labor force, the growth of output per worker slows.

SUPPLY-SIDE POLICY IMPLICATIONS AND PROPOSALS

An immediate policy concern of supply-siders is to redress the destructive effects of policies created by demand management and regulatory strategies over the post-war era, particularly since the early 1960s. This redress involves slower monetary expansion, regulatory reform, tax reduction and tax reform that reduce the disincentives to produce, work, save and invest.

To deal with the disincentives created by inflation, many supply-siders recommend indexing the tax system. For example, replacement cost accounting would permit firms to deduct from receipts the true cost of depreciation in computing income, avoiding the disincentives to invest posed by inflation. Second, inflation premia in interest rates could be excluded from taxation for firms and individuals. Finally, tax brackets for computing the individual income tax can be tied to the inflation rate to avoid bracket creep.

To reverse the disincentives created by past policy, some policymakers influenced by supply-side economics have recommended large reductions in tax rates on additional individual income, specifically a Kemp-Roth tax rate cut of 10 percent per year for 3 years. To reverse disincentives due to under-depreciation in the past, they have recommended a "10-5-3" capital cost recovery plan that accelerates the depreciation of physical assets to 10 years for structures, 5 years for business equipment and 3 years for cars and trucks used by business. Since capital expenditures under this plan are deducted from receipts as an expense sooner than otherwise, the additional income accruing from new capital expenditures is smaller in the earlier years of the life of an asset and larger later on. For the same additional receipts over the useful life of an asset, measured income is unaffected by accelerated depreciation; less of the income, however, is measured in the early years, while more is measured later. Therefore, taxes on income from assets are postponed, providing a greater incentive to invest today.

These two tax proposals have been the subject of controversy for several years. The intensity of the debate has increased dramatically since the proposals became the centerpeice of the initial tax package of the Reagan administration. It is ironic that the debate has become so tightly linked to arguments about supply-side economics. While both of these proposals arose out of concern for the disincentive effects of bracket creep and historical cost depreciation in an inflationary environment, neither confronts the source of the disincentive—nominal income taxation. Instead, both are aimed at redressing the disincentives created by past inflation.

The Kemp-Roth plan focuses on the importance of cutting "marginal tax rates," the rates applied on additional income, instead of simply cutting average tax rates. This distinction is of critical importance to supply-siders. The average tax rate is simply the total tax paid divided by the tax base, the adjusted gross income in the case of the individual federal income tax. For the income tax, the tax rate (marginal) on successive dollars of income is a rising percentage of additional income. The tax rate applied to additions to income (marginal rate) exceeds the average tax paid at any level of income. The *marginal* tax rate is the rate that influences decisions to earn more income by increasing work or savings. A rise in the marginal rate from 20 percent to 30 percent means that an additional $100 of income will net only $70 after taxes instead of $80, so the incentive to forego leisure or consumption to work or save to earn this $100 is reduced.

Chart 1 shows measures of the marginal and average tax rates over the past two decades. The average tax rate has changed little over the years shown. Periodic tax reductions have offset the effect of bracket creep on the average tax bill. The marginal rate, however, has risen sharply since 1970.

The Kemp-Roth proposal, however, does not legislate automatic insulation of marginal rates from the inflation rate, a fundamental tenet of supply-side economics. Moreover, the "10-5-3" proposal, a simplified accelerated depreciation plan, is unrelated to the continuing disincentives created through the use of historical cost accounting in an infla-

Chart 1   Personal Tax Rates in the United States

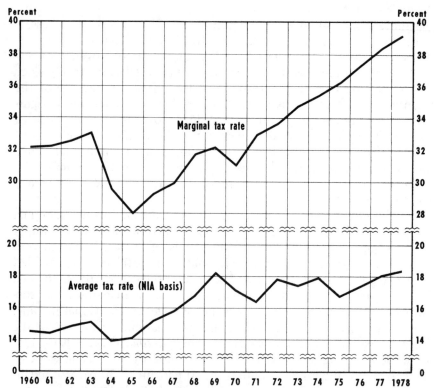

Source: Steven Braun,"Discussion of the Evans Paper,"The Supply-Side Effects of Economic Policy (Federal Reserve Bank of St. Louis and Center for the Study of American Business, 1981), p.95. The marginal tax rate series is that computed by Michael K. Evans. Both series includes state and local taxes and social security taxes.

tionary environment.[5] Neither of these proposals insulate current or future taxes from the ravages of inflation.[6]

Perhaps the greatest irony of the debate over these two proposals is that neither proposal is a path-breaking supply-oriented innovation. Many claim that such policies are unproven and that their effects are unknown. While this may be the case for some supply-oriented policies, it is untrue of the Kemp-Roth proposal or "10-5-3." Experiments with these two types of tax changes were the hallmark of the "New Economics" of the sixties. Much was written before and after such changes about their effectiveness. While supply-siders differ in the analytical approach to such tax changes, the evidence is certainly available.[7]

THE SUPPLY-SIDE RECORD

What has happened to the supply side of the economy during the last 30 years? A review of the record should show whether the changes in

[5]There are alternative proposals that reflect concern over these supply-side issues. For example, the Black Caucus proposes indexing tax rates on so-called earned income while the Jorgenson-Auerbach plan embodied in House Resolution 2525 attempts to eliminate the effects of inflation on depreciation expenses and business tax burdens. On the former, See Bureau of National Affairs, Inc., *Daily Report for Executive,* DER No. 82, April 29, 1981, p. LL-12; the Jorgenson-Auerbach proposal is discussed in Dale W. Jorgenson and Peter Navarro, "10-5-3: 'Deeply Flawed'," and the accompanying editorial "Real Depreciation, Real Inflation," *New York Times,* May 5, 1981. Note that, unlike the President's proposals, these two proposals are aimed at avoiding future supply-side effects of inflation but not at correcting for past disincentives.

[6]The spirit of the tax proposals in correcting for past inflation effects rather than breaking the link between inflation and tax rates can be seen in Paul Craig Roberts, "For Supply-Siders, The Focus is Incentives," *Washington Post,* April 13, 1981, where it is emphasized that the administration plan ". . . doesn't turn the tax clock back to 1965, but it is a big step in the right direction." Roberts notes that the marginal rate faced by the median-income family of four was at most 17 percent in 1965 and a family with twice the median income faced, at most, a 22 percent rate. These figures will rise to 32 percent and 49 percent, respectively, in 1984, without the President's proposal, according to Roberts. These figures, Roberts notes, ignore social security and state taxes and their increase since 1965.

[7]Unfortunately the existence of such evidence does not mean that it has been intensely scrutinized or, if it has been, that there is a consensus among policy analysts about the effectiveness of past policies. In the case of accelerated depreciation, business tax cuts, or investment tax credits, debate usually centers more on the relative merits of the three. See, for example, Richard W. Kopcke, "The Efficiency of Traditional Investment Tax Incentives," *Public Policy and Capital Formation,* (Board of Governors of the Federal Reserve System, April 1981), pp. 163-75. There is little question that these three policies temporarily increase the pace of investment. Whether such tax cuts *temporarily* reduce the inflation rate as supply-side arguments imply, leave it unaffected, or raise it, as Keynesians might expect, has been largely neglected.

economic policy of the past two decades have yielded evidence of the disorders discussed by supply-siders. At the same time, such a review can indicate whether the removal of the disincentives accumulated in the past could radically affect the economy. There is no question that the growth of supply of the nation's output has slowed markedly, at least since 1973, in large part due to the stagnant growth of productivity. This stagnation is supply-related, in that it arises from the astronomical rise in the price of energy resources relative to the price of business output and consequent losses in economic capacity (an inward shift of the production possibility frontier). This analysis has been detailed elsewhere, along with an examination of the potential contributions of traditional sources of productivity growth to this stagnation.[8] The emphasis here is on the past macroeconomic policy effects on supply.

Chart 2 shows the civilian labor force and the stock of nonresidential private structures and equipment available since 1947.[9] The civilian labor force has grown more rapidly since the mid-sixties. From 1948 to 1965, the labor force expanded at a 1.2 percent annual rate. From 1965 to 1980, it accelerated to a 2.3 percent rate. Capital stock growth shows about the same acceleration up until 1973. From 1948 to 1965, the stock plant and equipment rose at a 4.1 percent rate. Such growth accelerated to a 4.9 percent rate from 1965 to 1975, then dropped to a 3.0 percent rate from 1975 to 1980.

Thus, when one looks at growth rates of available resources, there appears to be no major deterioration in the economy's aggregate supply until after 1975. Indeed, from 1965 to 1975, supplies of resources were expanding much faster than before. The factors cited by supply-siders that reduce resource availability (such as the increasing regulation of both technology and the pattern of resource employment, inflation, rising marginal tax rates on income, and a growing share of government spending and transfer payments) do not seem to have seriously impaired resource availability, at least not before 1975.

Although this analysis is crude, a more detailed analysis shows essentially the same patterns. In particular, labor force growth is a crude measure of labor resource availability because it is heavily influenced by population trends rather than short-term economic factors. Supply-side policies can change the willingness of a given population of labor-force age to work by increasing their participation in the labor force or by increasing the effort of the labor force. Chart 3 shows the percentage of

[8]See John A. Tatom, "The Productivity Problem," this *Review* (September 1979), pp. 3-16, and the references cited therein.

[9]The stock of plant and equipment is the constant dollar net stock of fixed non-residential private capital, see John C. Musgrave, "Fixed Capital Stock in the United States: Revised Estimates," *Survey of Current Business* (February 1981), pp. 57-68.

Chart 2   Supply of Capital and Labor in the United States

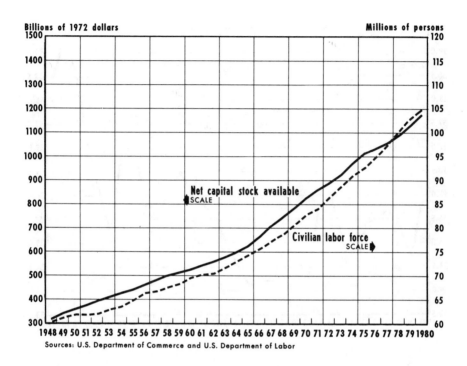

Sources: U.S. Department of Commerce and U.S. Department of Labor

the population over age 16 in the labor force. There has been no apparent deterioration in overall participation in the labor force.[10] Supply-side policies could also affect labor resource availability by altering the supply of work effort of a given labor force, for example, by changing the average hours worked per worker. Average hours worked have shown a significant downward trend throughout the post-World War II period, but this trend has not significantly accelerated in recent years. Nonetheless, studies of labor supply indicate that higher marginal tax rates have small negative effects on working hours, especially for wives with children.[11]

[10] In a detailed study of the labor force participation rate, Leonall C. Andersen, "An Explanation of Movements in the Labor Force Participation Rate: 1957-76," this *Review* (August 1978), pp. 7-21, found that an individual income tax rate cut would have a small transitory effect of increasing the participation rate. He also observed that social security tax cuts would have small permanent effects, *lowering* participation, and that reduced social security benefits would have permanent effects raising participation.

[11] See Jerry A. Hausman, "Labor Supply," in Henry J. Aaron and A. Joseph Pechman, eds., *How Taxes Affect Economic Behavior* (Brookings Institution, 1981), pp. 27-83. Detailed statistical analysis is required to support these results because the effect is relatively small, given

Chart 3   Labor Force Participation Rate

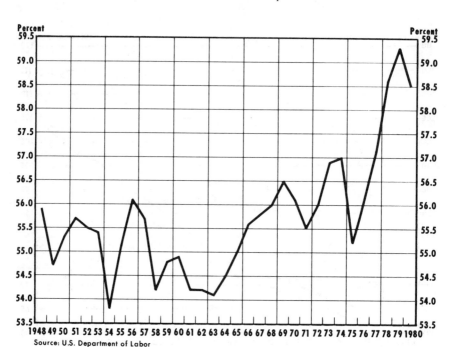

Source: U.S. Department of Labor

Finally, the available supply of labor need not have kept pace with the expansion of the labor force if the unemployment rate associated with full employment has risen significantly. While most analysts agree that the unemployment rate associated with high employment conditions has risen over the last 25 years, even the largest estimates of this increase would not reverse the pattern of accelerated labor resource growth shown in chart 2. More important, there is scant evidence that the rise in such a "full-employment" unemployment rate has been associated with growing supply-side disincentives.[12] Some policies presumably lead to a withdrawal from the labor force of workers with relative-

the increases in marginal rates that have occurred in the post-war period. For reductions in marginal rates to 1965 levels, the tax effect on labor resource availability would be correspondingly small and difficult to observe by simple statistical analysis. In addition, unless the reductions were repeated in subsequent years, the modest increase in hours would be of a once-and-for-all variety.

[12] See, for example, Daniel Hamermesh, "Transfers, Taxes, and the NAIRU," in *The Supply Side Effects of Economic Policy.* The NAIRU is the non-accelerating inflation rate of unemployment and is comparable to (usually used as synonomous with) the "natural rate of unemployment," or the full-employment unemployment rate.

ly high unemployment rates while others lead to withdrawal of individuals with relatively low unemployment rates. An example of the former is the rising minimum wage that reduces opportunities for the young, resulting in their dropping out of the labor force. An example of the latter is the effect of an increasingly generous social security system that induces older workers who normally have a more favorable employment record to quit earlier. Changes in the composition of the labor force due to demographic changes have been the primary source of the increase in the full-employment unemployment rate.

Another factor often accused of creating supply-side problems is the rapid growth of government activity. The expansion of the role of government in the economy can draw resources away from the private sector where productivity growth tends to be greater. Thus, the rate at which the production and consumption possibility curve shifts could be lowered. This view, however, misstates the pattern of government growth in the economy in recent years. Chart 4 shows the share of federal government purchases of goods and services in total output (GNP)

Chart 4   Federal Government Share of Output and Employment

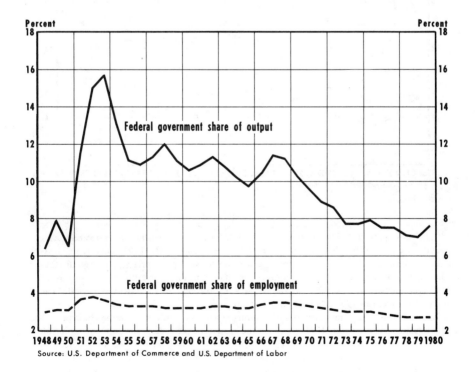

Source: U.S. Department of Commerce and U.S. Department of Labor

and the share of federal employment in civilian employment. Both of these measures peaked some years ago.[13] It is difficult to show that government has constrained output growth by altering the allocation of resources away from the private sector.[14]

How, then, has growth in the size of government adversely affected the supply side of the economy? Chart 5 shows the growth of federal

Chart 5   Federal Government Expenditures and Transfer Payments
As a Share of Output

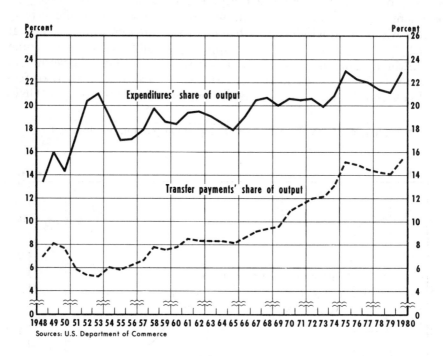

Sources: U.S. Department of Commerce

[13] The same pattern holds for state and local governments. The share of state and local government purchases of goods and services in GNP rose steadily until 1971 when it reached the 13 percent level. In 1973-75, the share surged upward to over 14 percent, and has subsequently declined to below 13 percent. Employees on state and local government payrolls as a percent of the civilian labor force also climbed steadily throughout the post-war period, peaking at about 13 percent in 1975, then declining slightly.

[14] Other forms of capital formation, including government, show the same showing as that in the business sector. From 1960 to 1973, the growth of the federal government capital stock was at a 1.1 percent rate; from 1973 to 1980, this growth rate declined to a 0.4 percent rate. For state and local governments, the decline was from a 4.8 percent to a 2.0 percent rate from 1973 to 1980. The growth of the residential housing stock declined from a 4.0 percent rate from 1948 to 1965, to a 2.7 percent rate from 1973 to 1980. Thus while inflation and the tax

the supply side of the economy? Chart 5 shows the growth of federal government expenditures (purchases of goods and services plus transfer payments) and transfer payments alone, with both measured as a share of GNP. The share of expenditures has grown due to the extremely rapid growth of transfer payments. The growth in transfer payments is the only likely candidate as a major source of government disincentives for production and growth.

Moreover, it is this type of fiscal development over which there is the greatest difference between demand and supply analysts. Demand analysts presume that tax increases to pay for increased transfer payments simply redistribute purchasing power with no real effects on demand, prices or aggregate output. From a supply analyst's view, such a policy produces a "double whammy," as both increased transfers and taxes provide disincentives to supplying resources in the market. But it must be emphasized that the trends in growth of resources do not indicate that the growing share of transfer payments has severely affected aggregate resource supplies.

THE OUTLOOK FOR SUPPLY-SIDE EFFECTS

While the past record does not indicate the possibility of revolutionary developments on the supply side of the economy, supply-oriented policies could modestly affect resource availability, economic efficiency and growth. As noted earlier, for example, higher marginal tax rates have negative effects on work effort. Thus, reductions in marginal rates should increase labor resource availability. In addition, supply-side policies can have modest *temporary* effects on investment and productivity growth.

Investment

The chart of the capital stock accelerated mildly (chart 2) following a move toward accelerated depreciation and the introduction of the investment tax credit in 1962, and the cut in individual and business marginal tax rates in 1964-65. Similar actions in late 1971 also appear to

system combined to reduce capital formation in business and divert some capital formation toward the housing sector, there was a slowing there. Even in owner-occupied housing, the sector with the greatest relative attractiveness, the growth rate of the housing stock declined from a 5.0 percent rate from 1948 to 1965 to a 3.2 percent rate from 1973 to 1980. See Musgrave, "Fixed Capital Stock" for data on these sectors.

have led to a mild subsequent acceleration. When the investment tax credit was suspended from October 1966 to March 1967 and again from April 1969 to December 1971, real producer durable investment slowed. From the third quarter of 1966 to the first quarter of 1967, real investment in equipment declined at a 3.0 percent rate, substantially slower than the 14.1 percent rate of expansion over the prior year or the 16.7 percent rate of the prior two years. From the first quarter of 1969 to the fourth quarter of 1971, such investment slowed to a 3.7 percent rate of growth. Over the prior year, such investment had risen at a 10.1 percent rate; it rose at a 9.6 percent rate for the two years ending in the first quarter of 1969. In the year following the end of each of these two suspensions, real investment in producer durables accelerated—to a 9.1 percent rate of growth in the first case, and to a 17.9 percent rate of growth in the second. From the end of 1962 to 1974, the constant dollar net stock of private nonresidential fixed capital rose at a 4.8 percent rate, much faster than the 3.5 percent rate of the prior decade, or the 3.0 percent rate from end of 1974 to the end of 1980.

Productivity

Accelerations in capital formation affect productivity growth. Nonetheless, improvements in the quantity and quality of plant and equipment do not yield massive changes in aggregate productivity. Most estimates of the impact of faster growth of plant and equipment show that a 1 percent increase in the growth rate of the capital stock adds no more than 0.3 percent to the growth rate of productivity. Thus, a 3 percentage-point increase in the pace of capital formation, extremely large by historical standards, would likely add less than 1 percent to the rate of advance of output per worker, or output per hour.

Also, most programs to cut the cost of plant and equipment for firms or to increase returns from investing in new capital only temporarily affect capital formation. Essentially, such policies raise the optimal amount of plant and equipment available per worker. According to economic theory, investment will accelerate to reach the optimal proportions, but is subsequently unaffected. This is important because it indicates that any added productivity growth from supply-oriented policies is temporary.

Inflation

The greatest controversy concerning recent supply-oriented proposals concerns the effect on inflation. Some advocates of supply-side economics contend that supply-oriented policies will contribute to the elimination of inflation.[15] The source of confusion in this analysis is a standard mark-up view of inflation that equates the inflation rate ($\dot{P}$) to the rate of increase in wage rates ($\dot{W}$), less the rate of productivity growth ($\dot{X}$). In this view, if productivity growth accelerates, then the rate of inflation slows (given the rate of increase in wages, $\dot{W}$). Even were this view correct, supply-oriented policies would provide little assistance for the anti-inflation effort. For the massive acceleration in capital formation and productivity growth in the example above, the pace of price increases would slow by less than 1 percentage point; even this gain would be as temporary as the acceleration in productivity growth.

But this mark-up view of inflation really has little to say about inflation. Instead, the equation tells something about the wedge between inflation of product prices and the rate of increase in resource prices, especially prices of labor; that is, the rate of increase in the purchasing power of wages, ($\dot{W} - \dot{P}$), equals the rate of increase in productivity, ($\dot{X}$). Consequently, faster productivity growth will increase the pace of growth of the purchasing power of wages, with little or no effect on the pace of wage and price inflation, *per se*. Since inflation is solely a monetary phenomenon, the only workable solution is to slow the growth in the supply of money.

At the other extreme, some supply-side critics argue that tax cuts, like those in the administration proposals, will lead to an increase in inflation.[16] This conclusion is based on the argument that tax cuts increase demand for the nation's output, since only part of the proceeds of a tax cut is saved, while the rest is spent. Two corollaries of this view are that a tax cut raises the deficit and that it causes higher interest rates. *Given* the nation's income or tax base, it is easy to see that the deficit increases. Also, the government must replace the funds involved in a tax cut by borrowing (assuming government expenditures remain the same), but only part of the cut is available for lending, that is, the portion saved. Consequently, interest rates will tend to rise to attract the additional lending required and to bid funds away from private sector borrowers.

The conceptual shortcomings of this view are equally well known. The burden of government expenditures on household budgets is not measured by current taxes, but rather by the expenditures themselves. If current taxes are insufficient to pay for current expenditures, then either future taxes must be raised to pay the interest costs on a larger

---

[15] See, for example, the analysis in the Joint Economic Committee, *Outlook for the 1980's*, pp. 11-14.

[16] An example of this argument is found in "Ease Off Kemp-Roth," *The New York Times*, May 15, 1981.

debt, or the debt can remain the same, if the Federal Reserve finances the additional portion by expanding the money supply faster. In the latter case, households pay the remainder of current taxes through higher inflation rates. Since the wealth and income of the economy is unaffected by a tax cut, it cannot lead to higher spending. A second problem is that even if individuals incorrectly perceive their wealth as larger after a tax cut and attempt to spend more on goods and services, a tax cut would indeed imply a shortage of funds in financial markets to finance the larger deficit. Interest rates would have to rise by enough to reduce spending to its original level.

For example, if taxes were cut $50 billion and neither government expenditures nor the Federal Reserve's holding of government debt were changed, the government would have to borrow an additional $50 billion. Now if individuals initially planned to spend $40 billion while saving only $10 billion of the tax cut, the excess borrowing requirement would be the amount of increased private spending, $40 billion. As the government attempts to raise the additional $40 billion in credit markets, interest rates would rise to increase household savings or reduce the borrowing and spending of other borrowers. Whether the $40 billion is attracted through more saving (less consumer spending) or less business borrowing (less investment spending), total spending will tend to be unaffected by the tax cut. In summary, a tax cut may cause interest rates to rise, but is unlikely to affect total spending demands and, therefore, inflation.

The difficulties encountered by the higher deficits/interest rates/inflation argument are not simply logical shortcomings. First, the tax cuts envisioned by the administration are accompanied by spending reductions, so there will tend to be little effect on the deficit or on interest rates. Second, the Kemp-Roth "cuts" in taxes are likely only to offset bracket creep over the next three years; thus, they are not really cuts in current taxes at all, simply offsets to keep average and marginal rates from rising due to current and prospective inflation.[17] Finally, the experience surrounding the 1964 Kennedy tax cut and the 1975 tax cut would not support the higher deficits/interest rates/inflation scenario even if the administration were proposing a cut in taxes. In the 1964 case, the deficit rose very slightly and briefly, but interest rates did not

---

[17] This argument has been made by, among others, Martin Feldstein, "'No Real Tax Cut' in Administration Plan," *New York Journal of Commerce,* May 21, 1981. This point has also been made recently by Walter H. Heller, "Supply-Side Follies of 1981," *Wall Street Journal,* June 12, 1981. Heller uses this point as part of an argument against the Kemp-Roth cuts. The cuts would keep marginal rates from rising further, however, so they would avoid a further deterioration in incentives over the next few years. This argument merely indicates that Kemp-Roth type cuts will have to be much larger to eliminate the impact of past inflation on marginal tax rates and incentives, not that such cuts are ineffective.

rise until well after the tax cut.[18] Inflation did begin to worsen, but only in response to the acceleration in money growth that began in 1963.

In 1975, federal taxes were reduced by increasing exemptions and the standard deduction. In that instance, the deficit rose sharply but interest rates did not. The 1975 tax cut was not associated with a more expansionary monetary policy. Instead, the growth rate of money stock for the year ending in the fourth quarter of 1974 was 4.7 percent; for 1975 it was 4.9 percent. These rates followed the rapid pace of monetary expansion at a 6.1 percent rate during the previous five years (ending in IV/1974). Consequently, inflation (GNP deflator) slowed, declining from a 7.7 percent rate in the year ending in the fourth quarter of 1974 to 4.7 percent in the year ending in the fourth quarter of 1975. Thus, even when a tax cut does not lower marginal rates, and/or the deficit increases as in 1975, it is not the case that interest rates must rise or that inflation must accelerate.[19]

CONCLUSION

Traditional macroeconomic policies affect the allocation, efficiency and growth rate of the supply of resources in an economy. These effects have been central to discussions of stabilization policies for centuries, but with few exceptions have been ignored in the post-war era. The reemphasis of these effects is what "supply-side economics" is all about.

There is little evidence to support the notion that supply-oriented policies will work miracles in restoring productivity growth or in reducing inflation. Indeed, it is difficult historically to see any major disruptions of aggregate resource supply or allocation that are sufficiently profound to explain the stagflationary performance of the U.S. economy since the early '70s. Only in the area of recent capital formation is there a clear resource supply shortfall and this is fully explained by supply forces other than government policy (energy price increases).[20]

---

[19] On the tenuous link between budget deficits and inflation, see Scott E. Hein, "Deficits and Inflation," this *Review*, (March 1981), pp. 3-10.

[20] The principal determinants of stagflationary developments since 1973 and 1979-80 have been sharp increases in the relative price of energy—supply shocks. These increases fully account for the post-1973 decline in the pace of capital formation as well. For a more detailed discussion, see John A. Tatom, "Energy Prices and Capital Formation: 1972-77," this *Review* (May 1979), pp. 2-11, and Tatom, "The Productivity Problem."

At the same time, however, the historical record clearly indicates that supply-oriented policies can modestly affect resource availability, especially capital formation. Also, economic theory indicates a number of disincentives created by the tax system in an inflationary environment. While the magnitude of these disincentive effects is difficult to establish empirically, few economists or policymakers disagree with the importance of remedying these defects in macroeconomic policy.

The administration's economic policy proposals have incited a great popular debate over supply-side economics. Ironically, the proposals are quite modest in their supply-side orientation. The initial proposals address the disincentive effects of past policy and are not aimed at breaking the link between inflation and the supply of resources and output. Moreover, the proposed individual income tax cuts are sufficiently small so as to maintain marginal tax rates at current levels, rather than lower them.

No doubt, the issues raised by supply analysts will be of central importance for some time to come as policymakers face the continuing challenges to break the inflation-supply linkage, as well as to stay ahead of the deterioration in incentives to work, save and invest due to the cumulative effects of past fiscal, regulatory and monetary policy. It is likely that, when the smoke clears, it will be impossible to say that one can disregard the supply effects of policy any longer. But then the exaggerated claims or hopes of some supply analysts will be forgotten as well. Over a decade ago, Milton Friedman noted that, "In one sense, we are all Keynesians now; in another, no one is a Keynesian any longer." It is likely that a similar characterization will soon be an apt description of supply-side economics.

33

Supply-Side Economics:
What Chance for Success*

ARIS PROTOPAPADAKIS[†]

The economic success of the 1960s gave way to unfulfilled expectations in the 1970s. The U.S. economy failed to deliver the price stability and the generally high growth of real income that had come to be expected. Perceiving this as the failure of Keynesian economic policies, some economists have advocated tax cuts and reductions in government regulations as the solution to the economic malaise that threatens to dominate the 1980s. These supply-side prescriptions represent a resurfacing of economic thinking dominant before the Great Depression.

The likely impact and success of supply-side economics were an important feature of the tax reform debate in the 1980 Presidential campaign. The emphasis on tax cuts in the campaign as well as the tax proposals of the new Administration reflect inroads of supply-side economics on the policymaking process. Whether this approach will work, however, is not clear.

THE 1970S: INFLATION AND SLOW GROWTH

During the 1970s, the U.S. economy experienced a high rate of inflation and a low growth rate of output. The growth rate of productivity (output per hour worked) came to a halt in the later 1970s, in contrast to the 1950s and 1960s. Furthermore, the share of income that the Federal, state, and local governments took through various taxes was

*Reprinted from *Business Review*, May/June 1981, Federal Reserve Bank of Philadelphia.
†Aris Protopapadakis is Research Officer and Economist at the Philadelphia Fed. He received his Ph.D. from the University of Chicago.

higher in this decade than at any other time (Figure 1), resulting in a decline in the per capita real income that goes to the private sector in the latter part of the decade. The average rate of inflation as measured by the CPI also was higher in this decade, and it increased alarmingly in 1977-79.

Figure 1   Productivity Growth Flattens Out . . .

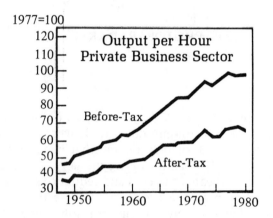

Source: Survey of Current Business.

. . . As Government Takes More in Taxes

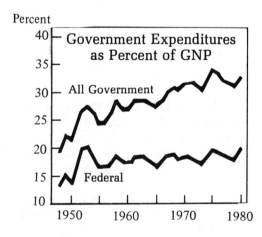

Source: Calculated at the Federal Reserve Bank of Philadelphia.

Inflation has been viewed both as a direct source of the economic malaise and as the reason for the poor output performance of the economy. Most economists and businessmen believe that at least in the short run the performance of the economy is not independent of the rate of inflation. Inflation is viewed as causing increased uncertainty in the business environment, higher and more volatile interest rates, automatic increases in taxes, and depreciation of the dollar vis-a-vis other currencies.

Though most people agree that stagnating productivity and high inflation are undesirable, there is much less agreement about their causes and cures. Some argue that the low and falling investment rate causes productivity to stagnate, which worsens inflation. Others contend that the high inflation rates reduce incentives to save while the accompanying uncertainty reduces incentives to invest, sapping productivity growth. Causes and consequences are hard to sort out.

One school of thought, generally referred to as supply-side economics, recently has gained attention with tax and expenditure cut proposals. The basic claim is that the economic stagnation of the 1970s is a result of increasing taxes on all forms of income that have reduced incentives to produce and invest, and that reducing these taxes will restore productivity growth.

DEMAND MANAGEMENT VS SUPPLY-SIDE ECONOMICS

Supply-side economics is firmly rooted in classical economic theory. Until the Great Depression, economists believed that government could increase the level of ouput only by implementing policies that increase financial incentives to produce. But economists were unable to reconcile the high and persistent unemployment of the Great Depression with the teachings of classical economic theory. They eventually came to conclude that a slowdown of the growth of output was evidence that labor and capital were not being fully utilized because they were *involuntarily* idle, so that increasing financial rewards to production would not increase output or reduce unemployment. The policy prescriptions of classical economics were viewed as bankrupt and demand management was born.

Demand Management. Economic policy since World War II has been dominated by demand management policies. Demand management (often referred to as Keynesian economics) is the attempt to increase output by increasing demand for it, through government policies.

There are two fundamental premises of demand management. One is that the level of economic activity can be affected in predictable and persistent ways by fiscal and monetary policies. The other is that the economy often experiences under-utilization of labor (unemployment) and capital as a result of the failure of markets to work satisfactorily. Since these underutilized resources could be put to work if more demand were forthcoming, Keynesians argue that it is up to the government to design policies aimed at increasing aggregate demand.

The two traditional tools of demand management are monetary and fiscal policy. To expand aggregate demand through monetary policy, the Federal Reserve increases the growth rate of the money supply above its longer term trend. This temporarily decreases the cost of borrowing to firms, which spurs investment and increases consumption demand as consumers try to spend the excess money. To expand aggregate demand through fiscal policy, the government can increase expenditures or reduce taxes. Demand increases directly, as government buys more goods and services or leaves more disposable income with consumers, part of which they choose to spend.

These traditional economic policies appeared to work reasonably well until the late 1960s. Since that time, it has become increasingly clear that the economy does not consistently respond in the way Keynesian economists predict; indeed, sometimes the response seems opposite to what they expect, as during periods when inflation and unemployment have risen simultaneously. This suggests that low productivity growth and high inflation might persist in spite of—some say because of—demand management policies.

The Supply-Side View.   The main claim of supply-side economics is that aggregate economic behavior will respond measurably to changes in financial incentives, and in particular to those incentives that are affected by the economic policies of the government. Why? Because all the goods and services in the economy are produced by people. People are hired by firms or are self-employed; in either case they use tools, machines, computers, and communication systems to produce those goods and services. In a decentralized economic system the number and kinds of tools, machines, computers built, and how much each person works are a result of individual decisions in response to financial incentives in the markets. The cost of borrowing to finance investment, wages earned from employment, and the tax rates on income are three examples of financial incentives. As any of these incentives is changed, individuals may change their decisions about what kinds of jobs they want and how hard they want to work, while firms may change their investment and employment plans.

Recent economic research has shown some reasons why the level of output is not likely to respond to demand management policies in predictable ways.[1] It argues that increased production requires the perception of higher rewards for working and investing—that output does not respond automatically to higher demand. If no additional incentives to produce are generated, increased demand is more likely to lead to higher prices than to more output. Proponents of supply-side policies therefore argue that the obvious remedy to stagnating growth is to concentrate economic policies on restoring the incentives to work and save, since it would be the only reliable way to increase aggregate output and productivity.

The principal supply-side policies that are currently advocated are reductions in tax rates on labor and capital income. Supply-siders claim that lower tax rates on wages, interest, dividends, and corporate income will increase output by increasing the incentives to work, increasing the supply of labor, and by increasing the incentives to save and invest. They also argue that the rapid increase in tax rates since the 1964 tax cut is largely responsible for the fall in the growth rate of productivity because it has diminished incentives to work and save. Thus, decreasing taxes will restore these incentives and cause an expansion of output.

Many economists are skeptical about these supply-side prescriptions. They believe that cutting taxes will significantly increase neither the supply of labor nor the supply of saving. What is the evidence? What, for example, have economists found out about the effect of taxes on labor?

REDUCING TAXES ON LABOR INCOME

There are many economic studies of how the work force in the U.S. has behaved as wages have changed.[2] Since a tax cut results in an after-tax increase in wages, these studies may offer a guide to how the labor force will respond to a tax cut.

Studies to date generally agree that prime-age males do not measurably alter the number of hours they work in response to changes in their wages over time. But other groups, which comprise an increasing share

---

[1] See Donald J. Mullineaux, "On Active and Passive Monetary Policies: What Have We Learned from the Rational Expectations Debate?" *Business Review,* Federal Reserve Bank of Philadelphia, November/December 1979.

[2] Harvey Rosen, "What is Labor Supply and Do Taxes Affect It?" *American Economic Review 70,* 2 (May 1980), pp. 171-176, and Jerry Hausman, "Income and Payroll Tax Policy and Labor Supply," paper presented at a conference on "The Supply Side Effects of Economic Policy," Washington University and the Federal Reserve Bank of St. Louis, October 24-25, 1980.

of the work force, appear more responsive to wage changes.[3] One recent study, for instance, shows evidence that married women vary their
work habits in response to changing wages: a 10-percent increase in the
wage rate increases the number of hours they work by more than 10
percent. The number of workers also appears to respond differentially
to tax rate changes. One estimate suggests that a percentage-point reduction in personal income taxes will increase the primary labor force
by only 0.05 percent, but the secondary labor force rises 0.37 percent.[4]
The net increase in employment hours (stemming from more workers
and some people working more) from the same tax reduction is estimated
at 0.5 percent.

There are other points to consider. The decision about when to retire
appears to depend on after-tax income. If the tax rates are high, take-
home pay is low relative to retirement pay and people choose to retire
early. Thus a decline in the tax rates may expand the supply of labor by
postponing retirement plans. Also, evidence from a study done on self-
employed individuals shows that both their hours worked and their intensity of work are highly sensitive to after-tax income and therefore to
tax rate cuts.[5]

To put things in rough perspective, a tax cut that would induce a 10-
percent increase in the supply of labor would result in a 7-percent to
10-percent increase in output, spread over the time period necessary for
the adjustment to be completed (which could take several years.[6] In
current dollars, this represents only a $190-billion to $270-billion increase in the full-employment GNP. Under optimistic assumptions, such
an increase could be obtained through a decrease of roughly 14 percentage points (roughly a 40-percent reduction in the marginal tax rates
on labor income).[7] These estimates are subject to a large margin of error.
It is also the case, however, that if the percentage of the secondary labor
force in the total labor force continues to increase, the responsiveness
of the total labor supply to tax cuts may well rise beyond the level assumed in this calculation.

---

[3] Prime-age males made up almost 70 percent of the work force in 1964 but only 56 percent
of the work force in 1977.

[4] Michael Evans, "An Econometric Model Incorporating the Supply Side Effects of Economic Policy," paper presented at a conference on "The Supply Side Effects of Economic Policy,"
Washington University and the Federal Reserve Bank of St. Louis, October 24-25, 1980.

[5] Terrance Wales, "Estimation of a Labor Supply Curve for Self-Employed Business Proprie-
tors," *International Economic Review* 14 (February 1973), pp. 69-80.

[6] The 7-percent increase in output will be a result of the increase in the supply of labor. The
additional 3 percent will be because as additional savings get converted into physical capital the
capital-to-labor ratio will return to its original value (K/L will initially fall as the labor force increases).

[7] This calculation relies on a simple Cobb-Douglas production function ($Y = K^{0.3}L^{0.7}$),
where Y is real income, K is capital, and L is labor. The increase in output would be 7 percent

What Kind of a Tax Cut? Taxes on labor income can be cut either by reducing the average taxes collected on income (the average tax rate), or by reducing the marginal tax rate on income—the tax a person pays on a dollar of *additional* income. Will these different ways of cutting taxes have different effects? To answer this question it is necessary to find out how changes in the wage rate affect the supply of labor.

A measure of the incentive that most affects people's willingness to work is the hourly take-home pay. Increasing the hourly pay has two separate and opposite effects on individuals. First, it results in more income for the same work, and this induces people to work fewer hours. But since the wage rate is higher, the income in additional wages people give up by not working more is higher. This induces them to work more hours. These two forces (the income effect and the substitution effect) work against one another.[8] Whether an increase in the hourly take-home pay will induce people to work more or less depends on which effect dominates.

Both the marginal and average tax rates on labor income affect how much people decide to work. (Progressive income tax schedules assure that the marginal tax rate is always higher than the average tax rate.) People will respond differently to changes in their marginal tax rates than in their average tax rates, because of the way in which the income and substitution effects operate. To see how this works, take a fictitious example of an individual who earns $25,000 a year, and whose total deductions come to $5,000. Also suppose that the tax rate for income between $15,000 and $25,000 is 30 percent, while for below $15,000 the rate is 20 percent. This taxpayer computes her taxes to be $4,500.[9] Her marginal tax rate is 30 percent while her average tax rate is only 18 percent.

Reducing her *average* tax rate but not her marginal tax rate can be accomplished by increasing her allowable personal deductions. If she

---

if capital remains fixed but 10 percent if the capital-to-labor ratio remains fixed. The primary labor force (55 percent of the total) is assumed to increase its work hours by .5 percent in response to a 10-percent increase in wages, while the secondary labor force responds with a 10-percent increase. The average marginal tax rate is taken to be 33 percent.

[8] Since work is the opposite of leisure, working reduces an individual's utility, everything else remaining equal. More income from increased wages for the same amount of leisure, therefore, will cause an individual to increase his leisure and utility. This is the income effect. The increase in wage rate, however, makes the opportunity cost of leisure (income foregone to obtain leisure) higher. If his income is kept the same, an individual will prefer to work more. This is the substitution effect. Whether an increase in the average wage rate results in an increase in the supply of labor depends on people's preferences and incomes. It is obvious that with sufficiently high incomes the utility of additional income will be sufficiently small so that an increase in the wage rate will decrease the supply of labor.

[9] She pays 0.2 × $15,000 = $3,000 on the first $15,000 reported income and 0.3 × $5,000 = $1,500 on the remaining $5,000. Her average tax rate is 4,500/25,000 = 18 percent.

were allowed to deduct $4,000 more, her total taxes would be only $3,300, her average tax rate would drop to 13.2 percent, but her marginal tax rate would remain at 30 percent. How would she respond to this tax cut? Since she has a higher income for the same hours worked, she will be likely to work less (income effect). Since her marginal tax rate hasn't changed, the substitution effect will not operate to counteract the income effect.

By contrast, a widening of the tax brackets will decrease her *marginal* tax rate but not her average tax rate—for instance income up to $25,000 may now be taxed at 18 percent. In this case, her average tax rate will remain at 18 percent but her marginal tax rate will drop to 18 percent. How would she respond? Since she will earn the same income as before by working the same number of hours, she has no incentive to reduce her hours worked. In other words, the income effect does not operate. But since her marginal tax rate has fallen, it is more lucrative to work more hours than it used to be (substitution effect), and she would be likely to work more.

The response of labor supply to a tax reform package is not easy to predict. If both marginal and average tax rates are reduced, then the overall effect on the supply of labor will come from the interaction of the income and substitution effects which is difficult to gauge. But if, as a result of the revenue loss, government services are reduced along with the tax cut, the aggregate labor supply will respond much as it would to a cut in marginal tax rates alone. The reason is that individuals will have to pay directly for services they are receiving through their tax dollars, so that the combination of the tax cuts and the reduction in government services will leave them with roughly the same income as before. Since the income effect is severely limited, the response of labor will reflect mainly the substitution effect, which should mean an *increase* in hours worked.

Most labor studies have not measured the income and substitution effects separately. Thus, we know very little about the magnitude of each effect alone. It is clear, however, that a tax cut that primarily reduces *marginal* tax rates rather than *average* rates will have the most impact, and almost certainly increase the supply of labor.

REDUCING TAXES ON CAPITAL INCOME

An additional way in which incentives to produce can be increased is to reduce taxes levied on the return to capital, or capital income. These are taxes collected directly from corporations via the corporate income tax and from consumers via taxes on dividends, interest income, and capital gains. The claim of supply-siders is that a reduction in taxes on capital income will increase the incentives to save by increasing the after-tax return to capital.

Taxes on the returns to capital have been growing steadily for two separate reasons. One is that income tax rates have been rising. The other is the way the tax code interacts with inflation. The existing tax code does not distinguish real capital gains (which occur only when the value of an asset changes *relative* to that of goods and services) from the rise in the dollar value of an asset caused by inflation. If the price of a share goes up by 6 percent while inflation is 10 percent, the real value of the asset has *declined* by 4 percent, but the tax system treats the 6-percent increase as a capital gain. The tax code affects interest receipts in roughly the same way. Interest receipts usually are treated as taxable income (interest on state and local securities is tax exempt), even though most if not all of them simply offset the rate of inflation. In an economic environment where the inflation rate is rising, as it was in the 1970s, the current tax code ensures that the tax rates on capital income will rise and the after-tax return to its owners will fall, for the same quantity of installed capital—plant and machinery.

Taxes on capital income reduce the return to the owners of the claims to this capital (stocks, bonds, and business loans). And this is equally true whether these taxes are collected from individuals in the form of income and capital gain taxes or from businesses in the form of profits taxes. Increasing the returns to capital may induce people to save more or less; the outcome again depends on a balancing of the income and substitution effects. A higher return to capital will make the future rewards from saving higher, which will encourage saving. This is the substitution effect once again. But higher returns mean that the future income from accumulated savings will be higher, so that people don't have to save as much or as long to get the same future consumption. This is the income effect, and it works to discourage saving.

While economists disagree about the impact of higher rates of return on savings, there is a consensus that the economy needs to generate more saving. Since gross saving represents the difference between what is produced and what is consumed in the economy, saving a higher proportion of income will make more resources available for the production of capital goods, increasing the amount of physical capital and research and development, both of which lead to higher per capita output in the future.

Economists have tried to find out how savings is likely to respond to higher rates of return by analyzing historical evidence. Early studies of consumption and saving found saving behavior to be insensitive to rates of return. A recent study by Boskin, however, has documented a substantial impact of after-tax returns on gross saving.[10] He found that a 10-percent increase in the real (actual returns adjusted for inflation) after-tax rate of return will result in an increase of approximately 2 percent to 4 percent in available savings each year, which would result in an overall increase in the full-employment GNP of 1 to 2 percent.[11] This means that halving of the tax levied on the returns to capital could result in a permanent increase in saving of 31 percent and an eventual increase in GNP of 10 to 17 percent (250 to 420 billion current dollars).[12] Evans also finds a significant correlation between savings and the after-tax real rate of return. He calculates that a one-percentage-point increase in this return would raise saving by $12 billion or by 2 to 3 percent.

Economists are far from agreeing on the magnitude of the impact of a tax cut aimed at stimulating saving. The estimates discussed here must be viewed as preliminary and probably optimistic. Changes in marginal tax rates again have a different effect on saving than changes in average tax rates. A decrease in the marginal tax rate will trigger the substitution effect response and will increase the supply of saving, while a decrease in the average tax rate only will operate through the income effect and will reduce the supply of saving. A tax reform designed primarily to reduce the *marginal* tax rates on capital income seems likely to result in moderate increases in the saving rate and in the full-employment GNP.

Can tax cuts increase the growth rate of productivity? How quickly will tax cuts work? How will they affect inflation? What will be the impact on the Federal deficit (see CAN TAX CUTS PAY FOR THEM—SELVES?)? These are the questions most often asked about supply-side economics. The answers are neither simple nor precise.

CAN SUPPLY-SIDE ECONOMICS WORK?

The supply-side logic and a small body of evidence suggest that reducing marginal tax rates on labor income will increase the supply of

[10] This study has come under some criticism and has been discussed extensively. For a good summary of the issues and criticisms, see Charles McClure, Jr., "Taxes, Saving and Welfare: Theory and Evidence," *National Tax Journal* 33, 3 (September 1980), pp. 311-320.

[11] This value is calculated from the same production function as before, but assuming that labor supply does not respond to the higher wages that will result from the increased productivity.

[12] This calculation is meant to be illustrative, because it is very difficult to take into account all the complexities of the tax laws. It is assumed that all returns to capital are taxed at a 35-percent average tax rate, that the inflation rate is 10 percent, and that the average return is 17 percent before tax. This implies an after-tax real return of 1.05 percent at 35-percent tax and 4.025 percent at 17.5-percent tax.

CAN TAX CUTS PAY FOR THEMSELVES?

Some supply-siders maintain that tax cuts will generate enough additional economic activity so that total tax receipts will not decline. A reduction in tax rates obviously will result in lower receipts to the Treasury at a given level of national income. But more tax revenue will be forthcoming if national income increases. If tax incentives increase income by enough, the new receipts will offset the losses from the tax cut, and the government budget will not show any additional deficits. This idea dates back to eighteenth-century economists, and has recently been revived by Professor Laffer as the "Laffer Curve."

There is no doubt that at sufficiently high tax levels this scenario can take place. But most economists are very skeptical that, at current tax rates, supplies of labor and saving will respond strongly enough to tax cuts to prevent an increase in the deficit. Fullerton, for example, calculates that even with optimistic assumptions about the response of labor, the average tax rate on wages would have to be well above 40 percent before tax cuts would pay for themselves.* And even if the deficit created by the tax cuts turned out to be small following all adjustments of labor and capital decisions, the deficits would be much larger in the beginning while the adjustment process gets under way, creating an interim need for large deficit financing.

There are some offsetting considerations, however. Some economists estimate the underground economy—that area of activity where transactions go unrecorded—to be as large as 33 percent of reported GNP.† If the reduction in the tax rates causes a significant portion of this economy to become legitimate, a tax cut might well pay for itself. In addition, individuals and corporations should find it less worthwhile to employ tax shelters at lower tax rates; if they report higher taxable income, Treasury revenues will increase. On balance, it doesn't seem likely that tax cuts will pay for themselves, though the resulting deficits are unlikely to be as disastrous as some opponents of supply-siders predict.

*Don Fullerton, "On the Possibility of an Inverse Relationship Between Tax Rates and Government Revenues," *National Bureau of Economic Research,* Working Paper No. 467, April 1980.

†Edgar Feige, "How Big Is the Irregular Economy?" *Challenge,* November-December 1979.

labor somewhat, while the same kind of reduction in taxes on capital income will increase the supply of saving and allow investment to rise. As a result of either type of tax cut, output will be higher in the future than it would be without the tax cuts. During the transition, as workers adjust their work habits and increased investment builds up the physical capital stock, the *growth rate* of output will be higher than it otherwise would be. For instance, it was noted above that a 14-percentage-point decrease in the marginal tax rates on labor income might result in as much as $270-billion total increase in output. In this scenario, output would grow by 3.5 percentage points more a year if the adjustment took as long as 7 years. Once the adjustment was complete, however, the *growth rates* of GNP and productivity would return to their longer term trend, though their *level* would always be higher.

The total marginal income tax rate has been climbing since 1964, in spite of periodic tax rate cuts (See Figure 2).[13] The principal reason is that as dollar incomes rise, individuals are pushed into higher tax brackets. This phenomenon, called bracket creep, will cause tax rates to continue rising automatically as long as inflation persists. Supply-siders argue that this continually growing disincentive is responsible for the low productivity growth in recent years. A tax reform that would reduce taxes, and more importantly keep them at the new rates, would allow productivity to grow permanently faster than it has in the recent past.

How quickly labor supply may respond to the tax cuts is hard to know. There are severe technical problems that make it difficult to measure accurately how quickly labor supply has responded to shifts in financial incentives in the past, as well as how quickly the U.S. economy has adjusted to the resulting changes in the supply of labor. The last question is important, because output will rise not because the supply of labor has increased but because more labor is employed. The circumstances surrounding the tax cut will affect the adjustment process and will determine whether and how output will respond in the short run. For instance, if people believe that tax cuts are likely to be reversed in the future, they will not significantly change their work habits or substantially change their consumption and saving patterns. Nor are firms likely to undertake major additional investments if they perceive the tax cuts as transitory. Unless tax reductions are viewed as permanent, there will be only a small response to the tax cuts at best.

Another important element in the adjustment process is the type of policy that accompanies a tax cut. The short-term impact of tax reductions is not likely to be the same as their long-term impact. Because the supply-side effects of tax cuts will appear slowly, the policies that accompany the tax cuts will, to a large extent, determine the economy's response in the short term. All tax cuts have demand-side implications.

---

[13] Michael Evans, "Reagan Plan Hinges on Tax Brackets," *The New York Times*, December 23, 1980, calculates that a 10-percent increase in personal income results in a 15-percent increase in personal income taxes.

Figure 2   Combined Marginal Income Tax Rate Continues to Rise

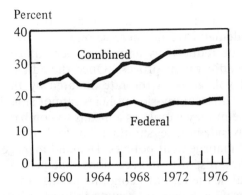

*The combined average marginal rate shown includes
Federal and state income taxes and social security taxes.
Most of the combined increase is made up of increases
in state income tax and social security tax rates.

A cut in taxes without a similar cut in government expenditures will probably cause an increase in the demand for goods and services, with higher prices and interest rates over the short term. This will facilitate the output adjustment by increasing the demand for labor and physical capital, but it will also likely mean a higher inflation rate and lower investment during the transition. If, on the other hand, government expenditures are reduced by roughly the same amount (to keep the deficit from growing), demand in the sectors that that depend on government financed programs will fall, while demand in the sectors dealing with consumers and business firms will rise. This will mean imbalances in employment throughout the economy that may take a while to work out, masking the supply-side effects of the tax cuts. But inflation during the adjustment would likely be lower than in the case where government spending is not reduced.

Can the supply-side effects of tax cuts help reduce the rate of inflation? The answer is disappointing: not by much. Over the long haul, inflation is basically the result of two economic forces. One is the demand for money (in terms of its purchasing power) and the other is the supply of money in dollars. If the real demand for money increases at 3 percent as a result of growth in output, stable prices require that the supply of money increase roughly by 3 percent. If however, the supply of money increases by 12 percent, then prices will increase by about 9 percent. It follows that tax cuts will reduce inflation at a given rate of money supply growth only if they increase the growth in the demand for money by increasing output growth. The consensus estimate from current studies is that a 10-percent increase in output will cause about a 6-percent increase in the real demand for money. Thus, if supply-side initiatives were to increase output by, say, 10 percent over a six-year period, money demand would increase one percentage point a year and inflation would be reduced by about one percentage point a year, but *only* during the adjustment process. Once the adjustment is complete, money demand will grow at the rate dictated by the long-run growth rate of output. Thus, supply-side policies cannot substitute for restraining growth in the money supply as a means to combat inflation.

Finally, supply-side policies should not be looked at to replace counter-cyclical demand-management policies. Demand management may be the appropriate policy response to recessions that periodically are brought about by special sequences of economic events. But these policies are ill suited to improving long-term growth in productivity and output, because they don't necessarily increase incentives to produce, save, and invest. Supply-side policies do precisely that, but they are likely to work slowly and therefore can't be used to combat recessions.

To sum up, the major claim of supply-side economics is that increasing incentives to produce and save by cutting taxes will increase the level of output and labor productivity and may temporarily reduce the rate of inflation. The available evidence indicates that such cuts, if properly designed, are likely to yield moderate gains in output and productivity. But once-and-for-all tax cuts should increase the growth rate of income and productivity only while the economy is adjusting to the new conditions. It is less likely that inflation can be significantly reduced through supply-side policies because the temporary increases in the growth rate of output are likely to be small and because they will have an even smaller impact on the demand for money. Money supply growth more in line with growth in real output is an unavoidable part of a viable anti-inflation policy.

34

"Demythologizing" Supply-Side Economics[*]

MICHAEL K. EVANS

It has now become painfully obvious that we are in the midst of another recession which will result in real Gross National Product declining 5% this quarter. Even if the economy snaps out of its slide in the next few months, we will still have budget deficits of $100 billion for the next two fiscal years. Does this mean a pauper's burial for supply-side economics?

Clearly much more has gone wrong than right in the economy this year. Yet the "voodoo economics" critics of supply-side policies are just as far off base in their own comments. They predicted that inflation would intensify if these programs were implemented, whereas it has declined sharply since the waning days of the Carter administration. The one thing nobody predicted was another recession coinciding with the onset of massive tax and spending cuts.

I have always stressed that it is foolish to expect overnight results from supply-side economics, that it would take two to three years before these programs would be translated into the realization of higher growth side by side with lower inflation. Yet their attempt to sell this program to the American public caused the Reagan administration, led by ersatz whiz kid David Stockman, to invent three myths. None of these has been found to have any basis in reality, and when taken together they have gone far to mask and even derail the true accomplishments of supply-side economics.

Myth No. 1: As soon as the financial markets saw the Reagan program, they would become so enchanted with the new plan that interest

*Michael K. Evans is President, Evans Economics, Inc., Washington, D.C. Reprinted from *The Cincinnati Enquirer,* December 2, 1981.

rates would drop immediately, even before the budget and spending cuts went into effect. This decline in interest rates would immediately be translated into lower rates of inflation, largely because of the importance of mortgage rates in figuring the Consumer Price Index. This would in turn lower inflation even further because of cost-of-liveing clauses and other similar relationships and we would reverse the vicious cycle of inflation overnight.

What actually happened, of course, was that the business and financial communities always had grave doubts about the new Reagan program, and the more they heard about it, the less they liked it. Consequently, long-term interest rates rose a full 3 percentage points from the time of Mr. Reagan's election until the verification of the recession in October.

Myth No. 2: The combination of tight monetary and easy fiscal policies could be used to bring about lower inflation and higher real growth simultaneously. Tight money would keep inflation down, and lower tax rates would be used to stimulate capital spending.

What happened to this theory was that, with its implementation, the housing industry virtually went out of business; car sales plummeted to 23-year lows and aggregate demand shirveled, capacity utilization plunged and profits collapsed. Production in key industries was as much as 25% below 1979 peaks as order backlogs shrank and the economy ground to a halt.

Myth No. 3: Businessmen would take the optimistic results of the Reagan program on faith and would increase capital spending in advance of the rise in demand and decline in interest rates.

In this case, new orders for capital goods had been increasing significantly as the Reagan tax package was building to a climax. Once the bill was actually signed, however, new orders did a 180% turn and plummeted more than 10% in the first two months after the tax cut was passed. This has been highlighted by the near-record 8% decline in durable goods new orders for October.

Now that these myths have been exposed, we can turn to a brief summary of how supply-side economics really works.

Personal tax cuts raise the rate of return on saving, hence increasing personal saving and reducing consumption. Higher personal saving is eventually translated into lower interest rates and higher investment. This increases productivity, which lowers inflation and fosters an increase in real income and economic growth. Providing that government spending declines in line with inflation, higher real growth eventually reduces the budget deficit.

All this sounds great—except that none of these reactions happens immediately. In the short run, the net effect is to *lower* growth and *increase* the budget deficit before the beneficial aspects start to take over, for an increase in savings means a decrease in demand before higher investment takes up the slack. If inflation declines, the deficit widens further, since tax receipts are based on incomes in nominal terms.

Despite the time lags involved before supply-side economics begins to show its positive side, we still could have had higher growth rates and lower deficits next year had the Fed decided to lower interest rates during the summer. However, as long as the administration was laboring under the handicap of Myth No. 2, rates stayed high while the economy withered on the vine.

Because these three myths dominated policy-making for much of the year, and because the original implementation of much of the supply-side program was delayed by almost a full year, we are now saddled with another recession instead of the great new vistas promised by the Reagan administration.

To return to the question raised at the beginning of this article, we are still likely to reap some of the benefits of supply-side economics in 1983 and 1984, with real growth averaging better than 4% and inflation stabilizing around 7%. However, it is unlikely that any more supply-side changes will be implemented in the future.

The unemployment rate will remain about 8% between now and the 1982 election and while real growth will pick up later in 1982, the economy will still be in lousy shape a year from now. This will present the Democrats with a tailor-made opportunity to increase their lead in the House and perhaps even regain the Senate, although the arithmetic works against them in the latter case. Thus Mr. Reagan could face a much more hostile Congress during the second half of his term, with the likely result that any further moves toward major tax and spending cuts will be stymied.

As a result, productivity growth will probably return to a 1.5% annual rate, clearly an improvement over present circumstances but far below the 3% average increase registered during the first 20 years of the postwar period. The rate of inflation will stabilize around 7% but will not decline to the 4% rate which was originally set as an "interim" target by 1984. The unemployment rate will stay above 8% in 1982 and 7% in 1983. With the continuing large budget deficits, the spread between short-term interest rates and inflation will remain in the 3% to 4% range instead of declining to the long-run historical average of less than 1%

Half a loaf is better than none and even the existing Reagan programs are certainly preferable to the bankrupt economics of the Carter administration, which led to permanent double-digit inflation and a virtual cessation of private sector saving. Yet the decision to sell supply-side economics like toothpaste, and the myths created by Mr. Stockman for this very purpose, have served both the Republican Party and the nation very poorly.

35

What Went Wrong With "Supply Side" Economics*

ARTHUR B. LAFFER

Q Professor Laffer, the economic picture now is far worse than President Reagan predicted when he came into office a year ago. What went wrong?

A The administration and Congress postponed the tax cuts. I put much of the blame on David Stockman, director of the Office of Management and Budget. This is the Stockman recession and the Stockman deficit. He was too concerned about budget deficits and watered down the tax cuts, which has slowed the economy. Stockman, with his talk of huge deficits, tax increases and more budget cuts, is fighting to bring back the days of Herbert Hoover. He's trying to scare people.

Deficits aren't the cause of bad economics; deficits are the consequence of bad economics. You never balance the budget when you have slow growth, high unemployment, high inflation and high interest rates, as we do now.

Q But Reagan's business-tax cut was not postponed, and the personal-tax cut was postponed for only a short period of time. Is the mechanism of "supply side" economics so delicate that even small changes upset it?

A I'll answer with an illustration. Suppose you have to go back to school and won't earn any income for a year. You have to decide whether to go this year when income-tax rates are high or next year when they are low. So which year do you go to school? This year, of course.

Now apply that to the tax structure. We have had a cut in personal income taxes so far of 1.25 percent in 1981. In 1982, we'll have a 10

*Reprinted with permission from *U.S. News & World Report,* January 18, 1982, copyright © 1982, U.S. News & World Report, Inc. Arthur B. Laffer is a professor of business economics at the University of Southern California in Los Angeles. A former chief economist of the Office of Management and Budget, he also is a member of the Economic Policy Advisory Board.

percent cumulative cut. The whole economy works on incentives like these. What's happening is that people are putting off investments and income-producing work now to wait for a more favorable tax situation.

As it is, the savings rate already has gone up substantially in response to new incentives. Businesses are certainly using the new tax-leasing arrangements in which firms with unused tax credits sell them, in effect, to other profitable firms that can use them and, in the process, lease back certain property. These leases may not have been the smartest step the government could have made, but people are moving very quickly to use the incentives that are there. Just think of the great shape we'd be in if the tax incentives scheduled to take effect in future years were in effect now.

Q Business is saying that high interest rates are what's keeping them from going ahead with new investment. Doesn't that situation preclude greater investment even if the tax cuts had taken effect earlier?

A Sure. Clearly, low interest rates, whatever the tax structure, would be better than high ones. Vice versa, with a given interest-rate structure, low taxes are better than high ones for investment purposes.

Q With the economic policies now in place, when is the recession going to end?

A Nineteen eighty-two will probably be sluggish, but not as bad as 1981. Then 1983 will be great, and 1984 will be phenomenal. Once the incentives to postpone taxes are gone, people will make production decisions immediately instead of waiting.

Q If 1983 and 1984 turn out as well as you are predicting, will the federal-budget deficit be shrinking, rather than ballooning as some estimates suggest?

A Yes. The deficit in and of itself is not a problem. It's a barometer of what's going on. Right now, it's an indicator that our economy is sicker than a dog. But the way you solve a deficit is to create economic growth and low inflation. These huge estimates are sabotaging Reagan's Presidency. It's strictly scare tactics. If you look back at estimates OMB has made in the past, they are never anywhere close to the later reality. Whoever is putting out these wild numbers is trying to unelect Reagan, the same way that Hoover was unelected.

Q Who's behind the numbers?

A The people who want to raise taxes. When you talk about a 182-billion-dollar deficit, it scares people. It also leads you to grasp for solutions. And the solutions they're grasping for are what they call revenue enhancers. I call them tax increases. These are the same people who fought the President's tax-rate deductions all the way. What they don't see is that the tax reductions are what it takes to get the economic growth we need to eliminate the deficits.

Q But Republicans in Congress are saying the same things—

A Then Republicans have serious problems in their own party. They have never been friendly to supply-side economics—it's just Ronald Reagan who is.

Q What should be President Reagan's strategy in the 1983 budget that will be unveiled later this month?

A The President should do all he can to spur economic growth. No. 1, he should make all the tax cuts effective retroactive to Janauary 1, 1982. No. 2, he should go back to convertibility—that is, a version of the gold standard—as fast as possible. He should restore some of the funds that have been cut for social programs. Finally, he should pressure the Federal Reserve to bring interest rates down. High rates won't solve our inflation problem.

Q If the President were to do all that, when would we begin to see results?

A You would see the benefits right away. It may take a long time to offset the total damage to the economy, but you wouldn't have hard times.

Q Why will 1982 be better than 1981? Won't people wait to invest until 1983 when there is a bigger tax cut?

A There will be some of that, but the tax situation nevertheless is better in 1982 than in 1981. That's why I was so strongly against post-poining the tax cuts. If it's good, it's good doing it now. If the President were to advance all the tax cuts to 1982, it would be a phenomenal year. And we would balance the budget by 1983 or 1984. The situation now is very close to what we faced in 1961-62. If you remember, in 1961 President Kennedy's popularity was falling, the stock market was falling. Then, in 1962, he came through with the first of a series of cuts that eventually included shorter depreciation, investment credits, a series of across-the-board individual-tax cuts, corporate-tax cuts, as well as his version of taking us back to the gold standard. The stock market hit its trough in the spring of the year, and then we started on the long, roaring '60s.

Q Inflation today is much higher than it was in Kennedy's day. Won't big tax cuts worsen the problem?

A In my view, inflation pushes people into higher tax brackets. Inflation is a tax increaser. So any tax-rate reduction that you would make when there is no inflation needs to be bigger if you have inflation. It takes a bigger tax cut now to get the same effect we had in the 1960s.

Reagan's Economic Forecasts: Hits and Misses

	Official Forecast for 1981 (Feb., 1981)	Actual Result in 1981	Original Forecast for 1982 (Feb., 1981)	Latest Forecast for 1982 (Sept., 1981)
Total national output (after inflation)	Up 1.1%	Up 1.8%*	Up 4.2%	Up 3.4%
Personal income	Up 11.0%	Up 11.3%*	Up 11.5%	Up 11.5%
Consumer prices (annual average)	Up 11.1%	Up 10.4%*	Up 8.3%	Up 7.0%
Interest rates (91-day Treasury bills)	11.1%	14.1%	8.9%	12.5%
Unemployment rate (annual average)	7.8%	7.6%*	7.2%	7.3%

*Estimates by *USN&WR* Economic Unit.

USN&WR table—Basic data: U.S. Office of Management and Budget, U.S. Depts. of Commerce and Labor

Q Do you see a need for deeper tax cuts than have already been enacted? And in what form?

A We surely never want a tax on corporate profits. It makes no sense at all. If a firm wastes resources and does poorly, the government bails it out; if a firm uses resources efficiently and makes a good profit, we tax the heck out of it. I'd favor a value-added tax at the corporate level to substitute for an income tax. We also should do away with progression in the tax code for individuals. It makes no sense to tax incomes at very high rates, because it destroys incentive to earn and invest.

Q Would you end deductions and exemptions?

A Sure. I'd like to have a flat value-added tax under which taxes are included in the price of goods and everyone who buys something winds up paying the same tax rate.

Q Why did you say Reagan should restore some of the budget cuts in social programs?

A I'd never risk the security of Americans in order to balance the budget. If there is waste and fraud, cut it out. But you don't solve the deficit problem by cutting off food stamps to people who are out of a job. You just don't do that, on moral or political grounds. It's offensive.

I surely would like to change some of the social programs, but you do it when you don't need them—in a growth economy. A boom is the necessary condition for any social-spending changes. Furthermore, you don't keep the safety net in place and then cut the welfare benefits of everyone outside the net. It creates disincentives. It's not worth it to go to work if you're a ghetto dweller. It's more advantageous to stay home and collect all the safety-net benefits that you can.

Q What about the defense budget? Is it too big?

A It depends on what you think we need to spend for the security of the nation. I do know that if you don't have locks on your doors, you're in trouble. And if you have 17 locks on your doors, you're wasting your money.

Q Even if the tax cuts had come in exactly as you wanted, the government's reliance on monetary policy to contain inflation would mean continuing high interest rates. How do you expect business investment to pick up in the face of those rates?

A You don't. The purpose of monetary policy is to make money attractive to hold. The government has an obligation to the citizenry to guarantee the purchasing power of the monetary unit. If we made a contract for a 20-year loan, you should know what you're going to be paying me, and I should know what I would be receiving in real, inflation-adjusted terms.

In almost all situations where you find stable prices and good monetary policy, you find the government guaranteeing the value of the currency by making it convertible—backing it up with gold. That's the monetary-policy side of supply-side economics, not the high interest rates we see today.

Q Why would a gold standard work?

A When you have an unhinged paper currency, as we do now, it depreciates in value. People don't hold paper because they like paper; they want to hold guaranteed purchasing power. Take a look at what's happened since August 1971, when President Nixon took us away from a fixed exchange rate. The purchasing power now of an ounce of gold is five times what it was in 1971. At $800 an ounce, it was 10 times higher. When you see the price of gold going from $35 an ounce to $800 an ounce, it tells you something is wrong with money. Gold is the first refuge of the cautious.

What you're really doing with a gold standard is conferring on a dollar bill all the qualities of gold. If you have a good money, the price of gold tumbles. What we have done by making an inferior money is to subsidize the chief producers of gold—South Africa and Russia—with billions of dollars in gold purchases. The price of gold has shot up as the value of our money has declined. If you want the price of gold to tumble, make the dollar as good as gold.

Q How do we do that? Don't we first have to cut inflation?

A No, just the reverse. If you look at what's been done in Europe to stop hyperinflation, you go to gold to restore the value of money. What ensues is rapid economic growth, and budgets are balanced quickly. In the U.S., the last time we stopped a major inflation problem was in

1946. What did Harry Truman do? He went to a modified form of gold convertibility and cut taxes on personal and corporate income. What we had in the years just after World War II was an unemployment rate that never went as high as 6 percent. The budget was balanced four out of five years. Enormous economic growth took place in the private sector.

The way you stop inflation is by growing out of it, not by contracting the economy. I don't know of any major inflation that has been stopped by a recession, by tight money and by high interest rates. It takes economic growth to solve the problem, and you can't get growth and investment with those policies.

Q If we went back to gold, wouldn't the Federal Reserve lose some of its power to control the money supply?

A The Fed doesn't have complete power over the money supply now. But the answer is that you'd put that power in the hands of the private sector. Gold has nothing to do with the quantity of money; it is just a barometer of attitudes about money.

It would work this way: When the Fed sees people selling gold to get dollars, it would know it didn't have enough dollars in circulation, so it would go into its open-market operations and buy government bonds in order to get more dollars in circulation. Then people would stop buying dollars with their gold.

Likewise, when people are turning in their dollars for gold, you know there are too many dollars outstanding, so you sell bonds on the open market until they stop. You use gold as the indicator of policy.

Obviously, you never go to the point where you let gold run your world. Suppose, for instance, someone discovers a new way to produce gold at $5 an ounce in unlimited quantities. In that case, you go off gold for a while and reset the price. I don't want a pure gold standard. But let's go back to a blended system where we use it when it serves us and we don't use it when it doesn't.

Q Then what's the point of switching? Aren't you still saying the Fed has to step in and use its judgment? That's no different from the situation today—

A The difference is that today we are not using any of the beneficial aspects of a gold standard. My proposal would specify in advance the conditions under which gold convertibility would be suspended and later re-established. Adjustments will be likely, and they should be done without destroying the system. The essential point remains that we need a money whose value is guaranteed, so that when I make a 30-year contract with you I will know what that currency will be worth at the end of the contract. It's nonsense to think that the current policy of slowing growth in the quantity of money will slow inflation. The reason is that the demand for money is just as important as the supply of it.

To show you what I mean, substitute apples for dollar bills. If I grow a bumper crop, the quantity of apples increases and the price of each falls. If there's a shortage, the price or value of each goes up. With money, the faster it grows, the higher inflation; the slower money grows, the lower inflation.

Now look at the other side of the equation. Say scientists discover that apples have strong aphrodisiac qualities. There's a huge increase in demand, the price goes up, apple growers pick their trees cleaner and grow more varieties. There's an increase in the quantity of apples as the value of each unit goes up.

Take a second situation. The surgeon general announces that apples cause a dangerous illness. Demand disappears, the price tumbles and the quantity tumbles.

I'm saying there is a demand curve and supply curve in every market, including money. Every classical economist knows that when you make a good money, you have more of it. If we made the dollar as good as gold, the quantity of money would increase enormously because we would have finally made money desirable. I want to see the quantity of money double, not because the Federal Reserve has more printed but because money is in demand.

Q How good a job is the Federal Reserve doing today?

A The Fed has no control over the quantity of money at all. I'd like to see the board reduce its taxes on the domestic banking system—that is, lower the interest rate on borrowed reserves, reduce the discount rate and reduce reserve requirements on banks. The point is to make money more attractive to banks, to increase demand for it.

Q Just what is supply-side economics, in your view?

A It's basically looking at incentives. People base their actions on incentives. When you change those incentives, they change their behavior. For instance, people don't work to pay taxes. They work to get what they can after taxes. The after-tax return determines whether a person works, or sits on the beach at Malibu, or changes jobs. People don't save to go bankrupt. They save to augment their wealth, not reduce it. Therefore, it's the after-tax rate of return on savings that determines the volume of savings, not the level of income.

In today's environment, supply-side economics means changing the tax structure so that productive investment gets the same or a better rate of return than nonproductive ones, such as investing in a law firm or in gold hidden in a basement or a Bermuda offshore corporation. The real problem is that today you make more money with those kinds of investments than in building steel mills, cement plants and asphalt factories.

Q Aren't you promising a free lunch for the economy—that we can achieve high growth and low inflation without any pain?

A Well, that is the whole purpose of economics—to create added value. Every time you make someone better off, it doesn't mean that someone else is worse off. If you develop a new widget that does its job twice as well, you're better off and every widget purchaser in the world is better off. You have created free lunches.

Q Do you feel your supply-side theories have been abandoned by the Reagan administration? Do we now have a jerry-built economic strategy in place? And will it work?

A Our policies haven't been abandoned. Reagan didn't back down on tax cuts. Sure, they're not as fast as I'd like to have had them. But they are on the books. Now we just have to sit and wait. Postponing them won't improve the situation. But 1983 will come and 1984 will come, and the economy will be in great shape.

Q What is your view on why Wall Street doesn't seem to believe the program will work?

A Wall Street probably has a good chance of being right. The chance of Stockman's winning this battle and dismantling the supply-side tax cuts is reasonably high. Stockman was the guy who put the plank in the Republican platform on gold; now he talks it down. He's the guy who advocated all the tax cuts; now he wants tax increases. He whispers one thing to the *Atlantic* monthly magazine and says other things publicly— both of which are quite different from what he tells people privately.

There is one supply-side "mole" in the White House. It's the President. He's the only guy who wants it.

36

The Education of
David Stockman

WILLIAM GREIDER

• • •

While ideology would guide Stockman in his new job, he would be
confronted with a large and tangible political problem: how to resolve
the three-sided dilemma created by Ronald Reagan's contradictory
campaign promises. In private, Stockman agreed that his former congressional mentor, John Anderson, running as an independent candidate
for President in 1980, had asked the right question: How is it possible
to raise defense spending, cut income taxes, and balance the budget, all
at the same time? Anderson had taunted Reagan with that question,
again and again, and most conventional political thinkers, from orthodox
Republican to Keynesian liberal, agreed with Anderson that it could
not be done.

But Stockman was confident, even cocky, that he and some of his
fellow conservatives had the answer. It was a theory of economics—the
supply-side theory—that promised an end to the twin aggravations of
the 1970s: high inflation and stagnant growth in America's productivity.
"We've got to figure out a way to make John Anderson's question fit
into a plausible policy path over the next three years," Stockman said.
"Actually, it isn't all that hard to do."

The supply-side approach, which Stockman had only lately embraced,
assumed, first of all, that dramatic action by the new President, espe-

Editor's Note: This reading contains excerpts from an article that appeared in *The Atlantic
Monthly*, December 1981. The excerpts were chosen because they pertain to supply-side
economics.

cially the commitment to a three-year reduction of the income tax, coupled with tight monetary control, would signal investors that a new era was dawning, that the growth of government would be displaced by the robust growth of the private sector. If economic behavior in a climate of high inflation is primarily based on expectations about the future value of money, then swift and dramatic action by the President could reverse the gloomy assumptions in the disordered financial markets. As inflation abated, interest rates dropped, and productive employment grew, those marketplace developments would, in turn, help Stockman balance the federal budget.

"The whole thing is premised on faith," Stockman explained. "On a belief about how the world works." As he prepared the script in his mind, his natural optimism led to bullish forecasts, which were even more robust than the Reagan Administration's public promises. "The inflation premium melts away like the morning mist," Stockman predicted. "It could be cut in half in a very short period of time if the policy is credible. That sets off adjustments and changes in perception that cascade through the economy. You have a bull market in '81, after April, of historic proportions."

• • •

The original apostles of supply-side, particularly Representative Jack Kemp, of New York, and the economist Arthur B. Laffer, dismissed budget-cutting as inconsequential to the economic problems, but Stockman was trying to fuse new theory and old. "Laffer sold us a bill of goods," he said, then corrected his words: "Laffer wasn't wrong—he didn't go far enough."

• • •

Artful as it was, the Jones resolution was, according to Stockman, a series of gimmicks: economic estimates and accounting tricks. "Political numbers," he called them. But Stockman was not critical of Jones for these budget ploys, because he cheerfully conceded that the administration's own budget numbers were constructed on similar shaky premises, mixing cuts from the original 1981 budget left by Jimmy Carter with new baseline projections from the Congressional Budget Office in a way that, fundamentally, did not add up. The budget politics of 1981, which produced such clear and dramatic rhetoric from both sides, was, in fact, based upon a bewildering set of numbers that confused even those, like Stockman, who produced them.

"None of us really understands what's going on with all these numbers," Stockman confessed at one point. "You've got so many different budgets out and so many different baselines and such complexity now in the interactive parts of the budget between policy action and the economic environment and all the internal mysteries of the budget, and there are a lot of them. People are getting from A to B and it's not clear how they are getting there. It's not clear how we got there, and it's not clear how Jones is going to get there."

●   ●   ●

In political terms, Stockman's analysis was sound. The Reagan program was moving toward a series of dramatic victories in Congress. Beyond the brilliant tactical maneuvering, however, and concealed by the public victories, Stockman was privately staring at another reality—a gloomy portent that the economic theory behind the President's program wasn't working. While it was winning in the political arena, the plan was losing on Wall Street. The financial markets, which Stockman had thought would be reassured by the new President's bold actions, and which were supposed to launch a historic "bull market" in April, failed to respond in accordance with Stockman's script. The markets not only failed to rally, they went into a new decline. Interest rates started up again; the bond market slumped. The annual inflation rate, it was true, was declining, dropping below double digits, but even Stockman acknowledged that this was owing to "good luck" with grain harvests and world oil supplies, not to Reaganomics. Investment analysts, however, were looking closely at the Stockman budget figures, looking beyond the storm of political debate and the President's winning style, and what they saw were enormous deficits ahead—the same numbers that had shocked David Stockman when he came into office in January. Henry Kaufman, of Salomon Brothers, one of the preeminent prophets of Wall Street, delivered a sobering speech that, in the cautious language of financiers, said the same thing that John Anderson had said in 1980: cutting taxes and pumping up the defense budget would produce not balanced budgets but inflationary deficits.

Was Kaufman right? Stockman agreed that he was, and conceded that his own original conception—that dramatic political action would somehow alter the marketplace expectations of continuing inflation—had been wrong. "They're concerned about the out-year budget posture, not about the near-term economic situation. The Kaufmans don't dispute our diagnosis at all. They dispute our remedy. They don't think it adds up . . . I take the performance of the bond market deadly seriously. I think it's the best measure there is. The bond markets represent worldwide psychology, worldwide preception and evaluation of what, on balance, relevant people think about what we're doing . . . It means we're going to have to make changes . . . I wouldn't say we are losing. We're still not winning. We're not winning."

• • •

Stockman was wrong, of course, about the bull market. But his misinterpretation of events was more profound than that. Without recognizing it at the time, the budget director was headed into a summer in which not only financial markets but life itself seemed to be absolutely perverse. The Reagan program kept winning in public, a series of well-celebrated political victories in Congress—yet privately Stockman was losing his struggle.

Stockman was changing, in a manner that perhaps he himself did not recognize. His conversations began to reflect a new sense of fatalism, a brittle edge of uncertainty.

"There was a certain dimension of our theory that was unrealistic. . ."

"The system has an enormous amount of inertia. . ."

"I don't believe too much in the momentum theory any more. . ."

"I have a new theory—there are no *real* conservatives in Congress. . ."

• • •

The supply-side effects would still be strong, Stockman said, but he added a significant disclaimer that would have offended true believers, for it sounded like old orthodoxy: "I've never believed that just cutting taxes alone will cause output and employment to expand."

Stockman himself had been a late convert to supply-side theology, and now he was beginning to leave the church. The theory of "expectations" wasn't working. He could see that. And Stockman's institutional role as budget director forced him to look constantly at aspects of the political economy that the other supply-siders tended to dismiss. Whatever the reason, Stockman was creating some distance between himself and the supply-side purists; eventually, he would become the target of their nasty barbs. For his part, Stockman began to disparage the grand theory as a kind of convenient illusion—new rhetoric to cover old Republican doctrine.

"The hard part of the supply-side tax cut is dropping the top rate from 70 to 50 percent—the rest of it is a secondary matter," Stockman explained. "The original argument was that the top bracket was too high, and that's having the most devastating effect on the economy. Then, the general argument was that, in order to make this palatable as a political matter, you had to bring down all the brackets. But, I mean, Kemp-Roth was always a Trojan horse to bring down the top rate."

A Trojan horse? This seemed a cynical concession for Stockman to make in private conversation while the Reagan Administration was still selling the supply-side doctrine to Congress. Yet he was conceding what the liberal Keynesian critics had argued from the outset—the supply-side theory was not a new economic theory at all but only new language and argument to conceal a hoary old Republican doctrine: give the tax cuts to the top brackets, the wealthiest individuals and largest enterprises, and let the good effects "trickle down" through the economy to reach everyone else. Yes, Stockman conceded, when one stripped away the new rhetoric emphasizing across-the-board cuts, the supply-side theory was really new clothes for the unpopular doctrine of the old Republican orthodoxy. "It's kind of hard to sell 'trickle down,'" he explained, "so the supply-side formula was the only way to get a tax policy that was really 'trickle down.' Supply-side is 'trickle-down' theory."

● ● ●

The final pasted-together measure would be several thousand pages of legislative action and, Stockman feared, another version of the Trojan horse—"a Trojan horse filled full of all kinds of budget-busting measures and secondary agendas."

● ● ●

Stockman's dour outlook was reinforced two weeks later, when the Reagan coalition prevailed again in the House and Congress passed the tax-cut legislation with a final frenzy of trading and bargaining. Again, Stockman was not exhilarated by the victory. On the contrary, it seemed to leave a bad taste in his mouth, as though the democratic process had finally succeeded in shocking him by its intensity and its greed. Once again, Stockman participated in the trading—special tax concessions for oil-lease holders and real-estate tax shelters, and generous loopholes that virtually eliminated the corporate income tax. Stockman sat in the room and saw it happen.

"Do you realize the greed that came to the forefront?" Stockman asked with wonder. "The hogs were really feeding. The greed level, the level of opportunism, just got out of control."

● ● ●

Where did things go wrong? Stockman kept asking and answering the right questions. The more he considered it, the more he moved away from the radical vision of reformer, away from the wishful thinking of supply-side economics, and toward the "old-time religion" of conservative economic thinking. Orthodoxy seemed less exciting than radicalism, but perhaps Stockman was only starting into another intellectual transition. He had changed from farm boy to campus activist at Michigan State, from Christian moralist to neo-conservative at Harvard; once again, Stockman was reformulating his ideas on how the world worked. What had he learned?

"The reason we did it wrong—not wrong, but less than the optimum—was that we said, Hey, we have to get a program out fast. And when you decide to put a program of this breadth and depth out fast, you can only do so much. We were working in a twenty or twenty-five-day time frame, and we didn't think it all the way through. We didn't add up all the numbers. We didn't make all the thorough, comprehensive calculations about where we really needed to come out and how much to put on the plate the first time, and so forth. In other words, we ended up with a list that I'd always been carrying of things to be done, rather than starting the other way and asking, What is the overall fiscal policy required to reach the target?"

That regret was beyond remedy now; all Stockman could do was keep trying on different fronts, trying to catch up with the shortcomings of the original Reagan prospectus. But Stockman's new budget-cutting tactics were denounced as panic by his former allies in the supply-side camp. They now realized that Stockman regarded them as "overly optimistic" in predicting a painless boom through across-the-board tax reduction. "Some of the naive supply-siders just missed this whole dimension," he said. "You don't stop inflation without some kind of dislocation . . . Supply-side was the wrong atmospherics—not wrong theory or wrong economics, but wrong atmospherics . . . The supply-siders have gone too far. They created this nonpolitical view of the economy, where you are going to have big changes and abrupt turns, and their happy vision of this world of growth and no inflation with no pain."

The "dislocations" were multiplying across the nation, creating panic among the congressmen and senators who had just enacted this "fiscal revolution." But Stockman now understood that no amount of rhetoric from Washington, not the President's warmth on television nor his own nimble testimony before congressional hearings, would alter the economic forces at work. Tight monetary control should continue, he believed, until the inflationary fevers were sweated out of the economy. People would be hurt. Afterward, after the recession, perhaps the supply-side effects could begin—robust expansion, new investment, new jobs. The question was whether the country or its elected representatives would wait long enough.

Appendix

Other Books About Supply-Side Economics

Bartlett, Bruce R. *"Reaganomics" Supply-Side Economics in Action.* Westport, Ct.: Arlington House Publishers, 1981.

Boskin, Michael J. (Editor). *The Economy in the 1980's: A Program for Growth and Stability.* New Brunswick (USA): Transaction Books, 1980.

Hailstones, Thomas J. *A Guide to Supply-Side Economics.* Richmond, Virginia: Robert F. Dame, Inc., 1982.

Laffer, Arthur B. and Marc A. Miles. *International Economics in an Integrated World.* Glenview, Ill.: Scott, Foresman and Company, 1982.

The Supply-Side Effects of Economic Policy. St. Louis: Federal Reserve Bank of St. Louis and The Center for the Study of American Business, 1981.

Wanniski, Jude. *The Way the World Works.* New York: Simon & Schuster, 1978.

About The Author

Dr. Thomas J. Hailstones is Professor of Economics and Dean of the College of Business at Xavier University. Before Xavier he taught at the University of Detroit, St. Louis University and Notre Dame. He was an economist for the Office of Price Stabilization during the Korean Conflict and has lectured throughout the United States and abroad. He has been a summer visiting professor at several universities, including Harvard, Loyola, Gonzaga, Colorado, Hawaii and Chaminade of Honolulu. He has conducted economic seminars for numerous companies, such as Cincinnati Milacron, AT&T, Bendix, IBM, Fujitsu, Whirlpool and Control Data, as well as many management and professional organizations. For a dozen years he was an adjunct professor at the General Electric Company Management Development Institute and an affiliate professor at the Japan-America Institute of Management Science (Honolulu). For several years he has given economic seminars for the U.S. Army, U.S. Air Force, the U.S. Civil Service Commission and the CIA.

He wrote a weekly newspaper column on *Economic Trends* for 10 years and during five of those years had a weekly radio broadcast on Economic Trends. Dr. Hailstones offered the first Economics course for credit on education TV more than 25 years ago and has since made numerous TV appearances.

He was Chairman of the Mayor's Full Employment Commission, (Cincinnati) Chairman of the Federal Manpower Development and Training Commission for the Southwest Ohio Region, Regional Chairman of the Advisory Board for the Ohio State Employment Service and Treasurer of the Cincinnati Community Action Commission. Dr. Hailstones has considerable experience implementing federal employment and anti-poverty programs at the grass roots level.

Dr. Hailstones is past national president of the Association for Social Economics and past president of the Midwest Case Research Association. He is a member of the board of directors of Clopay Corporation, Gradison Cash Reserves, Inc., The Ohio National Fund, and Student Loan Funding Corp. He has been an economic consultant to many companies, both large and small.

In addition to numerous articles for academic journals and trade periodicals, Dr. Hailstones has authored a number of textbooks, including: *Economics: An Analysis of Principles and Policies* (2nd Ed.); *Basic Economics* (6th Ed.); *Readings in Economics* (4th Ed.); *Contemporary Economic Problems and Issues* (6th Ed.); *Introduction to Managerial Economics* (1st Ed.); *A Guide to Supply-Side Economics;* and *Viewpoints on Supply-Side Economics.*